Once I Was You

A Memoir of Love and Hate in a Torn America

Maria Hinojosa

ATRIA BOOKS

New York   London   Toronto   Sydney   New Delhi

ATRIA
BOOKS

An Imprint of Simon & Schuster, Inc.
1230 Avenue of the Americas
New York, NY 10020

Copyright © 2020 by The Hinojosa Corporation

First Atria Books hardcover edition September 2020

ATRIA BOOKS and colophon are trademarks of Simon & Schuster, Inc.

For information about special discounts for bulk purchases, please contact Simon & Schuster Special Sales at 1-866-506-1949 or business@simonandschuster.com.

The Simon & Schuster Speakers Bureau can bring authors to your live event. For more information or to book an event, contact the Simon & Schuster Speakers Bureau at 1-866-248-3049 or visit our website at www.simonspeakers.com.

Interior design by Dana Sloan

Manufactured in the United States of America

5 7 9 10 8 6 4

Library of Congress Cataloging-in-Publication Data
Names: Hinojosa, Maria, 1961– author.
Title: Once I was you : a memoir of love and hate in a torn America / Maria Hinojosa.
Description: New York : Atria Books, 2020. | Includes bibliographical references and index.
Identifiers: LCCN 2019057657 (print) | LCCN 2019057658 (ebook) | ISBN 9781982128654 (hardcover) | ISBN 9781982128678 (ebook)
Subjects: LCSH: Hinojosa, Maria, 1961– | Television journalists—United States—Biography. | Radio journalists—United States—Biography. | Hispanic American journalists—Biography. | Hispanic American women—Biography.
Classification: LCC PN4874.H495 A3 2020 (print) | LCC PN4874.H495 (ebook) | DDC 070.92 [B]—dc23
LC record available at https://lccn.loc.gov/2019057657
LC ebook record available at https://lccn.loc.gov/2019057658

ISBN 978-1-9821-2865-4
ISBN 978-1-9821-2867-8 (ebook)

Para Ceci, mi papá y Maritere,
who taught me to find joy in every moment.

And to all the children who grow up in a country that
isn't their own. You are not invisible. I see you because
I still am you. Te veo porque aún me veo en ti.

Contents

Introduction

A Letter to the Girl at McAllen Airport

In February 2019, I was kneeling down on the nasty gray carpeting of the McAllen airport, nine miles from the border of Texas and Mexico, looking for a plug to charge my phone. I knew I looked silly. A grown woman on all fours at seven in the morning in a relatively empty airport. My hair was pulled up in an unruly bun and I was wearing my black-rimmed glasses and a beat-up gray cashmere turtleneck—my low-maintenance travel outfit. But I was still a self-respecting Latina. So I had on a dab of Selena's lipstick, my gold hoops, and of course, my cashmere sweater bought at a discount store.

That's when I caught you looking at me. At first, I thought you were curious, like any other kid staring at a strange woman in an airport. Except that you looked at me as if I wasn't there. I just happened to step into your line of sight by mistake. You were staring into nothing because nothing made sense anymore.

At least, that's how you looked. Exhausted. You didn't even seem scared. It's as if you had been there, done that. Fear didn't serve you.

Now you were just the numb girl, the one with the gaze of nothing-ness, of just barely being human, because that's how you have been made to feel these past weeks (or was it months?). It's as if you had been anesthetized by some mysterious poison that kept you alive on the outside but dead on the inside.

Could you really be telling me all of this with one empty stare?

When I saw you looking at me, or rather, through me, I stared back with concern but also an all-encompassing curiosity, which al-most immediately became an intuitive, maternal kind of warmth. Did you feel that? Was it the first time since you had crossed into this hell of a place that anyone had looked at you with affection?

You might have been ten years old, but your eyes looked like the ones from my old Barbie doll, Midge—the one with tightly curled brown hair and 1960s cat eyeliner. That's what you looked like at seven in the morning, your beautiful eyes like a movie star's.

Your hair was long and so pitch-black that it shone. You had soft, undulating curls rolling down from a high ponytail and just a wisp of bangs. Your skin was the color of toasty-warm milk chocolate, but it had a gray, ashy pallor, like it had been deprived of sunlight for a very long time.

Then, thirty or forty-five seconds into our mutual staring, some-thing happened. For just a second, your shield of numbness broke and you smiled at me. First, it came from your eyes, a slight little wrinkle along the would-be cat eye, and then it spread to your small mouth, the edges turning up for a second, and it softened you. Now I could see a ten-year-old girl who is used to smiling at people, because wher-ever you live in Honduras or El Salvador or Guatemala, I imagine, is a small town and everyone there knows one another. And there, even though it might be one of the most dangerous places in the world, people still smile at each other.

I don't know how I knew that this exchange was not a regular passing morning gesture at the airport, like the hundreds of random niceties I have shared with strangers while traveling across the country. But from the moment my eyes caught yours, I understood not to look away.

I surveyed the situation. You were one of nine children being taken from the border by two chaperones on this flight to Houston, and then, who knows where you would end up or what your collective fate would be. I realized then that this was my chance to speak to one of the children who we have been told over and over again present a secret threat to our country. These are the children President Trump called animals, who must be kept out of the country at all costs because "They look so innocent. They're not innocent." I had a recorder with a built-in mic already set up because I was about to call a source and record our conversation, as per usual. But now I was ready to hear your voice, mijita. Ready to hear your story.

"Hola."

"Hola."

"¿Cómo estás?"

"Bien."

When you spoke, I could barely hear you. It's as if they had taken away your ability to speak. How many times had they told you to be quiet? Yelled it at you for speaking or laughing? Now I was asking you to speak, and your voice was as timid as one could be without being a silent whisper, without me having to read your lips.

"¿Acabas de llegar? ¿Tienes miedo?" (Did you just arrive? Are you scared?)

"Un poquito." (A little.)

"Un poquito. Y tus papás, ¿dónde están?" (A little. And your parents, where are they?)

"En Guatemala." (In Guatemala.)

"¿Viniste sola?" (You came by yourself?)

"Con mi tío." (With my uncle.)

"Y esa gente, ¿es tu familia? ¿Estás solita, solita, solita?" (And those people, are they your family? Are you all alone, alone, alone?)

"Aquí no . . ." (Not here . . .)

"¿Te pusieron en un centro de detención? ¿Una casa súper grande, súper-súper grande?" (Did they put you in a detention camp? A very big house—very, very big?)

"Sí." (Yes.)

I took a breath. I was trembling inside. I was bearing witness in the gentlest of ways—a quiet, intimate conversation—to one of the greatest modern horrors of the USA: the holding of innocent children; the transporting, trafficking, kidnapping of children by a government. Children like this little girl who clearly had no idea what was going on or why.

Suddenly, the woman chaperone stood up and you immediately jumped up mid-sentence, because by now you knew; after weeks in that super-big detention building, you had been trained to respond quickly to the adults around you, to follow their orders, follow their lead.

I stood at a distance for a moment as the children all formed a line, surveying the situation, recording verbal notes into my phone:

"So, let's see, how many kids do I see? One kid looks like he's probably eight years old, another boy who looks like he's ten, a boy who looks like he's maybe four or five, a boy who looks like he's fifteen, another boy who looks like he's a teenager, a little girl, another boy, and another small boy. I'm going to go talk to them, because they are obviously wondering what's going on with me. And I shouldn't have any fear. Let me go talk to them, see what happens."

I walked up to the woman and said, "Hey, I know you're wondering who I am. My name is Maria Hinojosa. How are you?" She was Latina herself and quickly told me to speak to her supervisor, the

Latino man who was leading the group. I introduced myself to him as a journalist and as I did so I spoke in Spanish to the kids, saying, "No tengan miedo. Soy periodista, es todo." ("Don't be afraid. I'm a journalist, that's all.")

The man leading this group of clearly disoriented children looked blankly at me and said in a kind of monotone, "There's a media person that you need to contact and they can give you all that information. . . ."

"Yeah, I got it," I said.

And then he became nervous and defensive, as if knowing that there really was something wrong with what was happening. Two adult strangers taking a group of children not related to them on plane rides to undisclosed locations, and the kids have no idea what's going on? Almost as if he knew what I was thinking, he added, "But we're not . . . We're just doing our job. That's it."

I had heard that excuse before.

"I get you," I responded, "but you understand as somebody who lives in this country who is a journalist watching this story unfold, I have to be able to ask questions. That's *my* job."

"I know," he repeated flatly. "But my job is to tell you to call that number for the media person so you can get your answers."

"I understand," I said, although I didn't at all. Not really.

I looked at the kids, who were numb and anxious, and with tenderness I spoke in Spanish to the chaperone, but my words were really meant for the children. I wanted them to know:

"Lo único que yo quiero es que ellos sepan que hay gente que está muy interesados en que ellos estén bien, que los estén cuidando, que estén protegidos; que sepan que hay gente que los quiere, que los queremos en este país, que los queremos mucho. Eso lo único . . . ¿no?" (The only thing I want is for them to know that there are people here who are very interested in making sure that they are okay, that they are being looked after, that they are being protected; for them to know that there are people who care about them, who want them in this country, who love them very much. That's all . . . no?)

"That's all I can tell you," he interrupted me.

But I continued, speaking to the kids. "¿Ellos tienen el derecho de decirle lo que quieran a una periodista o no? Quiero decirles que estamos al tanto. . . . Que traten de no tener miedo. Que ustedes no son los enemigos." (Children, you have the right to speak to journalists. You are wanted. You are not the enemies.) I said all of this in Spanish because I wanted you to understand me, to hear my voice and know that I saw you.

I see you, because once I was you.

Chapter 1

Land of False Promises

It was four o'clock in the morning and the full moon was shining through Berta's bedroom window. Her beloved Colonia Narvarte, which was usually a cacophony of sounds—the street sweepers, the knife sharpener's panpipe, the silver almost-church-bell sound of the garbage truck, the barking street mutts of all shapes and sizes—was eerily silent. Not even the birds she fed regularly were up. Berta got out of bed and looked at the clothes she had laid out the night before. This would be the outfit she would travel in as she said goodbye to her birthplace. It had to be perfect and memorable. Berta wanted people to see her just like in the parties. She wanted them to see the arrival of this New American. She wanted people to do a double take when she walked by and not because of the four children she would be bringing with her.

In front of her lay a white satin button-down shirt and a black velvet skirt and the off-white lace petticoat slip that went underneath. She studied her pearl drop earrings and opaque pearl choker. Then her eyes were drawn to the floor, where her pair of black patent leather slingbacks were at the ready. She smiled to herself.

Berta, my mother, was not worried about leaving her country behind. For six months, she had been preparing and processing. She knew my father, Raúl, was struggling to comprehend the enormity of his impending American citizenship, something that he was required to commit to as part of his new job. But Berta knew Mexico would always be her home, no matter what. She would always have her green Mexican passport and an American green card. For her, there was no contradiction.

After staring at her clothes in a daze, the moon now beginning to set and the light blue of morning beginning to brighten over the Popocatépetl volcano, Berta realized she wasn't just smiling. She felt ecstatic. For a full month, the butterflies that were usually a sign of a baby kicking in her belly were now in her tummy because of the thrill of this upcoming adventure, and it was finally here. Still, a small part of her felt ashamed. She was having a hard time understanding exactly why she was so happy about leaving everything she knew behind. Why was this so much easier for her than it had been for Raúl?

Quiero ser más libre. No quiero que nadie me controle. Ni mi mamá, ni mi papá, ni mis hermanos. Yo quiero ser yo. Amo a Raúl y él me ama como soy. Quiero ver el mundo y criar a mis hijos a ser independientes. Quiero ser una mujer entera y no sé si lo puedo lograr aquí en México. (I want to be freer. I don't want anyone to control me. Not my mother, my father, or my brothers and sisters. I want to be me. I love Raúl, and he loves me as I am. I want to see the world and raise my children to be independent. I want to be a complete woman, and I don't know if I can do that here in Mexico.)

One by one, she woke up her children, starting with the oldest, Bertha Elena, who was seven. Berta helped her get dressed, all sleepy like a rag doll, but soon she perked up and assumed her role as her mother's helper. She combed her thick jet-black hair and added a pink barrette. She pulled her white button-down sweater over the black dress Manuela, her abuelita, had made special for her just for this trip, and then she put on her frilly white socks and white leather shoes.

My mom took care of me, dressing me in an off-white baby dress she had sewn with a delicate crochet hem she'd designed herself. I was a crawler, so Mom carried me everywhere that morning as she did every day. Even as she supervised my two brothers and sister, she never let me go.

She called me her chicle, her gum, because I was always stuck to her.

I was her little baby girl, the last one she would have because, unlike my siblings, I was not planned or expected. There would be no more babies, so Berta doted on me. Every minute. With my brothers and sister everything had been a bit utilitarian, but with me, she savored every moment. She wanted to raise me in slow motion, making every memory with her final baby last as long as possible.

Hours later we were on the first leg of the plane ride to Chicago to meet my father. I fell asleep in Berta's arms for the entire flight, while my older sister looked out the window as small tears rolled slowly down her cheeks, thinking about her friends left behind. After close to five hours, we finally landed in Dallas, where we had to change planes and then catch our second flight up to Chicago. We would go through customs and immigration at this airport in Texas.

Berta was petite and stunning, carrying me in her arms with my flowing lace dress draped over her strong, slender arm, my sister holding each of my brother's hands, all three coiffed and shiny, arriving to this fascinating new place with glee all over their faces.

Berta walked up slowly to the immigration agent standing behind a lectern and handed him our five green cards. She knew these cards were more valuable than the temporary visas she had stamped in her Mexican passport. These little pieces of plastic gave Berta legitimacy in her new country. But there was a history to them that Berta didn't know.

In 1940, when something called the Alien Registration Act was passed, noncitizens were required to register with the government for the first time to obtain documentation of their status. What does it say about us immigrants that the government called us aliens from the very beginning? Green cards, as they were commonly referred to, granted immigrants legal residency and work authorization. At the same time, though, this system allowed the government to surveil and track them.

Berta understood that this card meant she had a right to be in this country.

She had seen the immigration agent from afar, his hair the color of white corn tinged with yellow, a thick mustache, and so tall Berta felt like she was looking up at one of the hundred-year-old trees in Chapultepec Park. At five feet tall, she had to touch the back of her head to the top of her spine in order to see his face. Even so, Berta was not nervous.

She imagined his voice would sound like the gentlemen from the Hollywood romance movies she loved, but at first he didn't say a word. As each second passed, Berta saw that his demeanor visibly soured, his nostrils flaring and mouth pursing in disdain. He was scanning our faces to match them with our cards, again and again, and then peered all over our bodies. What exactly was he looking for? Still in her arms, I began to pick up on Berta's increasing anxiety as if I were absorbing it by osmosis.

Then the agent turned to me. His eyes combed over every inch of my tiny body and Berta pulled me even closer. He was fixated on a small reddish patch of skin on my arm, where a rash had developed from the substitute blanket I had been using the last weeks at home (since my own blanket had been packed away and shipped north). It was a minor allergic reaction to the wool from the Mexican highlands. The agent looked at me, then turned to my mom and shook his head.

"Ma'am, your baby looks like she has German measles," he said in a thick Texas accent. "Which is contagious, so we are going to have to put her in quarantine. The rest of you are okay to come in with your green cards. But the little baby, we are going to have to put her in quarantine and keep her."

For my mom, those two words sent her reeling: *keep her*. Her knees almost buckled, and she felt the urge to run away as fast as she could. How could she be feeling both impulses at once? She had to force herself to take control of the situation. This man wanted to take away her chicle! Berta had never before been told that someone was going to keep one of her children.

Her heart was beating so fast it felt like she had a hummingbird in her chest. She wanted to unleash a bloodcurdling scream right then and there. It felt like someone had just sliced her open, reached in, and tried to rip out her heart like in one of the sacrificios de los Aztecas.

Berta took a deep breath. Cálmate, she told herself, while at the same time she instinctively looked around her for allies and saw that she had no one to come to her aid. A petite woman with nothing but her own guts to call on, she would have to defend herself.

"*Sir!* I am Berta Hinojosa. I am the wife of Dr. Raúl Hinojosa. My husband was invited by the president of the University of Chicago and if you don't believe me, you can call him yourself."

I've often imagined that moment when my mom's inner voice of maternal strength and anguish came shooting up from within her in the form of an anaconda that wrapped itself around the immigration agent's biceps and started squeezing, out for blood, coming in for the kill, like a mother tiger protecting her cub.

"Under no circumstances will I allow you to keep my child be-hind, and our paperwork is all in order, and I know we have the right to come into this country."

And in that moment, the sexy, dainty mom in kitten heels trans-formed into a monster twice the size of the agent. With a powerful voice, she yelled up at the man who looked like a tree and said firmly in her thick, unmistakably Mexican accent, "I am coming into this country with ALL FOUR OF MY CHILDREN, SIR! DO YOU HEAR ME?! YOU CANNOT KEEP MY CHILD, SIR! DO YOU HEAR ME, SIR?"

The agent shrank away from the verbal assault, suddenly looking very small. Berta had never wielded this tone before. After her impas-sioned speech, when the fear and anger had been released and the adrenaline drained away, her body began to shake all over, her little ankles knocking against each other. She realized her own voice—strong, assertive, fearless—had made this man, tall like a Chapultepec tree, shrink to a shrub.

The man was stunned. No one had spoken to him like this before.

"Why, yes, ma'am. Yes, ma'am . . ." he said, not quite knowing what else he could do.

I imagine he had thought my beautiful mother would be quiet and compliant. How many others had been? I couldn't have been the first to have been scrutinized and deemed too dangerous to enter the coun-try. Was there a secret nursery in the Dallas airport in 1962 where they kept all of the "diseased" and unworthy children? My mom had stood up to him, though, and because of her, I wasn't taken and held with other quarantined children who were scared numb.

It had to have been a mistake. That's what I told myself my whole life. But I was wrong. In fact, there was a room for babies like me, and I would discover that as I was writing this book. It wasn't just a room. It was an entire system decades in the making.

The immigration agent waved us all through the checkpoint with his big, brawny hands as he said, "Yes, ma'am. Correct! You may *all* come into the USA. Welcome. Come on in!"

In 1961, a year before embarking on our journey to the United States, I was born in the metropolis of Mexico City. My country of origin, Mexico, was a beautiful product of the chaos of confrontation between the advanced civilizations of the Mayans and Aztecs clashing with the arrival of the Spaniards, with their massacres and rapes and the Africans, some free and some enslaved, they brought with them. Mexico was a multicultural puzzle made up of people who had already been there for centuries and those who had come from afar to claim it. But Mexico did not define itself or its value as being a country of opportunity for immigrants. That was never Mexico's national narrative.

My adopted country, the United States of America, was founded by immigrants who had no papers or permission to come but who were seeking a new beginning with boundless potential. This was central to their raison d'être, their grand mission, the great plan, a collective narrative of its people. America has always put forward a public veneer of loving immigrants and their role in this country, but in reality, the underside of immigration, the hidden hatred and internalized oppression and silence, has made our relationship with the notion of being a nation of immigrants much more embattled; a permanent secret war of words and hatred against itself.

History shows us the truth. Or rather, one version of US history told from a limited perspective reiterates the "truth" that they want us to believe. In school, we were taught that the first settlers were English-speaking Europeans seeking religious freedom. In fact, the first colonial settlements in the territory we now consider the United States were not in Jamestown or Plymouth Colony. The Spanish, led by Pedro Menéndez de Avilés, arrived at St. Augustine in what is now Florida in 1565; Plymouth was not founded for another fifty-five years, when the first Puritan pilgrims landed in 1620. In 1610, only three years after English colonists backed by the Virginia Company founded Jamestown, Spanish colonists built a settlement in what is now Santa Fe, New Mexico. Yet our public education system focuses only on the English settlements, almost completely overlooking those of the Spanish, "the originals."

History is written by the victors, which means we should question the version of history that has been handed down to us—by teachers, the media, and authority figures. The victors certainly have not labeled themselves or the people they descended from who arrived on this land without papers or permission as the very first "illegal aliens." Instead, we are taught that this is a land that welcomes immigrants (passive indigenous people just wanting to share . . .), a place where the idea that we are all created equal is a self-evident truth (though written during slavery), that we are each endowed with unalienable rights (except voting, if you were a woman, till 1920), including life, liberty, and the pursuit of happiness. Perhaps the most important document for immigrants in this country, the Declaration of Independence, says we all have a right to exist and to fight for our existence (but mostly if you were a white man).

In reality, our attitudes toward the immigrants who come here to work, either by choice or by force, are double-edged. Twelve and a half million innocent people were enslaved and brought to the New World from Africa as early as the 1500s. Of the 10.7 million Africans who survived the journey, 305,000 arrived in the US. The history books written from the perspective of white male privilege call this tragedy the slave trade, but perhaps we should call it what it is—an international, government-sponsored human-trafficking ring. It was a sanctioned, forced migration that dehumanized and stoked hatred toward black bodies in order to justify the labor force driving America's economy.

When the US won the Mexican-American War in 1848, Mexico was forced to cede nearly half of its territory—land that later made up California, Nevada, Utah, Arizona, New Mexico, Colorado, and Wyoming—for $15 million as part of the Treaty of Guadalupe Hidalgo. The people living there did not cross any border or migrate anywhere. Instead, the border crossed them, forcing US citizenship on them overnight with the promise they could keep the land they owned. That promise didn't stop businessmen and railroad companies from stripping Mexican Americans of 20 million acres in the decades that followed, resulting in a massive transfer of wealth away from Latino families, creating a legacy of poverty for those who had lost everything.

In the 1860s, railroad tycoons like Collis Potter Huntington and Charles Crocker recruited thousands of Chinese laborers to help build the transcontinental railroad. Because the exchange rate between the US and China worked in their favor and Chinese laborers were eager to repay the merchants who had paid for their passage to America and begin sending money home to their families, they were often willing to work for less pay. The competition for jobs provoked tensions with other immigrant groups, like the Irish, who felt squeezed out by the Chinese. So the California state government attempted to curtail Chinese immigration with a number of racist and exclusionary measures. Leland Stanford, the founder of the university with his name on it, a former California governor, and one of the railroad tycoons who had depended on Chinese labor to finish his railroad, said in a message to the legislature on a cool January day in 1862, "The settlement among us of an inferior race is to be discouraged, by every legitimate means. Asia, with her numberless millions, sends to our shores the dregs of her population. . . . There can be no doubt but that the presence of numbers among us of a degraded and distinct people must exercise a deleterious influence upon the superior race."

Those words and sentiments on racial superiority helped pave the way for Congress to pass the Chinese Exclusion Act in 1882, which banned Chinese laborers from immigrating to the US. But it was Asian women who were the first people ever legally excluded from this country with the Page Act of 1875, which prohibited women from China, Japan, or other Asian countries from landing on these shores. The white man's version of history says they needed to be kept out because they would come only to work as prostitutes, but isn't it more plausible that they were just like my mom, coming to a new country to reunite their families?

Increasingly restrictive immigration policies reinforced the ideology of the eugenics movement and the belief that the human race could be improved through genetics and breeding—by admitting the right kinds of immigrants and keeping less desirable ones out. One headline from the *New York Times* in 1921 read: "Eugenists Dread Tainted Aliens; Believe Immigration Restriction Essential to Prevent Deterioration of Race Here."

By 1924, amendments to the Chinese Exclusion Act had effectively banned all immigration from China and other Asian nations.[1] The law was not repealed until 1943 (after being on the books for sixty-one years), when the US needed China as an ally against the Japanese during World War II. In one fell swoop, the Chinese became our friends and the Japanese our enemies. We carted off our own citizens, Japanese Americans, made them leave behind family homes and businesses, their entire livelihoods, and put them in thinly disguised prisons called "internment camps." These are the histories the victors don't want us to study so that we won't recognize the fact that history gets repeated again and again.

The conversation around immigrants in this country has revolved around the question "Who is fit for our society?"[2] That question naturally lends itself to a binary, often schizophrenic, perception of immigrants—which is why we are always having a conversation about "good" immigrants versus "bad" immigrants. When immigrants are convenient and beneficial to our economy or political agenda, we use the words *hardworking, deserving, courageous,* and *freedom-loving.* When our economy dips and jobs are suddenly scarce or we hear too many people speaking languages other than English on the street and "our way of life" seems threatened by "the other," immigrants become *menacing, criminal, contaminated,* and *a drain on society.*

In 1962, my family moved to Los Estados Unidos at a time when the country was once again redefining its relationship with immigrants. President John F. Kennedy, the grandson of Irish Catholic immigrants, embodied a new perspective when he spoke about the pilgrims and immigrants in the same breath: "The endearing qualities of Massachusetts—the common threads woven by the Pilgrim and the Puritan, the fisherman and the farmer, the Yankee and the immigrant—are an indelible part of my life, my convictions, my view of the past and my hopes for the future."

His deep connection to his own Irish Catholic roots and his keen sense of identification with the other and the outsider led JFK to pave the way for the Immigration and Nationality Act of 1965, legislation that would finally repeal the quota system instituted in the 1920s. The US was also looking for skilled workers—people like my father, who were experts in their field, brilliant professionals who could maintain the country's competitive edge in science, technology, and business.

It turns out that my mother's unexpected pregnancy and my subsequent arrival in this world had everything to do with my family's decision to leave Mexico. With three kids, my dad might have been able to piece together a professional life in Mexico, but with a fourth?

My dad, Raúl Hinojosa, was a huge nerd. Born in 1932, he grew up in the then-small city of Tampico with his two sisters, his mom, and my abuelito, a Mason bureaucrat with a ranch with cows and horses outside of town. Tampico was an oil and port city that smelled like shellfish and tar. It had tropical heat and the university didn't have air-conditioning, but still my dad spent all of his time in the musty libraries reading medical books about surgery and the inner ear.

Soon Raúl was a small-town boy living in the big city all alone, the first in his family to go to college, and now he was in medical school. His parents didn't really understand his big sueño of becoming not just a doctor, but a doctor who doesn't even see patients and instead does research. He was not as cosmopolitan as the young men from Mexico City who were his fellow students, nor was he a partier. But one night, some of his medical school friends invited him to a low-key gathering in the Colonia Narvarte and he decided to go, surprising even himself that he had said yes.

The party was for my mom's older sisters and their friends, but she often tagged along. Berta was the youngest person there at only sixteen, but she needed to be the center of attention, to be seen by everyone. When Dad walked in, she was dancing. Smiling. He spotted her immediately. He liked that she seemed unafraid as she swung her hips in her black-and-white polka-dot wraparound dress.

Raúl asked her to dance and Berta was immediately smitten. Who was this dark, handsome man with a black mustache and skin that looked like he had just come from the beach?

By the second time he saw her, at a chaperoned visit to the blue house on La Calle Pitágoras, Raúl knew he was in love. Berta liked Raúl, but she had other suitors, some of them from very wealthy families, and that was part of what Berta understood, at her young age, that marriage was about: a smart, strategic decision often not based on love. A family decision.

In the days after he met her, Raúl was suddenly doing things he never imagined he would. He gathered all of the money he could spare and went to Plaza Garibaldi in downtown Mexico City, the plaza of the for-hire mariachi bands, and hired the best one he could afford. Together, they all went to La Calle Pitágoras and, in the early morning light, Dad stood under the front window of the blue house with a bouquet of flowers while the mariachis played the trumpets as loud as they could and the sun came up over the mountains in the distance.

Berta jumped on her bed, unable to contain her excitement during this singular moment—going from deep sleep one minute to suddenly having a band of a dozen men playing their instruments and singing their hearts out just for her in the next.

Berta knew that once she pulled back the curtain from her bedroom window overlooking the band (an act of acknowledging and therefore accepting the serenade) that it was almost certain that Raúl would propose to her soon after. She had found the man she loved, and her life was going to change in an instant.

In those first busy years of their marriage, Berta and Raúl had two kids and went to Europe. Soon after, Raúl accepted fellowships at Harvard, Johns Hopkins, and finally, the University of Chicago. Research scientists around the world had begun to hear about his work and his ideas about studying the temporal bone as a clue to restoring hearing.

Mom and Dad were the first in their families to leave Mexico, and were learning about the world together. It always frustrated my father that in order to be respected and given the resources he needed to continue his research he had to leave his homeland. It bothered him deeply that he felt like his own country didn't love him as much as other places.

To support his wife and, now, four kids, Raúl was teaching to pay the rent, along with seeing patients in a clinic (the thing he did not want to be doing anymore), and then, when everyone was asleep, he would drive back to his laboratory and spend hours into the night looking into his microscope and writing up his research. He could not lose this edge, he would say to himself on the cool nights driving through the thick, moonlit palm trees of the Colonia Roma and Narvarte. He could not drown in taking jobs here and there just to pay the rent.

Raúl's forehead was increasingly shriveled like the prunes he ate every night. He worried about paying bills all the time. It was Berta who convinced him to finally say yes to the University of Chicago. She read every single letter stamped from Chicago, and as she did, her mouth would start to hang open. They were offering Raúl a full-time position in an established ENT laboratory with a solid salary, and they would pay to relocate him and his family. But there was one major hitch that Raúl had not banked on. And it was this that made him keep saying no.

In order to take the job, the university explained, Raúl would have to become an American citizen right away. He would have to pass the test, of course, but because of his extraordinary abilities, he would be fast-tracked. In order to do this, he would have to give up his Mexican citizenship. Practically speaking, this was like asking Raúl to cut out his heart and hand it to the United States like some twisted proof of gratitude.

Choose your passion and your future or your country and the past. Imagine him handing over his Mexican passport to someone at the American Embassy!

Raúl did not want to go through that humiliation.

"No, Berta," he would say. "I'm not going to do it. ¡Yo soy mexicano! ¿Cómo se les ocurre?" (How can they even suggest it?)

Raúl stayed up many nights with his borderline migraine headaches and ran this proposal through his head on long walks in the city he now considered his home—his crazy, colorful, tormented, and yet loving Ciudad de México. He had just found his footing as a city man and now these people had the audacity to ask him to not only leave his country but leave behind his nationality and heritage?

There was no name for brain drain back then, but this is what it looked like. The United States was willing to bring the best to their country from anywhere. Emma Lazarus was speaking to the masses, but this was not about the tired and weary being invited to safety. This was a country hungry and betting on the future, and another country, Mexico, acting like modernity and competing with the rest of the world didn't matter.

I imagine the tens of thousands of immigrants, just like my dad, who took similarly long walks in the night to make the decision to leave their birthplace behind, a thing that can feel more terrifying than exciting. In 1960, the year my dad arrived, 265,398 people immigrated to the US and became legal residents. These were 265,398 people detangling themselves from their past and trying to plant new roots in the United States.

On the mornings after his sleepless nights, Berta could swear that Raúl had lost more hair overnight. He was becoming fully bald in plain sight because of the stress. His constant anxiety about the future was his biggest character flaw and emotional handicap. And every day there was no escaping it because of his other Achilles' heel: his stubbornness.

No me voy. I'm not going. I'm not leaving Mexico, he would tell Berta, in an even more serious tone than usual; he would not leave and become an American. Berta was having a hard time hiding her disappointment.

She laid out all of the arguments why going made sense. He was getting a chance to do the thing he was passionate about and get paid for it. He would be able to support his family with one job, not three. And we would all be together in a modern and advanced city in a beautiful neighborhood called Hyde Park. Raúl would have to become a citizen, but everyone else would get green cards and be able to keep their Mexican citizenship. We could come back to Mexico every year.

After almost eight months of courtship, on the day that President Mateos confirmed that the research hospital where Raúl dreamed he might one day work would not be built, Berta convinced Raúl to say yes to the University of Chicago. It was his dream job, if not in his dream country.

———————

Flying was for the rich. Instead, Raúl took the bus from Tampico, where he and Berta had moved temporarily to save money, and crossed the border in Matamoros by foot with his Mexican passport stamped with an official US visa from the university. Then, in Brownsville, Texas, he caught a direct bus and headed up through Texas toward Chicago.

Once Raúl got to the Brownsville bus stop he immediately boarded and off they went on the flat, brown roads of southern Texas. Dad had never traveled this way in the US and had never traveled through Texas by land, so he was at first excited to see the landscape, but then bored by the sameness of the view outside his window. Hours later the bus made its first stop on the US side of the border, still in Texas. When Raúl got off and made his way to the bathroom off to the side of the gray gas pumps, he was suddenly confronted with the original sin of this country.

In the back of the small station there were two bathroom doors, but it wasn't one for men and one for women. Here, above each rickety door, was a sign painted on a wooden panel hanging by a rusty nail. One sign said WHITE. The other said COLORED.

Raúl sighed. Was he white or colored? And if he wasn't one or the other did he even exist in this country?

The question humiliated and disgusted him.

He knew he was not white, which in my dad's mind meant American: "gringo," blond hair, blue eyes.

And he had never heard of this word *colored*. What did it mean?

Obviously it meant anyone who was not white.

He had heard people use another word, Negro, but negro in Spanish meant "black," and while he wasn't black, he also wasn't white.

He was confused. And upset. Angry.

Instead of just being on a journey to make his scientific research dreams come true, he realized he might also be on a journey of erasing who he was in order to assimilate to the norms of this strange country. In Mexico, Raúl was respected and looked up to as a man of honor and success. But in this country, he was reduced to the color of his skin whenever he needed to use the bathroom? How degrading could this modern nation be?

If he felt invisible at this very moment as a medical doctor, how would his wife and kids feel here? Respected? Or would their youngest daughter end up internalizing all of her father's insecurities, which now ran through his body like an electrical shock wave? At the desolate bus station Dad realized he needed to make a decision. So, in an act of self-preservation or complicity or fear, but one that also felt deeply deceitful, my father chose privilege and walked into the "white" bathroom.

In that moment, he realized he didn't fit in this country, and that maybe he never would. Whiteness became an unspoken privilege that always felt like it should never have been his or ours. We were not Americans, but if we kept our mouths shut, sometimes we might be able to pass.

Chapter 2

How I Became American

In Chicago, we lived in a three-bedroom, walk-up rental in Hyde Park that became our family cocoon. We spoke Spanish, and most of the people who my parents hung out with spoke Spanish, too. As we settled into our new life in America, we clung to some traditions, while opening ourselves up to new ones.

My parents liked both neighbors the same—one was a Jewish family in which the boys wore yarmulkes and they strictly observed the Sabbath; the others were liberal psychologists from South Africa who kept copies of *Playboy* magazine on their coffee table—and so did us kids. Their kids were weird and so were we, that's the way I saw it as a six-year-old. We had been in the country only five years. I was the most American of all my family. The first years of my life had been here in the United States, in Chicago, with gray skies, frigid winters, caves and hills made of ice, steamy humid summers, black people, and Motown. Not Mexico City, with palm trees and the Popocatépetl, street vendors, and my tías and tíos and primos.

I was the youngest of four, and I was happy. I had my family unit and I had my mom, my protection. I watched her navigate being a woman in the United States. Because my siblings were in school and I wasn't, sometimes she and I had these moments together where it was just the two of us figuring out this new place. The day John F. Kennedy was shot, she and I watched the tragedy unfold on our clunky black-and-white TV set rimmed in wood. I saw Mom cry for the first time in front of a TV set showing important-looking men who spoke perfect English and were the narrators of this new country of ours that we were still trying to understand. I will never forget that the first man I ever saw cry was Walter Cronkite as he delivered the tragic news.

The six of us entertained each other at home. The only family friends we had were other immigrants—a family from Chile and another from Mexico. That was about it. Every night we shared a home-cooked meal together, all six of us. Albondigas or lengua or bistec empanizado or enchiladas de pollo, and always a glass jar with chile chipotle. I was sure no one else outside of our home knew what the words *pollo*, *tortilla*, or *chipotle* meant. The words were delicious in my mouth. When I said them I felt an ancient connection to Mexico I could not name.

My older sister and brothers had started going to school in Mexico. In the US, they were learning to perfect their English day by day, their Spanish textbooks replaced by *Dick and Jane*. The day Mom walked into the principal's office with her four Spanish-speaking kids, the principal and vice principal and the secretary actually applauded. "You are from Mexico!" they squealed. "How exciting! Welcome to our school! We now have Mexicans at our school! Welcome!"

Things made sense at school because even though there was no one else who looked like me there, my classmates came from diverse backgrounds and that made me, for some reason, feel safe. There were black and white kids along with a girl whose last name was Takeuchi and a boy named Tahir. By now I spoke English, but that didn't help me make sense of the strange things we had to do, like walk single file to the basement, put our heads against the walls, and then rest on our folded arms for something called an air-raid drill. I understood the words individually but not what they meant all together.

Our Hyde Park neighborhood was a multicultural oasis (before anyone used that term) in an otherwise intensely racially segregated city. When we left our community, though, that all disappeared. I didn't see the black faces of my neighbors and friends from school anywhere north of downtown Chicago on Lake Shore Drive.

On car rides, I would look out the right-side window and see the foreverness of Lake Michigan, its grayish-blue waves with white tops, and then through the window on my left, my eyes would land on massive, brown cement towers, twenty floors of fencing around balconies and doors. No windows. My parents told me they were called the projects. I wondered why they had no windows even though they were built overlooking this beautiful lake. It seemed like a purposeful punishment.

Linda, a classmate, and I used to walk home from school together in first grade. One day in late summer, that delicious time in the Midwest when it's warm and cool at the same time, this little Mexican immigrant girl and her friend, a little Jewish girl, hatched a plan on their walk home. Linda was carrying her empty lunch box as we made our way along Fifty-Fifth Street. I was carrying my button-down bunny sweater perfectly folded in my arms.

It was 1968. A man by the name of George Wallace, the popular governor of Alabama, was running for president. He was a Democrat who supported segregation, but left the party to run on his own independent ticket. When he won his first governorship in 1962, he famously declared, "Segregation now, segregation tomorrow, segregation forever." The country knew him as the man who stood in the doorway at the University of Alabama to block three black college students from registering for classes in 1963. That's when his famous scowl ended up on the front page of all the papers. It was an unforgettable image because he looked like an angry, growling dog. I remember seeing real dogs, too; German shepherds pulling on their leashes held by bullying white police officers. I didn't need words to understand the hatred on his face.

In his eyes I saw the images of black people, my neighbors, bodies up against a wall, water from hoses pounding onto the backs of teenage girls who were my sister's age. They got tossed and turned against the wall. The hoses never missed their human targets, aimed so precisely like water cannons. Only a man filled with hatred could do this to people simply because they were different from him.

In the aftermath of the assassination of President John F. Kennedy, the country was in a vulnerable place. Politicians fed on voters' fears that the country was descending into chaos, threatening the stability and safety of middle-class life. Wallace never called himself a racist, but he peppered his speeches with dog whistles that appealed to white southern voters who felt that civil rights were an attack on their way of life—his presidential campaign slogan was "Law and Order." NBC News correspondent Douglas Kiker, who reported on Wallace's campaign, observed, "It's as if . . . George Wallace had been awakened by a white, blinding vision: they all hate black people, all of them. They're all afraid of them, all of them. Great God! That's it! They're all Southern! The whole United States is Southern!"[1] Wallace had made it clear which side he stood on in a country that was still fighting against the outcome of the Civil War a hundred years later.

That day on our way home, we talked about where we would hide if George Wallace was elected president. "My basement is nicer, but yours is much bigger," Linda said in a matter-of-fact tone for a six-year-old. Linda lived in one of the tallest buildings in Hyde Park at the time with about eighteen floors. Our three-floor walk-up sat in the shadow of their building.

"I think we should do mine. It's going to get crowded if we stay at yours. And mine is easier to get in and out of, for food and stuff." We both knew that because we had played games down there: hide-and-go-seek, "show me yours," indoor kickball when it was raining.

"Okay," said Linda. "Let's not tell anyone. Not yet."

"I hope he doesn't win," I said.

"Me too," she said. "I hate him."

"Me too. I hate his guts," I said with emphasis because I was the older one.

It didn't come up again and he didn't win. But the damage had been done. Wallace won more votes than anyone expected him to and demonstrated that divisive politicking could work; his campaign inspired a large number of conservative Democrats to leave the party, who later became known as Reagan Democrats.

Of course, Mom and Dad had no idea I had a secret plan to keep my family safe. I had to take care of them because I was the one who understood this place. A place I needed to learn to protect myself from.

Dad wore his lab coat with pride. On the left side, in delicate, hand-embroidered red lettering was my father's name: Dr. Raúl Hinojosa, MD. It even had the accent over the *u* in Raúl. As a little girl, I knew that the reason I was in this country had everything to do with that lab coat, that crisp, almost uncomfortably starched white coat that my father loved because it defined him.

In fact, my dad was part of the opening of this country toward some immigrants. It was the University of Chicago that wanted him and so, like a basketball player, he was drafted. And it was the university that applied for and processed our green card applications. They did it all because my dad was a highly skilled immigrant. This kind of pawn they wanted.

Only three years after we immigrated to the US, Lyndon B. Johnson successfully pushed the Immigration and Nationality Act (INA) of 1965, also known as the Hart-Celler Act, through Congress. This sweeping immigration reform bill, which President Kennedy had laid the groundwork for before he was assassinated, overturned the decades-long national origins quota system that had been put in place in 1924 by the Johnson-Reed Act. The restrictive quota, which only granted immigration visas to 2 percent of the total population of each nationality present in the US as of the 1890 census, favored Western and Northern European immigrants and made it nearly impossible for people from Asia, Africa, the Middle East, Eastern Europe, and Latin America to immigrate in meaningful numbers. For example, in the 1950s, more than half of all immigrants were European and only 6 percent were Asian. With the passage of INA, the quota system was abolished and replaced with a preference system based on family relationships and professional skills and education.

The legislation was an important turning point in America and a moment of opening toward outsiders. My family didn't know that there was an ebb and flow to this American immigration fairy tale. They didn't know about the various anti-Chinese, anti-Jewish, anti-Italian, anti-Irish, and anti-Mexican waves when we were called wops (without papers) and greasers and ungrateful infiltrators. Anti-immigrant feeling was and has been a naturally occurring, cyclical phenomenon in this country. It's not a Republican or Democrat thing; it's an American thing (until we decide it's not).

For example, immigration to the US surged from 1880 to 1914, with more than 20 million immigrants arriving in a country that had a population of only 75 million.[2] A majority came from Italy, Russia, and the Austro-Hungarian Empire, and they were poorer and less educated than earlier arrivals from Northern and Western Europe. This eventually lead to a backlash against immigrants and the strict quota system that was put into place in the 1920s, pausing immigration from everywhere except Western Europe.

When the economy plummets, the rhetoric and policies against immigrants are usually not far behind. During the Great Depression, President Herbert Hoover announced a national program called "American jobs for real Americans." Local laws were passed that prohibited companies from employing people of Mexican descent, even citizens; Mexican Americans and immigrants who did not have the proper documentation were detained and deported; public raids amplified the message to motivate others to leave of their own accord.[3]

But World War II sent all the able-bodied American men overseas and the US once again found itself hungry for immigrant labor. In 1942, the Bracero Program was launched, recruiting millions of Mexican "guest workers" to do low-paying, backbreaking agricultural jobs.[4] The good immigrant/bad immigrant narrative comes and goes with the tide. After nearly forty years of restrictive quotas on immigration, big change was on the horizon in the 1960s.

The mood around INA, however, was tempered to appease the fear that foreigners might suddenly overrun the country. President Johnson attempted to play down the change it would bring—"The bill that we sign today is not a revolutionary bill," he pronounced. "It does not affect the lives of millions. It will not reshape the structure of our daily lives."[5] In actuality, the law had an immediate and dramatic impact on immigration. The number of green card holders rose from 297,000 in 1965 to an annual average of 1 million by the 1990s. My family had simply been ahead of the curve when we arrived in the US in 1962.

As for Dad, he loved everything about his work, except the country he was doing it in. He smiled all the time in his public interactions and was very kind to everyone, albeit serious, but he was only fluid and relaxed and full of easy laughter in Mexico. Still, here he was looking at molecules, at the tiniest of particles of humans, without having to understand much else about them, and that brought him not joy but total ecstasy.

If he wasn't looking into the electron microscope, slicing temporal bones, he was in his office writing the grants to do this work. His research was so cutting-edge that the National Institutes of Health (NIH) consistently funded Dad, and that's why he had to become an American citizen after five years. But the insecurity of his position came with a huge cost. Every three years, Dad would almost develop an ulcer worrying about his grants getting funded. Every three years it was heartache in our home as Dad waited to hear about grant approvals. More than once, we talked about leaving Chicago if grants didn't come through. The university had lured him there, but it hadn't once discussed tenure with Dad. We lived grant to grant.

Berta wondered to herself why the University of Chicago didn't offer him tenure and security. But if she harped on this at all with her husband, it might not be long before he would probably say that they should just leave the United States altogether.

Everyone back in Mexico teased Dad for becoming an American citizen. They said he had turned his back on his country, a vendepatrias—literally, a man who sells his country. They called him a gringo and a gabacho.

Dad understood them. He understood their love/hate for this country. Since that first day at the Texas bus stop when he had to choose a bathroom, Dad had witnessed so many other versions of the same thing. This was the shameful part for Dad. If he was a citizen of the United States, he had to own the bad along with the good.

Distrustful of America as he was, Papi still found things about his new country that he loved and embraced. Over our first eight years in the United States, little by little Dad had saved enough money to make one of his lifelong dreams come true: buying a new car. A green Dodge station wagon, to be precise.

By now it was 1969. Saigon had fallen, soldiers were dying in Vietnam, activists were challenging sexism and war, and every day the country felt like it was being shaken from the stupor of imperialism and racism. But for the Hinojosa clan in the immediate term, the new car altered many things. It was mobility for us as we drove fearlessly through Chicago at thirty-five miles an hour and watched segregation manifest across the city.

We learned about who we could become in this country by getting out and about. And so, on many weekends, the six of us would climb aboard our alligator-green station wagon and sail along the smooth highways to the arboretum to admire the trees that changed colors with the seasons, or to the Field Museum of Natural History to stare in awe at the dinosaur bones, or to the Oriental Institute, where we examined texts from the cradle of civilization.

We made regular trips to Pilsen, the Mexican barrio on Eighteenth Street, a place that became so familiar it was an extension of our third-floor cocoon. We were welcomed by the rhythm of rancheras and the warm scent of chicharrón. When Mom two-stepped in, the butchers, cashiers, and clerks addressed her as usted, and while I didn't understand it, I liked it. They called her Señora Berta and welcomed her in a singsong Spanish that I struggled to keep up with. The flirting was low-key, but even as a child, I caught the smiles, the winks. Mom grinned back, her eyes made up perfectly with her jet-black Maybelline pencil.

One time on another shopping trip, we drove even farther west from Chicago to a suburb called Cicero, where no one was black or Mexican. This stood out to me as different. My mom and dad, como si nada, sauntered in like they belonged in this all-white neighborhood. As usual, Mom and Dad were speaking Spanish in the market aisle while pushing a cart, talking over me as I walked between them.

Suddenly, I felt like we were in a circus and everyone was looking at us. I was horrified. Why did I feel this way? I told them to stop. My mom responded with a mini-slap upside my head.

"No seas tonta," she said. She had never called me stupid before and so I never forgot it. I made a mental note to never say anything about feeling ashamed about speaking Spanish.

There was also the slow realization that there were more of us Spanish speakers in Chicago. Puerto Ricans and Colombians and Venezuelans and Chileans and Argentinians. And so many Mexicans. And there was also this other group of people I was a part of. The group that had moms and dads who spoke with thick accents. People from all over the world who didn't speak English at home, and who, like us, were born someplace outside of the United States. They were everywhere in our neighborhood because of the university. They were Dad's coworkers from India, Korea, Japan, and Spain, and my mom's best friends, one who was from Uruguay, and another, Slava, who had a tattoo on her left inner forearm, a child survivor of Auschwitz. My mother told me never to stare at it, but I did. I couldn't help it.

In her thick accent, Slava talked to my mom about how lucky she felt that the US let her in. Twenty-five years prior, she explained, the United States had turned away many refugees. In 1939, her friends had been on the SS *St. Louis*, a luxury ocean liner that had left port in Hamburg, Germany, with nine hundred Jewish, mostly wealthy, passengers. They were among the last to leave, in part because they would lose all of their assets if they left Germany, and in part because they never thought the Nazis would come after them—the blond-haired, wealthy, assimilated Jews. But they had. They paid a lot of money to buy those boat tickets, but once they crossed the Atlantic, they were denied entry, first by Cuba, and then by the US and Canada.

After being at sea for several weeks, the passengers were sent back to Europe, where, through the persistent and unrelenting insistence of the ship's captain, as well as American Jewish allies, they were taken in by a number of nations including Belgium, Britain, France, and the Netherlands. For many of them, refuge was short-lived; the Nazis surged into most of these countries, and ultimately, 250 of the original 900 passengers died during the Holocaust.

People from all over the world were a part of my American life on the South Side of Chicago, which was likely an outgrowth of immigration reform. In 1965, 84 percent of the US population was of European descent, while Latinos only accounted for 4 percent and Asians were just 1 percent. The following years saw new waves of immigrants, often highly educated and skilled, arrive from China, Mexico, India, the Philippines, Vietnam, El Salvador, Cuba, South Korea, the Dominican Republic, Guatemala, and more. By 2015, Latinos made up a whopping 18 percent of the population and Asians another 6 percent. That change wouldn't have been possible without INA.

In fact, the idea of "Hispanic"—a people united by their Spanish-speaking heritage—was not conceived of until the mid-1970s, when the National Council of La Raza and others began lobbying the Census Bureau to create a category that would more accurately account for people from Latin America. The 1980 census was the first to include the term *Hispanic*, with options to check off further subcategories such as Mexican, Mexican American, Chicano, Puerto Rican, Cuban, and others. Before this, Mexicans and Puerto Ricans had been counted as white. Activists used the new data from the census to advocate for funding for job-training programs and social services, while the media took this data to blue-chip corporations to demonstrate the buying power of "Hispanics" as a consumer group. For better or worse, we now had a name, and that meant the government could keep all kinds of tabs on us.

Chapter 3

Is This What Democracy Looks Like?

Mexicans had long been considered outsiders who were expendable. According to William D. Carrigan and Clive Webb, between 1848 and 1928, at least 597 Mexicans were lynched in the United States. Anti-Mexican hatred has many roots. Some say it started in California during the Gold Rush because Mexican miners had more experience and were more successful than white miners. Between 1910 and 1919, Texas Rangers killed potentially thousands of Mexican and Mexican Americans and took their land, just like that. The Zoot Suit Riots of 1943 witnessed hundreds of US servicemen violently attacking Mexican and nonwhite youths on the streets of Los Angeles for dressing the way they wanted to, in zoot suits—"a swaggering subversion of middle-class conservatism first popularized by black jazz musicians."[1]

Signs popped up in the 1950s and '60s. NO DOGS. NO MEXICANS.

We had been invisible. Now we were animals.

More open immigration laws had ushered in an increase in people crossing without papers or official permission, which many understood as a misdemeanor that was rarely enforced. Industries were sending out recruiters to towns across Mexico spreading the word that there was work in El Norte and helping many to make the move.

President Richard Nixon seized upon this fear of the other and used it to justify his "war on crime." In 1968, he launched Operation Intercept and sent thousands of federal agents down to the southern border to search suspected drug traffickers who they believed were fueling the uptick in marijuana use. Agents primarily targeted Mexicans and movement between the US-Mexico border slowed nearly to a standstill. Large-scale raids and deportations were implemented in Mexican communities, which contributed to the 2,014,334 deportations under Nixon's watch—a huge increase compared to 740,175 people deported while Johnson was president. On January 2, 1971, Nixon signed into law the Omnibus Crime Control Act of 1970, which officially paved the way for stricter enforcement of US borders and immigration.

That same year, the *Los Angeles Times* ran an editorial that used the word *wetback* in its headline. *Wetback* was a commonly used term back then; President Dwight D. Eisenhower had even named his campaign to deport Mexicans in the 1950s Operation Wetback. But a group of Chicano law students at UCLA balked at what they saw as a racial slur and wrote to the paper to propose the adoption of the term *illegal alien* instead. The new term stuck and could increasingly be heard on the lips of politicians and newscasters in the 1970s.[2]

I must have been in high school when the term first came into my consciousness, but I focused on the part that was me. I was an alien as per the government definition. I was used to presenting my green card and passport at the border for inspection whenever we drove back from Mexico from our annual trip there. One time I found myself examining the green card more closely, staring into the faint, squiggly lines printed on it to prevent counterfeiting, and read the words *Resident*

Alien. I squinted and then scoffed. *How ridiculous*, I thought. *Whoever wrote this must be old and completely out of touch. Resident alien* was not something that described me in the least. I could never have imagined that, as an older woman, I would finally realize people were and are still looking at us—immigrants—as aliens. I didn't know then that the word *alien* can be traced back to the very beginning of our country's history. The Naturalization Act of 1790, which President George Washington himself approved, stated that American citizenship could be granted only to an "alien" who is a "free white person." When the Chinese started coming to the US in the 1850s, many called them "celestials"—beings so foreign they appeared to be from another planet.

––––––––––

One day, Mom said, "Raúl, there is an apartment for sale and I want you to come and look at it with me." Mami was asking Dad to commit to Chicago. To the United States.

Dad worried about putting down stakes. Mom saw something else.

A home. Something permanent. Dad was skeptical during the entire apartment tour—until they got to the final room of the massive 3,500-square-foot, four-bedroom apartment. Inside the room was a brand-new study with wooden shelves on all four walls. Not even Mom knew that Dad had wanted a room like this his whole life. In Tampico, alone in his bedroom in high school, he dreamed of a study like this one, with shelves for all of his books. He looked at my mom and said yes.

Mom had convinced Dad again. There was no dreaming here. This was understanding that owning something not only grounded us as a family but also that my parents were playing into the economic power dynamic in their new country. Staying in America, putting down roots in this country, despite the disrespect and constant low-grade fear about our second-class status, meant we would always have more money to return home with—more money than my dad could ever make in Mexico—as much as it meant an investment in the United States.

Berta was making a savvy business decision, but when she was alone with her thoughts in the middle of the night, she would think about Mexico. Things were getting ugly in the US, but they were way uglier in Mexico when just two years earlier the government had massacred nonviolent student protesters in what became known as La Noche de Tlatelolco and then tried to pretend like it never happened. Those would be the moments when Berta would feel small and lonely thinking about Mexico. She was torn because, in her new country, they were killing political leaders. But then she would think about her kids, how happy and settled they were, their perfect English, her many friends in Hyde Park from all over the world.

When I asked Mom in 2019 about making the decision back then to buy an apartment in the middle of so much political, racial, and economic uncertainty, she said, "Well, back then they assassinated politicians. It was targeted violence. It's different from what's happening now, which is terrorism against immigrants and Latinos and Mexicans because the threat is everywhere and it can happen anytime to any of us who look or sound different."

We didn't have any extra money, so we bought the apartment as is, and it had just been remodeled by an Iranian doctor and his wife. The apartment was high 1970s modern with a touch of Middle Eastern wealthy kitsch. The living room had gold wallpaper and the dining room had this strange dragon motif in dull shimmer green. And then the kitchen was just insane.

One woman who was looking to buy the place before us walked into the kitchen and ran out with a migraine. The wallpaper in the kitchen was like walking into an exploding bouquet of red, pink, blue, green, purple, and yellow flowers that looked as if they were drawn by a six-year-old, in lots of circles around one bigger circle. It was so over-the-top that it was disconcerting.

My mom loved the fact that we would have an eat-in kitchen. Damn that wallpaper. We would not paint over it. We would use it as a badge of honor. If you can't take this color, then maybe you can't take us.

It was in the kitchen with the crazy wallpaper as our backdrop that we would spend most of our time together as a family around a table for six. And now that we could, we became that thing we feared. A family that watched TV during dinner. Mexican families, *our family* in Mexico, did not have TV sets in their kitchens, much less in their dining rooms. What could be more offensive and more gringo than that?

From the TV, my middle-class Mexican immigrant family learned about a Mexican guy named Cesar Chavez, who picked crops on the other side of the country and now was organizing workers and asking people to stop buying grapes in Chicago to support farmworkers (and also to not buy Gallo wines), and so we did. We started boycotting grapes immediately.

There were times I stood up to watch the TV and held my face so close to the twelve-inch screen that I could see all of the little light bubble particles that made up the back of the screen. The colorful lightbulbs and twisted wires hypnotized me.

Watching TV became my private little ritual. Before we would sit down for family dinner, I would watch the evening news. As a little girl I saw the bloodied and mangled bodies and busted-up heads of the soldiers in Vietnam being carried on stretchers through the jungle and loaded into helicopters. I saw police lift their wooden batons and come down with all of their might on the skull of someone who looked like my own brother. I remember standing there in 1973 with my face glued to the TV set, watching as La Moneda in Santiago, Chile, went up in flames with President Salvador Allende inside of it.

60 Minutes changed our lives. On Sunday nights at 6:00 p.m., we watched the news program as we were eating dinner. It was family time with disturbing headlines about Vietnam, wounded soldiers, war in the Middle East, or bombings in Belfast.

There was corruption in the government. And there was Woodward and Bernstein and Deep Throat and the Pentagon Papers. At our dinner table, we talked about politics and what we called police brutality, local politics, Mayor Richard Daley and his Chicago machine—the words *fascism* and *racism* came up a lot. We talked about the news around the world and in Hyde Park and everywhere in between. In Spanish and English.

On *60 Minutes*, every report was more riveting than the one before it. Watching them made me believe in this country and made me love journalists for their service, for challenging the people in power. We became a news-consuming family, and that defined us as an American family. We were awake and informed, and that is what you do in this country, we understood. Because in order to participate in democracy, we had to know what was going on.

And yet, as a Mexican immigrant family, we were invisible. Aside from Cesar Chavez and the United Farm Workers, we never saw anyone that looked like us on TV. The newsrooms that were making choices about what to air and what to talk about and how to talk about it at that time in the turbulent 1960s and '70s were largely made up and led by white men with class privilege and private educations.

I looked for myself everywhere. I was twelve years old when I remember watching *American Bandstand* every Saturday at noon after my morning babysitting job. I would scan the dancing teenagers in the crowd—all these young hippies and *Brady Bunch* girls. The prime-time drama *Julia*, starring Diahann Carroll, featured a black woman

who played a nurse, and for a minute, women of color and their ubiq-
uitous power was seen on TV screens everywhere. The show lasted
only three seasons, ending in 1971, but I felt like Diahann was mi tía.

I insisted that my sister take me with her and her boyfriend to
watch the prime-time TV premiere of *West Side Story* with all of her
friends. I could also chaperone my sister (to satisfy my dad) so that she
wouldn't be alone with her boyfriend the whole night.

I tingled with anticipation. For me, *West Side Story* mixed something forbidden with romance. I had heard there were a lot of men
dancing in provocative ways, swinging their hips, though less jerky
than Elvis Presley. The men who danced that way spoke Spanish
like I did. When the women appeared, all of them sounded like my
mom and looked like my tías in Mexico. But it was also a cultural
milestone—a story about race, violence, and interracial love was being
aired on national television to millions of Americans. All my classmates would be watching it.

Their neighborhood with fire escapes and clothes hanging out to
dry reminded me of Eighteenth Street, but I'd never heard anyone
speak about gangs in Chicago's Mexican barrio. Not the carnicero or
the people from the tortillería. Not yet. But the characters sounded like
my family, and the star of the whole thing was Maria. Then the most
magical thing happened: Tony, a white boy, falls in love with Maria.

"Maria! / I've just kissed a girl named Maria / And suddenly I've
found / How wonderful a sound / Can be!" A white boy could fall in
love and kiss a girl like me, a girl named Maria? Was I the Maria from
the movie?

"Maria!" He kept saying my name over and over again. "I'll never
stop saying Maria!" I was in ecstasy. Finally, I saw myself reflected and
represented in popular media. And everyone else was seeing it, too.
It didn't matter that I had no other on-screen role models to fashion

myself after or that Natalie Wood wasn't actually Latina (they'd used orange pancake makeup to make her darker). It was uplifting and deeply confusing at the same time. In reality, a Mexican immigrant from Chicago had nothing in common with a Puerto Rican American citizen from Hell's Kitchen in Manhattan except speaking Spanish and her name.

Chapter 4

Nowhere to Hide

Once I hit puberty, my hormones took over. The music on the radio sounded like it was dipped in pheromones. Earth, Wind & Fire had their hit "Reasons" with its orgasmic a cappella high note midsong, Marvin Gaye was singing about "Sexual Healing," and the Rolling Stones screamed out "Let's Spend the Night Together."

Berta and Raúl saw none of this nor did they hear any of it. They never understood the lyrics anyway, and I knew that beyond bringing up a boy's name here or there, kissing and touching was off-limits. I did not talk about dates. I was well behaved and polite, and I loved my family very much—but boys! They were my magnet. My be-all. My new chicle.

I was fighting with myself, a boxing battle between my heart, my head, and the hot explosion between my legs. By now, my mother had already told me the parable of the crumpled rose petal: if you had sex before marriage, it was a permanent stain on your honor, like the rips and wrinkles of a trampled flower (a theme that would later be the centerpiece of the TV show *Jane the Virgin*). Mami used another metaphor to explain it—if you breathed too closely on a mirror, a foggy smudge would remain on the mirror. Being sexually active, a slut, a putita would leave a permanent stain on your family's honor. I was enjoying this new physical experience, but it was weighed down by the thought of disappointing my father for being a gringa and my mother for being a puta by leaving a foggy cloud over the entire family because a boy was feeling me up.

And yet, most of what I knew about being a woman came from Mexico. I watched how the middle-class women there behaved, dressed, and spoke to fulfill Mexican standards of womanhood. It's no surprise, then, that I wanted to be my own version of my mami, the one who was watched and looked at during the Mexico City parties of her youth. I wanted that attention. I wanted a boy to look at me. I was convinced that no boy could like a girl who didn't exist in popular media—not on TV, not in the history books, not in the news or novels, and not in movies. My feeling of invisibility was ingrained, a part of me, something I used to judge myself against others. If I was a bad Mexican daughter, and I was an invisible American girl, did I matter?

I had been taught throughout my life that being a woman was about attracting boys. That's what I learned from my cousins in Mexico, my first role models. They weren't playing dress-up. They were dressing up for real. I saw their Holy Communion pictures, the ones of them at seven years old wearing veils like they were getting married. I wanted a veil, too. I wanted the things my girl cousins had—white frilly dresses, white lace gloves, white patent leather shoes—but I was also repelled by them. They meant so many different things to me: spending money on frivolous things like clothes and makeup; play-acting the role of a bride from a young age; becoming educated and well-rounded enough to attract a husband.

In Mexico, I watched my aunts and cousins get primed for a night out in a way I never saw my own mother do. They waxed and did manicures at home the day before. Then there was the visit to the salon the day of, with lots of hairspray. It was Mexican women who taught me the art of being coqueta, of how to flirt with life, really.

There was an unmistakable message in all of this. Mexican women were beautiful and their bodies were on display even more than in the US. Huge billboards along the Periférico (the internal beltway in Mexico City) for bras and women's underwear made me and my brother Jorge blush. The X-rated magazines in every newsstand were visible for all to see. Women, mostly nonwhite Mexicans, nursed their babies and showed their breasts in public. Mexican women were smart but also alive in their bodies.

Women there also maintained a formidable feminine power. It was in Mexico, not Chicago, where I saw women delivering the news on TV for the first time. I also heard their smooth voices on Radio Educación reading the headlines or sitting in the anchor chair on the educational television channel known as Canal Once. I got another message: Mexican women are public thinkers, change makers, beings who are not afraid to be visible and take up space.

While my mami's side of the family was ultratraditional, Catholic, and politically conservative, a small group of my relatives on my papi's side were bohemians, leftists, and artists. One uncle was a journalist and editor in chief of a well-known magazine; one cousin wore only Mexican huaraches in an act of resistance and another was working toward a PhD in anthropology. They were radicals who smoked pot and dressed like hippies. They taught me about Gandhi and Salvador Allende, about communists and socialists, and Diego and Frida. Coupled with our yearly visits to Mexico City were trips to see the ancient pyramids and countless archaeological museums. There I learned about another side of Mexico's identity and saw an alternative to the voluptuous mexicana who lives for her hombre.

The adelitas, also known as the soldaderas, were women enlisted to support Emiliano Zapata and Pancho Villa's efforts during the Mexican Revolution. They cooked for the men fighting in the war, set up camp, transported supplies, and nursed the wounded, but they also played strategic roles as spies, propagandists, and armed fighters on the front lines.[1] Their badass courage spoke to me.

The story of La Malinche further complicated this dual narrative of women in Mexico. Cast at various times as both a native heroine and "the ethnic traitress supreme," La Malinche was an Aztec woman born to a noble family, but later sold into slavery (trafficked), where she ultimately "served" the Spanish conquistador Hernán Cortés.[2] She grew to be one of Cortés's most trusted advisers; her ability to translate indigenous languages and brilliance as a political strategist became indispensable. La Malinche famously saved Cortés by informing him of Aztec plans to destroy his army, helping clinch his victory in the Spanish-Aztec war of 1519 to 1521. Her detractors accused her of betraying her own people and helping the white man to slaughter them; more scandalous was the fact that she gave birth to Cortés's child, who might have been the first mestizo person.[3] Yet it was La Malinche who had been sold by her own people, her mother no less, into slavery and delivered to the enemy. Hadn't she simply used her feminine powers and intellect to survive despite the odds stacked against her?

My poet cousin gifted me a copy of Elena Poniatowska's book *La Noche de Tlatelolco*, a graphic account of the student protest in Mexico City during the 1968 Olympics that turned into a massacre when the military showed up. The book contained Poniatowska's interviews with people who had witnessed the event, and included photos, too, many showing the faces of bloodied students. I had never read a book like that before. It made me wonder, *Where did she get the nerve to uncover and write about something like this? And why did she look like a blond-haired American?* (Her family were Polish immigrants.) These Mexican heroines, journalists, and soldiers were also my first role models.

While I understood that beauty attracted boys and that if boys saw and affirmed me, then in my mind, I existed—I also knew that I had a voice and the power to control how I presented myself. I was going to make sure that boys saw me, in both Mexico and Chicago, but on my terms.

By this time, my cousins in Mexico were already getting engaged to their first boyfriends. I cringed at the thought. Marriage? No way! The American side of me wanted to have lots of boyfriends, like Marcia on *The Brady Bunch*. I would show my cousins, who I knew looked down on me for being a gringa, not only that I was fashionable and up to speed on American pop culture, but also that I was sexually liberated (even though I wasn't) and ambitious. I didn't need to hang on to a boyfriend at thirteen so that I could marry him at seventeen. That gringa girl inside of me was running away from the traditional mexicana girl as fast as she could.

———

When I finished grammar school, the question was raised of whether I would continue on to Kenwood Academy, a public high school that was majority black, like my sister, Bertha Elena, had, or follow my brothers to the University of Chicago Laboratory Schools, an elite private school affiliated with the university. Was Kenwood going to be a place where Maria was safe and could excel as a top student? The unspoken agreement in our family was that I would be safest if I went to Lab School with my brothers. It's hard to fault my papi for wanting to "protect" his daughters, but learned and now internalized anti-blackness fed into his worst fears. Kenwood was being abandoned by people who could afford private school and I was part of that. It had to do with race, class, patriarchy, and the dangerous habit of immigrants buying into mainstream narratives.

I had proudly cut my teeth in public school by dodging fistfights and participating in air-raid drills for the coming B-2 bombers. When I left Bret Harte Elementary School, I was leaving behind eight years of formative experiences. My whole grade school class had lived through the country's racial trauma as a unit. We were together when they shot Martin Luther King Jr., a hero we had seen speak on TV. My fellow students and I hugged one another because someone we loved had died, and the word *assassination* was now part of our collective vocabulary. We were together when a man stepped on the moon and when they shot Robert F. Kennedy. We were all mixed-up, the fast learners and challenged ones. The kids who threatened to kick my ass, the kids who were poor, they were black and also white. So were the well-off kids. My classmates were also Japanese Americans, the children of Chinese immigrants, and Jewish kids.

I was thrilled at the prospect of attending Lab School. It was part of the University of Chicago campus and housed in impressive Gothic-style buildings. The student body was much smaller and close-knit, less than eighty students to a class, and many of the kids there had been attending school together since kindergarten. I understood the status that came with a spot at Lab School, which I had miraculously tested into (I had been convinced I wouldn't qualify). I also knew it meant I was leaving the street kid behind to be one of the private school kids I used to make fun of. At Bret Harte, we teased private school kids for being too wimpy to deal with Chicago public schools and gritty South Side Chicago real life.

I had believed that only the super-rich sent their kids to private schools. Early on Papi clued me in to the fact that money translates into influence in this country. He was always talking about los ricos, a term that never included us. What I hadn't realized was that the children of professors paid only half tuition, which included my dad, so that way people like us could go there. But it was lost on no one in our family that Papi would be paying three tuitions for Lab School. That meant there would be nothing left over in the budget for anything special. "We're not buying you any new clothes. That is the price tag."

I should have been elated about going to Lab School, but instead I was overwhelmed with panic and anxiety because I was convinced I wasn't going to be able to keep up. My new classmates were not only the super-rich, but the super-smart, too.

Those first days of private school, I woke up ninety minutes ahead of time at 6:00 a.m., when it was still dark out. I would wake slowly, take out my portable mirror, and just like my mami, I would arreglarme la cara—fix my face. I was fourteen, so I'm not sure what I was concealing exactly, but I always used concealer first, then brown eye shadow, plus black eyeliner pencil on my top and bottom lids lightly, with two coats of mascara after curling my eyelashes with a strange contraption. The idea was to make my features stand out, not change them, or at least that's what Mami said and this is what I also knew from my mother. That you never show your face unless it's made up. American women went out in our neighborhood without being done up. Not the women in my family. Especially when there was no one at that school who looked like me.

It was in high school that my imposter syndrome first bloomed. Each morning, fully dressed, my mod neck scarf tied just so, my tight bell-bottom jeans hugging my behind, I would sit down and eat a bowl of Cap'n Crunch cereal. Five minutes later, my nerves would take over and attack my stomach. Without anyone realizing that I was having a panic attack, least of all myself, I would quietly go to the bathroom and throw up several times before reemerging.

This went on for about two months. Every day before school I would get so anxious that I couldn't hold down any food. I told no one. Often I was too hungry in my morning classes to pay attention. I knew I had to do something to stop whatever was happening to me. I didn't know how to reach out and talk to someone about this, so I tried my best to solve my own mental health issues. I suffered through vomit-inducing anxiety and a severe inferiority complex in silence until I was able to wean myself back to a normal routine by nibbling on Cheerios I carried around with me in a baggie. I learned that status came with suffering. Going to the Lab School gave me status, but I was too sick and paranoid to enjoy it. This status could only be seen from the outside looking in, though, because inside the school I had virtually no friends.

In grammar school, I had played one of the three witches in *Macbeth*. And ever since I saw Tony singing to Maria in *West Side Story*, I played with the idea of acting. I convinced myself to try out for our high school theater production and got the main role in that year's student-directed play, *Another Way Out*. I played a French woman from the 1920s who wanted to have an open relationship with her husband and was in sexy pajamas for the entire show. I found my tribe among the theater kids, the rowdy artists, several of whom were gay or queer, not the misfits of a school that celebrates the arts, but definitely the existential artistes and counterculture kids.

Papi came to our theater and watched me sit on the lap of a boy and kiss him on the lips. He was paying money for his daughter to do this? I could tell that Papi was proud of me—he showed up, after all—but it was yet another moment of mixed emotions between us. His pride was tinged with embarrassment because his daughter was publicly displaying her sexuality. I wanted to please him, but in a profound way I also enjoyed being an iconoclast. My intention wasn't to hurt Papi but to let him know I was not a good Mexican girl. I wasn't sure why, though.

At home, our family time still centered around dinner and the evening news, and on Sunday nights, *60 Minutes*. Everywhere on television I saw men delivering the news. Papi and I would watch *Meet the Press* together. We talked politics over dinner and argued about the mistakes the Democrats or Republicans were making.

I was one of the kids who brought a sack lunch to school to save money, but on the rare occasion I ended up going down to the cafeteria, I would pass by the editorial room for the award-winning high school newspaper. I'd see the cutout columns pinned on bulletin boards as mock-ups for the paper. I eagerly waited for our witty high school newspaper to drop each week, but I never thought I was good enough to work there. That job was for American men, the little voice inside me said.

For my family, journalists were more important than Hollywood movie stars because we watched them change the course of the country. Bob Woodward and Carl Bernstein were young men when I was in high school. They had helped bring down Nixon's presidency. They were superhuman, almost gods. My classmates at the school paper were not superhuman, but they did come from some of the richer families, including one that owned newspapers. I would walk by the newspaper office and wish I had the nerve to go inside.

My new school was mostly white and focused on getting students into college, specifically the Ivy League. We had a state-of-the-art gym, swimming pool, theater, and many other amenities, but these things only served to further reinforce the idea that I didn't belong there next to my designer-clothes-wearing classmates—well, the white kids wore only the best Top-Siders, Lacoste shirts, and khakis, while the black kids dressed to the nines. Not only was I hiding my Mexicanness—I studied French instead of Spanish and I no longer wrote essays about family trips to Mexico as I had in grade school—but I was also hiding the fact that my family wasn't wealthy. The only thing that kept my imposter syndrome at bay was appreciating all the things I had now. It was me, not Mami, who would say: "Look at everything around you and see how lucky you are to be here." This feeling of indebtedness must have come from overhearing talk all the time between Papi and Mami about how tight the family expenses were. When I struggled to write papers about Joseph Conrad and Sartre for my literature classes, I told myself that I should be glad I was being so intellectually challenged. It was better than not learning anything at an underserved public high school where people like me might not be seen as having intellectual value.

The grateful Mexican immigrant—who had somehow made it into the halls of an elite institution where there were no other Mexicans— was alive and well inside me. I understood that for my parents, sending me to the Lab School was a choice. It could go away at any point. I was thankful to them for paying for me to go to school when there was a free one down the street. But this place was also crystallizing many class contradictions for me; in fact, so many that I began to understand the term *class* and everything that came with it.

Part of my life was lived in Papi's library. That corner of our apartment made me feel close to him, to his seriousness. Visual media was influencing policy in a way that hadn't been seen before. A headline might not change the course of history, but a photograph could. Despite all the news reports on the use of napalm, even when there was footage of it being dropped and the ground under the palm trees lighting up like inverse fireworks, even when people knew that children were in those villages, things didn't change. Not until we all saw the photograph on the front page of the *New York Times* of Phan Thi Kim Phúc, a little Vietnamese girl running naked toward the camera, her back ravaged and burned, napalm dripping from her delicate fingertips. As a teenage girl, I was shocked and ashamed by this image. It felt disrespectful to show a little girl, not far from my own age, in that state; I would not have wanted my flat chest and hairless vagina to be seen by the whole world. But now we knew what napalm looked and felt like. The conversation changed inside the Capitol after that, and the photographer, Nick Ut, won a Pulitzer for the image.

I was sitting in the back of our local pizza joint in the summer of 1974, eating ice cream sundaes with my brother and his best friend, when Nixon resigned live on television and the whole place erupted in applause. We had gone there on purpose to celebrate. The corruption was finally laid bare for us to see and Nixon represented it all. He was gone. And later, under President Gerald Ford, the gruesome body-count stories from Vietnam stopped and the war finally ended. Other wars raged on in faraway places like Belfast (between Irish Catholics and Protestants) and Palestine and Israel (between Jews and Arabs, Palestinians and Israelis). But the social and political unrest that had characterized the late sixties and early seventies in the US had dissipated. The soldiers were gone. The Black Panthers were gone, in part because of the FBI and COINTELPRO's infiltration. Chavez's grape boycott was over.

The TV news was no longer focusing on protests by hippies and feminists. Instead, night after night, we saw Vietnamese people. Although the story was about them, they were always in the background. Someone was always speaking for them or over them. It was as if they didn't have voices or that news executives thought that nothing they said was deemed worthy of translation. They were nameless, angry, crying. For years, the nightly news had led with stories about a war involving people we never met. Sometimes they were referred to simply as "the enemy." The student protests against the war weren't so much about fighting for the humanity of the Vietnamese people as they were about bringing American soldiers home.

As a young person watching the TV evening news religiously, the narratives were confusing. All of this turmoil in the United States, the narrative went and so it seemed to many, had been stirred up by the Vietnamese. And now they wanted to come here? In fact, some said they had the right to be in the United States. First they were the enemy. Now they were refugees. I kept hearing that the country was "full," but we actually never heard from the Vietnamese themselves. Was the US really full? Wasn't there a lot of wide-open space in the middle of the country, which I had seen traveling by car from Chicago to Mexico? I wondered about the words I had learned that were on a statue I had not yet seen with my own eyes: Isn't this what Lady Liberty was all about? Weren't we supposed to be a nation that welcomed those seeking refuge?

The entry of the Vietnamese to the US en masse was the first televised refugee crisis in history. The media had been instrumental in telling Americans how to feel about the war and its aftermath. Journalists like Morley Safer, Ed Bradley, and Ted Koppel—men who reported from the front lines in helmets and camouflage—covered the war in a way that was warlike. People could eat their TV dinners and watch American soldiers get blown up from their living rooms. News television today is much more censored and couched with trigger warnings. What we knew of the war was terrifying and no attempt was made to humanize the Vietnamese.

By the time the Vietnam War finally ended in 1975 after twenty years of combat, 58,000 US soldiers had died fighting in a war they barely understood. But that number hardly compared to the more than half a million Vietnamese, both military and civilian, who died defending their own soil. There was no official US policy on refugees at this time, but given the crisis—more than 3 million people were displaced by the war—and the country's role in it, the US agreed to evacuate and resettle 125,000 Vietnamese. By 1980, that number had risen to 231,000. Another half a million Vietnamese landed in Australia, Canada, and France.

With the Fall of Saigon came images of crowds mobbing the gates of the US Embassy, climbing over the barbed-wire walls, handing babies to strangers, and doing anything possible to make it onto the last helicopters taking off from the roof of the embassy. Others tried at sea, fleeing the Vietcong takeover in small fishing boats. American journalists labeled these desperate refugees—innocent families displaced by war—"boat people." "First Wave of Southeast Asian 'Boat People' Arrives," the *New York Times* reported in September 1977.[4] A few months later in the op-ed pages, the *Times* praised Carter's administration for allowing more Vietnamese to enter the US, but argued that the "hill people" from Laos were also in need of resettlement.[5] Boat people and hill people? Like truck people. Or car people. Should we call those waiting on the sidewalks at the border in Mexico concrete people? What's next? How else can we otherize people from different places?

Americans didn't want the "boat people" in their country. Polls done by CBS and the *New York Times* in 1979 showed that 62 percent of the country disapproved of the government's plan to increase the number of refugees admitted. California's then-governor Jerry Brown (yes, the same Governor Jerry Brown who declared California a "sanctuary state" in 2018 and passed legislation that would limit police cooperation with federal immigration authorities) was vehemently against allowing Vietnamese refugees into California, and he worked arduously—but unsuccessfully—to keep them out of the state.[6]

I remember watching news footage of shell-shocked human beings crowded onto docks somewhere in Asia. Survivors of war and torture, they now found themselves, due to government policy they had nothing to do with, living one on top of the other. Then the cameras would show one rickety boat docked next to another, a woman nursing her baby while holding the hand of a toddler in the other, an old grandma with a map of wrinkles on her face wearing a straw hat. There were other pictures of people in humiliating circumstances, wearing rags and crying—and these were the images we saw day in and day out with headlines asking, "Too Many?" Every day, journalists batted around the question of how many of "these people" to let in. Their objectivity was never questioned.

———————

It was a Saturday afternoon. At home, all was calm. I was in my bedroom finally taking down the life-sized Elton John poster that I had been too lazy to remove since eighth grade. I climbed down from my dresser and carefully rolled up the poster, kissing goodbye another moment in my American preteen life. I had borrowed my mami's old radio from the kitchen, a brown plastic one we had during our first Chicago years, the one that always sounded scratchy no matter what station it was on. And then, suddenly, I landed on a station—it must have been WBEZ 91.5 FM—and heard a voice like the ones on Mexican public radio. It wasn't an announcer or a DJ, but a journalist. Instead of yelling, he was speaking to me. Intelligently. My mind was exploding. I wanted to scream, but I needed to hear every single word and I was afraid that if I let go of the dial, the voice would disappear the way things sometimes disappeared on the radio, with the slight movement of the thumb and forefinger, then gone.

I moved slowly to bring my ear closer. They were talking about Latin America, a phrase I had only heard before in Mexico on the news in Spanish. It was like hearing Radio Educación–style radio in English in the United States and, to my surprise, they were reporting about Latin America. The experience was a revelation of sorts, perhaps spiritual. Two very different parts of myself had suddenly awakened and found themselves braided together, and now I knew what that sounded like. I knew that WBEZ existed on the dial, that at least at 2:00 p.m. on Saturdays I could tune into this place and hear this.

And so I did.

One week later, I sat in my room and played with the dial at that exact time and I found the station again. All the way to the left of the dial was my new community. This was where my ears wanted to live, listening to radio pública in English all alone in my bedroom.

At the end of my freshman year, I proved to myself and all the girls in my grade that I had arrived. My competition with them focused not so much on grades but rather on getting the boy. That's how I ended up on the phone with my first real boyfriend one night, the green curlicue phone cord stretched twenty feet from the kitchen into the dining room.

John was a graduating senior and the son of a wealthy second-generation banker. He was the star of the year-end play and, in my view, the most attractive and therefore most unattainable boy in the school. A cute, preppy white guy who wore salmon-colored Izod shirts, his sandy-blond hair with a natural flip, his lips upturned a little so he always looked like he was smiling coyly—why would that boy fall for me?

I was able to take the nausea from my early days at the Laboratory School and transform it into combustible energy. I had learned that sexiness, flirtation, and teasing were all effective with the opposite sex by watching women in Mexico. For them, it all came off so natural. The way they smiled broadly, throwing their heads back to expose their necks, or how they squeezed men on their biceps or pecked them on the cheek.

I wanted to learn how to do this, too. After some secret afternoon heavy-petting sessions in the middle of winter with a different sophomore boy, I felt more confident as an American teen. That got me to my boyfriend, John, the senior, and yet, so much of it felt like an act.

I proved to myself that I could be more American than the American girls, win at a game they didn't know they were playing with me, defy my father and mother, and distance myself from the unattainable virgin status of my cousins.

I was playing the role of a girl who liked to get down with boys, but I had no interest in getting married. I wasn't defining myself, as some other young women in my high school did, as sexually mature and in control and making decisions for themselves. I wasn't going to show off that part of myself so explicitly and be labeled "easy." Yet I didn't want to be seen as a prude.

John and I got together at the end of my freshman year. He graduated and we continued to hang out over the summer and into the fall, when he headed off to college. One frigid evening in December, my sophomore year, John and I were on the phone, hoping to make plans to see each other when he came home from college. While I played with the phone cord twisted along my middle finger, my ears were drawn to the Spanish that Mami and Papi were speaking to my brothers in the kitchen. At the sobremesa, my family was talking about our upcoming yearly trip to Mexico. We would pile into the station wagon, all six of us, the car packed so heavy the muffler would scrape in every pothole. This year we were headed to Oaxaca. We were going to sit in the main plaza on December 23 and, on La Noche de Rábanos, eat buñuelos on clay plates and then, as was custom, dash them down to the ground. All around us, everyone would be smashing plates together in the plaza, with a collective sense of awareness of one another's space, of when to break a bowl and when to wait.

It was the late seventies and people were increasingly talking about the border. President Gerald Ford's Domestic Council Committee on Illegal Aliens, which had been signed into existence in 1975 via executive order, had just delivered its report on the effects of undocumented workers in the United States. The report found that the population of undocumented immigrants had grown to nearly twice the number of people who had legally immigrated; 386,194 immigrants entered the country legally in 1975 compared to 679,252 people who were arrested or deported as "illegal aliens." The Immigration and Naturalization Service estimated there were between 6 to 8 million undocumented immigrants in the country, and the report indicated that most unauthorized immigrants came into the country through the southern border with Mexico.

The council argued that low-income Americans faced escalating competition for jobs from undocumented workers, and that a strain on welfare and other social services was likely to surge. But at the same time, they recognized that "massive deportation of illegal aliens is both inhumane and impractical," which led the council to conclude that preventive measures to block and discourage undocumented immigrants from entering the country in the first place would be the most effective course of action.

I had been crossing the border for years already. Every year we would drive from Chicago to St. Louis and to Memphis or Texarkana and then through Texas. The trip was an annual confirmation that we were not citizens. Except for Papi. His status was irrefutable. He had an American passport. The rest of us still had green cards. While we never had a problem with this fact, we also understood that getting back into the US when we crossed the Texas border would depend on the Border Patrol agent's mood.

I was reminded of how essentially powerless I was when the agent would walk away with our green cards as we waited in the car. I knew nothing about my arrival story in America at this point. The immigration agents looked tall and sounded very Texan to me. I always felt vulnerable at the border, as if my life could change with a random decision by some man wearing a uniform who was meeting me for the first time.

I was explaining to John my family's plans for the winter break—it turned out we would miss seeing each other by a few days—and that's how I got to talking about the border. I told him about having to show my green card to the Border Patrol in Texas in order to get back into the United States; how they could decide to hold us back if they wanted to.

"But you're American!" my boyfriend said.

"No, actually, I'm not. I'm Mexican," I said.

"No, you're not! You're really American! Why can't you just say so?" he insisted.

I was incredulous. John had met my family, had come over for dinner, heard us speak Spanish at the kitchen table. In Mexico, I was constantly having to prove I was both Mexican and American to my relatives. In the US, I never felt American enough, especially around my rich classmates at Lab School. How could John not see me as Mexican, one of the most essential aspects of my identity?

"Because I'm not," I finally said. "Yes, I've grown up here, but I'm Mexican. I've got a green card. I'm Mexican."

"No, you're not. You're American."

Now I was being challenged to prove my Mexicanness. How could I show him how un-American I often felt because of what I looked like and what my name was? Being binational required constant jujitsu to navigate the expectations of others, and it was exhausting. My life seemed to exist in defiance of, in relation to, in response to, either being Mexican or American, all the time. I broke up with John soon after.

In December 1977, a year after we broke up, I was sixteen and a half, I didn't have a boyfriend, and I hadn't had sex yet. I was going to spend the latter part of the month in Mexico with my parents because, as the youngest girl in the family, I had no choice where I spent my vacations. Yet my brothers were given the right of refusal and allowed to walk away from family time. Dad would never leave his daughter alone like that.

For this year's annual trip to Mexico, my parents and I would make our traditional drive in the station wagon and my sister Bertha Elena, who had graduated from Lawrence University in Wisconsin, was going to fly down for a week.

Four days of driving. Four days of just me and Mami and Papi when they were at their happiest. Once we crossed into Mexico, Papi sometimes became more serious. There could be soldiers along the roads, and he had to pay attention to the curves. Also, men stared at me. I would often stare back in defiance. Papi would get angry and say I was egging them on. Mami would say I was just a little girl, so how could I even understand what I was doing?

That year when we met up with my straitlaced tía and her daughters, I felt the noose of my Catholic, status-seeking Mexican family tighten. We were all spending Christmas together in an undiscovered, up-and-coming tourist district on the coast of Mexico. There was nothing there yet except for a tropical hippie beach club a few miles down, a huge thatched-roof open-air disco, and a bar on stilts built over the rocky shore beneath. The area where we were staying had six small bungalows on a large garden with a pool, common eating area, and kitchen.

Five minutes away, the disco music echoed off the ocean water; the pulsing beat accentuated by the moonlight. In the evenings, Mami and Papi stayed behind with the adults, but all of the teenagers went out dancing to the tunes of Donna Summer and Gloria Gaynor.

None of my primas' boyfriends were around, so they danced with one another. I had become friendly with Pablo, the twenty-four-year-old son of another family who was also visiting the bungalows. He flirted with me, and I knew how to flirt back.

Every night, our group would pile into two cars, my cousins in one, Pablo and his brother in another—they always drove separately. Most nights, the hardwood dance floor was almost empty. I danced barefoot because I didn't have to wear my heels there. My family knew my real height, so there was nothing to hide. We would order rum and Cokes, and dance in the salt air to the incessant thumping of the disco music for hours. After three nights of no adults and dancing till we were sweating, Pablo kissed me. He opened his mouth and let his tongue find mine. I found his right back, and then he grabbed my waist a little tighter. I liked the way that felt, like he was a grown man and not a sixteen-year-old boy.

The next night, in defiance of all Mexican social norms, I put my parents on the spot and asked them for permission to go alone with Pablo to see the new cabanas his family was building at the top of the hill. He wanted to show me the sunset. I forced my parents to confront their gringa daughter. Seizing on an opportunity to call out their hypocrisy and use it to my advantage, I prepared to strike. I had watched Mami celebrate how independent I was, showing me off to the conservative Guadalajara families gathered there. She didn't get to brag about all the great things I was doing as an independent American teenager and then not let me be independent. Although it was almost 7:00 p.m. and growing dark, I demanded and got Mami's permission.

I was totally into this boy and into this moment. I figured, what a way to lose my virginity. The thought of fooling around in such a romantic spot thrilled me. Pablo was nice enough, cute enough, but definitely not anything special. He was a mama's boy who still lived with his parents at age twenty-four and tagged along with them on their vacations. I'm not sure he had a job. But he was Mexican and, God, did that disco music really make me feel hot against the backdrop of the ocean, the shadows of the cliffs, and that deep blue midnight sky with the reflection of the moon. Gloria Gaynor was oh so right, I will survive.

I thought about how so many important moments in my life happened in Mexico and that having sex might now be added to the list. I calculated that I was only a few months younger than my mami when she lost hers. I wasn't focused on the fact that I knew nothing about this man. We hadn't exchanged more than twenty words.

We got in his car and he stopped at a small pharmacy on our way up to the top of the hill. While he jumped out, I took a moment to touch base with reality and think about what was happening. This boy hadn't given me a kiss in the car, and he'd barely said anything to me in the last ten minutes. I realized he hadn't made one romantic gesture toward me, not a peck, not a dreamy look, not a compliment, nothing. When he got back in the car with a brown paper bag, nothing again.

I began to get nervous. I thought I wanted this, but he seemed to have made up his mind about what was going to happen without asking me. I was a little angry that he thought he could just decide what he was going to do with me. Now I was getting exasperated and scared. I figured I could talk my way out of it and calm him down, but I definitely did not want to have sex with this guy tonight. Not for my first time.

When we got to the top of the cliff, he turned off the lights of the car. It was pitch-black outside, and I felt disoriented. I heard keys open a door. Things came slightly into focus. Inside one of the model homes his family had built to woo buyers, there was no electricity or furniture, but strangely a new mattress still covered in plastic wrap. I remember he sat me down abruptly on the bed. Then he started to kiss me. He pushed me back, and I thought for about fifteen seconds it was going to be fun, but then he became more forceful. I started to say no. And in my head, I was like, *What is going on here?* I was unable to push back.

He stopped being gentle. And I stopped being willing. What should have been a moment, a culmination of something special, turned into me being pinned down, in a dark room, on a bed with no sheets, my sensuously parted lips now feeling a tongue thrust down in my mouth. *Shouldn't I be happy that I'm about to lose my virginity? Isn't this romantic? What's the matter with me that I don't find this romantic? Am I not saying NO loud enough? This is really hurting now, no, no, no, no, no, and ouch, stop it, oh my god, it hurts! I'm burning!* And then it was over.

He rolled off of me. I didn't scream or slap him. I tried to think about how cool it was that I was no longer a virgin. But I was also in pain. I was angry and in shock. I was scared because I had been gone a long time and Mami and Papi would be upset. I was upset that I had just said no for what felt like eternity and this person didn't listen. *All boys are the same*, I thought. *But does he like me?*

How could it be wrong if I was wondering whether he liked me?

———

After the holidays, we drove back to Chicago. At school, I told my girlfriends that *it* happened, but not what really happened. I was ashamed, but I doubt anyone picked up on it. I didn't have the words for what I was feeling, so instead I didn't talk about it. And that was that.

My friends thought I took summer school classes because I was a nerd. They didn't know I took them because I was too afraid of taking tough English and politics classes during the year without failing. They thought I was a star student, but really I was just a scared one.

By the summer of my junior year of high school, I had saved enough money from my jobs as a salesperson in a jewelry store and as a waitress in the local pizzeria to pay my way to Europe. Two girlfriends and I slept on the streets of Edinburgh for fun, drinking malt beer and eating digestives. I traveled on to Paris, where I stayed on the top floor in the servants' quarters of a Uruguayan yogi widow. I was lost in so many ways. I had sex with two strangers, one in London and the other in Paris, and while it was not exactly fun, at least I wasn't saying no. I thought that was progress.

By senior year all of those dreary summer classes had added up. I had enough credits to graduate from high school six months early. I could save my dad the money for tuition, which made him happy. I would graduate in December and spend the first six months of the year studying theater and dance in Mexico City. I would live with my cool uncle and aunt, and I would finally tackle a personal challenge I had set for myself—this was the city of my birth and I had to conquer it.

For the December 1978 holidays, my brother Raúl had invited me to join him (my father trusted my older brother) for New Year's Eve on the beach in Oaxaca with some of his Mexican poet friends. One was a dancer who trained at the national Ballet Folklórico de México. I was getting closer to an image of myself as a young Mexican woman that had nothing to do with my prissy, religious cousins. The Mexican woman I was becoming was a proud mestiza, budding poet, and dancer who was fascinated by her indigenous roots and finding her own definition of feminism. It also had nothing to do with wearing a suit and being called Ms.

The fact that my brother was asking me, his little sister, to join him on an adult trip assured me that I was headed down the right path, shedding the high heels, makeup, and deodorant-wearing teen to become an earth mother, Totonacan indigenous artist. Mami and Papi liked that two of their kids had bonded, unlike the children of so many of their friends back in Chicago, where brother and sister were pitted against each other.

I brought a black sketchbook to mark the beginning of my extended stay in the mother country; it would be the longest amount of time I had been in Mexico since I was born there. Raúl and I sat in the back of a raggedy bus that drove six hours in the mountains through the night to get to the desolate coastline south of Puerto Escondido, and finally another bus to a hippie beach named Zipolite. We rented hammocks overlooking the coast and woke up with the sun.

It was New Year's Eve and the night before the one-year anniversary of me "losing my virginity," which is how I had come to refer to that night in 1977. Now here I was without a man, on a beach lit up by the stars, not disco lights. A year ago, I had been with status-hungry Mexicans who only cared about money. Tonight I was with a group of kindred spirits who were giving me a peek at the kind of adult I wanted to be. I was living in the Mexico I had imagined, hanging out with a ragtag group of anthropologists, dancers, poets, and a couple of tourists from Brussels. We wanted to be free on this New Year's Eve and we could do that on this secluded beach, smoking pot and sitting around a fire. The women went topless in the way European women always go topless on the beach. I felt so comfortable I took off my bathing suit top, too, and lay back on the sand to look up at the night sky. We thought this was the safest place on earth.

My mind wandered to the next six months of my plan to become more Mexicana. After that I might be headed to New York, since I'd sent an application off to a school there, but it felt so far away in the future, like something that might never happen. As my mescal-tainted mind floated, I thought of how I had fallen in love with Manhattan because of Woody Allen's film of the same name, and how much I loved Gershwin. I was enjoying the free association and border crossing that I always seemed to allow myself when I was at my happiest and most relaxed state of mind.

My thought bubble exploded with the *pop! pop!* of a pistol and the shine of a machete blade as two guys with bandannas tied around their mouths accosted us on the beach. The men kicked my brother and threw sand in our faces. The Belgian tourists screamed. I quickly pulled off the scarf tied around my head and wrapped it around my bare chest. Instead of raping us on this desolate beach, the men demanded our bags and wallets and then ran off with them.

When we called my parents from the police station, their words were like exploding firecrackers filled with anger and shock. *Boom!* They had trusted their son to take care of their baby girl. Instead, he had almost gotten her assaulted. *Crack!* Papi yelled at both of us, using every single word he could think of that made it clear I could have been raped without actually saying the word "rape."

"This could have been the most horrible thing," Papi said, "to have my daughter assaulted in Mexico. No man can touch my daughter here. ¡Ni se les ocurra!"

I closed my eyes and my mouth puckered as I thought, *If only you knew, Papi. If only you knew that it has already happened.*

As a result of the New Year's Eve fiasco, I would no longer be allowed to stay in Mexico for six months. The decision was final. The dream of finding my Mexican self died on the beach that night in a bloodless slaughter with a pistol and a machete.

I hadn't conquered anything about Mexico. Once more, Mexico had conquered me.

Chapter 5

Embracing a New Identity

Since I graduated from high school early and then was forced to move back to Chicago after the beach assault in Mexico, I had started waiting tables and taking acting classes, and I paid my own way to visit New York for the first time. And now here, in this dirty, crime-ridden city, I also saw what I wanted to be: an artist who performed on Broadway and then took the graffiti-covered subway home. Here was a career that called for a big ego onstage, and humility, too, when the lights went out.

I wanted to make New York City mine. And I wanted a stage. A fuerzas.

Even though I hadn't seen any Latino actors really, I was under the illusion that I could make it as a working actress. As insecure as I was as an artist, I still convinced myself that I should at least try. Plus, I had been paying for acting classes at the Victory Gardens Theater. That had to be worth something.

When I heard about the search for an actress that fit my description for a movie role, I prepared for my first major audition. I told myself that if I got the part, I would take it as a sign and tell my parents I would forgo college to start my acting career. I had worked myself up into a frenzy over this audition, convinced it was going to change my life.

The audition went fine. I didn't forget my lines and the three-person panel watching seemed interested. Then the director, a man in his late forties, asked to speak to me.

"Thank you for your fine audition. You did a good job. But I'm not sure I get you," he said as he looked at me. "You see, you're not white enough and not Mexican enough, you're not tall enough or short enough, you're not street enough but not sophisticated enough either, not light enough or dark enough—I'm sorry, but I just don't get you and I'm not sure the industry will get you, either. But thank you for trying. . . ."

His words confirmed everything that little voice in my head had always said: this gringa isn't really Mexican, she just acts like she is. I had no idea who he was or if he indeed was a big shot, but as a white male director, he represented the Hollywood establishment. I gave this stranger power over me because of that. I believed he was right. I didn't conform to what was perceived to be talented and beautiful.

Besides Natalie Wood, who wasn't actually Latina, there were very few examples for me to look to in popular media. Freddie Prinze, a young up-and-coming comedian, starred in the sitcom *Chico and the Man* from 1974 to 1977; the show was a hit but ended abruptly when Prinze took his own life. Cheech and Chong had also broken into the mainstream with their cult-classic film *Up in Smoke* in 1978, and Carlos Santana was a household name after he and his band performed at Woodstock. But they were all men and not the kind of role models I was searching for. Latinos were very much in the box, and most often portrayed as caricatures, not full-fledged people like normal Americans.

In that moment of rejection, my dream of becoming an actress began to die inside of me.

————————

When my sister, the oldest, was applying to college, she almost had to leave blood on the floor before Papi would let her go to Lawrence University in Appleton, Wisconsin, and live alone in a dormitory, away from her family in a strange city. From my father's perspective, there was no reason she couldn't go to college in Chicago or Mexico City, where we had family.

Those family fights over college happened nightly until Mami finally forced Papi to relent. My sister and then my brother Jorge both went away to school. My other brother, Raúl, lived at home and went to the University of Chicago, getting home-cooked meals throughout college. By the time I rolled around, it was a given that I was going to go away to college.

I made the craziest, most rebellious choice by moving to New York, the most dangerous city in the country, maybe in the world, to attend Barnard College. Crime was about to hit an all-time high. Murders were on the uptick with 1,733 homicides in 1979 (compare that with 292 in 2017) and robberies had skyrocketed from a previous record in 1976. "1980 Called Worst Year of Crime in City History," wrote the *New York Times* in 1981. In 1977 there had been an overnight blackout and mayhem had ensued, with people looting stores on Madison Avenue, assaulting women, and robbing apartments.

I'm not sure why I loved this ridiculously harsh place, but it didn't scare me. It reminded me of Mexico City. The pictures of the Columbia University students taking over Hamilton Hall and clashing with the police during the 1968 protests (these also reminded me of Mexico) were one of the reasons why I chose to go to Barnard, the women's college affiliated with Columbia. I wanted a campus that was engaged in the politics of the moment. I had looked up the definition of the word *radical*—it meant going to the root of things—and that was how I now saw myself. I was a pushy, radical young woman, and that's why I was going to New York City for college.

When my dream of going to Mexico, of looking south to define myself, had disappeared, I began to look east. New York was the farthest I could get from Mexico, where I had tried on different identities that both led to violent outcomes. I was going to a city that was part of the counterculture, dangerous, and gritty as a young woman all alone. I would be able to live on my own terms. Deep down, I knew that embracing New York was an intentional move to distance myself from Mexico, from societal expectations, and from Papi.

At the end of the summer of 1979, I packed up two suitcases with the clothes that would define me for the next four years. In August, I boarded a plane for New York and then got in an old yellow Checker Cab and we slow-rolled down 125th Street from LaGuardia Airport. Everything looked gray and empty and foreboding though it was the middle of the day. Almost every store was boarded up and the empty lots had piles of trash in a corner, some on fire.

Harlem looked like a more intense version of Sixty-Third Street near our place in Chicago. The neighborhood was predominantly black folk. Here the energy of the streets was electric, though everywhere you looked there were abandoned buildings, their empty windows like slices of endless darkness in a brick facade. There were many liquor stores and the occasional corner market. I saw kids playing in the street around a hydrant, squealing with glee, and then the immediately recognizable public housing complexes, architected to feel tall and menacing. We made a left turn on Broadway, drove past the gates of Barnard and Columbia, and then stopped at my women's dorm right on 116th Street—a dorm in the middle of New York City, just like I wanted.

The cab dropped me off at the lobby of a stately gray-brick building, my new home, that was buzzing with first-year students, all women, arriving for the weeklong orientation. My room was the ugliest in the entire dorm. I was on the second floor with a window that looked directly inside of the air shaft, so I heard every sound from the twelve floors above me: girls listening to the radio, arguing with their room-mates, practicing the cello. I heard it all but had no sunlight. Not one drop.

I had arrived to the suite I would be sharing with five other girls in the early afternoon and was unpacking my clothes when the phone rang. The person on the other end of the line asked for Cecilia, my stunning freshman suitemate who was showing off her long tanned legs in tennis shorts. She had sandy-blond hair reminiscent of Raquel Welch. She was an official American beauty, and in my mind, I thought I could never compete because of the light emanating from her.

"Cecilia! The phone is for you! Cecilia!"

I left the phone dangling off the hook by the cord and got back to unpacking. Then I heard this beautiful yet strange-sounding Spanish.

"¡Hola, mamá! ¡Sí, claro, che! ¿Vos vas a venir? ¡Shzyo estoy aquí feliz, mamá!" I heard Cecilia say into the phone in the other room.

As soon as she finished her call, I ripped open the door and squealed with excitement, "Where are you from?"

"Me? I'm from New Jersey," Cecilia calmly replied.

"I mean, where are you really from?"

"Oh, my parents are from Argentina," she said with distance.

This was a sign! She didn't understand my excitement, but to me, her entrance into my life affirmed that I was on the right path to fig-uring out my Mexican and Latin American identity. And I'd finally have a chance to work on my Spanish.

Later, Ceci would tell me that she took our meeting as a sign, too. Her dad had passed away six months before college and she was an emotional zombie. But I saw her light and it called on me to do things I had never done before, like crawl into bed with Ceci one day when I could feel her hurting. We became fast hermanas with much in common. She was born in Buenos Aires, I was born in Mexico City; she was raised in suburban New Jersey, while I was raised in Chicago; she had two brothers and a sister just like me; both of her parents spoke with thick accents, while she and I were trying not to lose our Spanish. We were high-achieving American girls and the youngest children from Latin American immigrant families at a Seven Sisters school where most of our jokes revolved around not fitting in. We were constantly navigating multiple worlds. We both passed as white in different contexts and we both came from a place of privilege that had been hard-won.

We studied Gabriel García Márquez, Eduardo Galeano, and Julio Cortázar together, along with Theda Skocpol and her theory of revolution. We listened to Mercedes Sosa and Silvio Rodríguez, and Ceci fell in love with an Argentinian gaucho bolero singer. She was the revolutionary comrade and twin sister I met and fell in love with at eighteen. Ceci was my new chicle.

Cecilia was also an actress, and her spirit hadn't been deflated like mine. In the fall of freshman year, she went on auditions, and I went to an orientation meeting at the Columbia University radio station WKCR instead. The number of guys over at Columbia, where they didn't accept women into the student body, except in the engineering school, was jarring. In just three days on the Barnard campus, I had begun to relish the all-women spaces, where everyone exhaled and let out their belts a notch or two to feel more at ease.

As I was leaving the radio meeting, a guy named Luis and a few others introduced themselves and said they heard I might be interested in Latin music. I said I might be but that I had nothing but the ten records of political music from Latin America that my brother had given me. And they weren't salsa, which was the only music blaring on NYC streets.

They didn't mind. They were excited that even one person who cared about any kind of Latin music had shown up. The three-hour time slot they ran on Wednesday nights on WKCR from 10:00 p.m. to 1:00 a.m. was radio prime time. Puerto Rican students, they explained, had fought for those hours as part of the social justice battles on campus post-1968.

When one of their DJs moved away, Luis called me up and asked me to fill in so they wouldn't lose their slot.

"But all I have is ten records!" I objected.

"It's ten more than zero, which is what that time slot has now. You don't really have a choice."

Luis made me see the role I had to play. Privilege means responsibility. It might be my voice that inspires another little girl who stumbles upon our program while she's playing with the radio dial. In a tattered notebook, I made a playlist for my first show with *Nueva Canción y Demás.*

————————

WKCR was essentially run by men, but now that I was at a women's college, I had a little voice inside me that would say, *If the guys can do a twenty-four-hour jazz festival or twenty-four hours of Bach on the air, then you have to do a twenty-four-hour Latin American music festival.* The voice implored me to ask for a twenty-four-hour festival because I was convinced they would say no to someone who barely had more than a year of experience on the air, but they said yes. The university sent me to Cuba on a research visa, although travel to Cuba was barred, and I recorded the Festival de la Nueva Canción in Varadero in 1981.

Fidel had just launched the Mariel boatlift, allowing 125,000 Cubans to flee to the US, including people whose family members had already resettled there and a number of persecuted gay people, many of whom had been previously imprisoned for what the Cuban government considered "dangerous behavior." President Jimmy Carter, who was known as a proponent of human rights, granted asylum to anyone who arrived at the Mariel harbor in Key West, Florida. Even though the US had been welcoming Cuban refugees in large waves since the 1960s and '70s—Lyndon Johnson's Freedom Flights had run planes from Cuba to Miami twice a day, five days a week, for eight years, bringing a total of 260,000 Cubans to the country—we've always had a love-hate relationship when it comes to refugees. The US government is selective and strategic about deciding who is allowed to come in, granting asylum when it is politically advantageous, as it had been during the Cold War against communist governments like Fidel Castro's. In this instance, the media grasped onto the fact that Fidel had released former inmates and people hospitalized in mental institutions in order to discharge them to the open arms of the US, characterizing this group of refugees as criminals and degenerates landing on our shores.

On my first trip to Cuba, I was a kid playing in dangerous political territory. I was getting involved with a country that was considered a US enemy, and I was giving voice to Castro supporters. When my report aired on WKCR, Omega 7, a right-wing anti-Castro terrorist group made up of Cuban exiles in Florida and New York, took notice and called us twice. We didn't take the threat seriously and never reported it.

Cecilia and I befriended a gay couple, both Afro-Cuban men who had left during Mariel and were now squatting in an empty building on 106th Street. They were stealing electricity and had a makeshift stove and electric heater in a building with no doors or windows. They weren't nameless refugees. They were our neighbors who were simply trying to eke out a living. We cooked together and they taught us how to make the best arroz con pollo (¡hechale una cerveza entera!).

We increased WKCR's coverage of Central America in response to the threats. We heard from the rebel radio station broadcasting from guerilla-controlled territory in El Salvador. US-trained death squads were picking off rebels and human rights activists; Archbishop Óscar Romero, an outspoken critic of the death squads, was shot dead as he was giving mass; and the US was now sending down soldiers and millions of dollars of military aid every single day. Four American nuns had been raped and murdered and American-trained soldiers had been implicated.[1]

Cecilia and I would buy the *New York Times* every day and scour the reporting on Latin America. We devoured everything written by Alma Guillermoprieto and Raymond Bonner on the front page of the paper. They humanized what had become another war story for most journalists. Alma and Bonner were doing the kind of journalism—eyewitness accounts, but with humanity—Ceci and I dreamed of doing one day. They disappeared from the front pages at around the same time we started hearing reports about a massacre in El Salvador from Salvadoran refugees in New York.

The Salvadoran army held the entire village of El Mozote hostage and interrogated villagers about the location of guerilla fighters, whom they had little or no connection to. All told, the Salvadoran forces, who had been funded and trained by the US, tortured, raped, and killed more than a thousand people. Blood flowed into the nearby river, turning the waters red for miles. That's how people first knew that a massacre had taken place.

Bonner and Alma published a story about the massacre in the *New York Times*, but Reagan's White House dismissed the report as exaggerated. The official US government line was that no massacre had ever occurred, and Alma and Bonner were chastised by their own paper. Cecilia and I were devastated. This was censorship in the United States at the paper of record.

In response, we invited the voices that weren't being heard in the mainstream media to speak on my radio show (Ceci was now one of the producers): people who had family members killed in the massacre; women who had been raped in prison and charged with being guerilla sympathizers because they worked with progressive church groups and wanted reproductive rights. One night we got a scratchy phone call from the rebel-controlled radio station in El Salvador. Another time Mercedes Sosa, the protest singer from Argentina, showed up. On another occasion a barefoot Mutabaruka, the spoken-word rebel musician from Jamaica, came by. There was always good music and laughter, but what we were trying to accomplish at our little radio show was much more serious now. Central America was in a state of all-out war and we were one of the lone voices challenging Reagan's administration and the *New York Times*.

Sophomore year of college I also fell in love with a leftist Salvadoran revolutionary named Alberto who had been recruited to play professional baseball and now worked in a high-end photo-finishing shop. At night we attended political meetings, long sessions of crítica y autocrítica, and learned about the number of people shot and killed by the US-supported Salvadoran army. During the day, I visited small groups of Salvadoran refugees who were on a monthlong hunger strike at the Interchurch Center, steps from Barnard. Their protest demanded that Reagan's administration recognize the Central Americans fleeing violence as refugees, end military aid to the region, and help negotiate a peaceful resolution to the conflict (sound familiar?).

In 1980, when President Carter was still in office, Congress passed the Refugee Act to standardize the admittance and processing of refugees into the US. The bill, which was largely in response to the successive waves of refugees coming from Vietnam and Cuba, and now Latin America, raised the annual ceiling for refugees admitted to the US to fifty thousand. It also redefined the term *refugee* based on UN conventions as an individual with a "well-founded fear of persecution."

The Chileans who had survived torture in the 1970s and come to the US as refugees were now helping the survivors of torture from El Salvador in the 1980s and supporting them through their hunger strike. After reading poetry from Pablo Neruda in class, I would walk across campus and stop by the hunger strike as a supportive witness. Sometimes I helped out as an impromptu media liaison to the press who turned up to cover the story, so I got to see journalists at work. The hunger strike was covered by news outlets worldwide. Meanwhile, I saw people I knew force smiles as they got weaker and weaker every day. Journalists from all over the world came to cover the hunger strikes at Riverside Church, including a reporter from Japan, but Ronald Reagan didn't seem to care. I would go home at night and be comforted by my guerilla lover who wore his hair in an Afro and cried while listening to boleros.

By the end of sophomore year, I had saved a thousand dollars from my multiple odd jobs—projectionist for an art history class, reshelving library books, babysitting—to join my brother Jorge on his travels to South America for the summer. I also splurged on the latest craze, a Sony Walkman radio/cassette player. The lyrics to the song "Lua de San Jorge" fell out of Caetano Veloso's mouth like pieces of coconut candy floating on a cloud as I traversed the streets of Rio de Janeiro with Jorge. We had decided we were going to make this part of the world our own. Jorge had been living in Rio for six months and I flew down to meet him so that we could travel together through Brazil, Paraguay, Argentina, Bolivia, and wherever the wind blew us.

In Salta and Jujuy, I wrote love letters to Cecilia telling her how I now understood her Argentinian melancholy and the stoicism of the gaucho ethos after seeing the purple mountains of the Cordillera. I fell in love with the most unexpected Latin American man—Ruben was blond-haired, blue-eyed, and the son of a Russian immigrant who was now an army general in Paraguay for the fascist Stroessner regime.

Jorge and I crossed into Bolivia and rode all night to the silver mines in Potosi, a city with one of the highest elevations in the world. Women were banned from entering the mines, but sometimes they made exceptions for tourists, and they allowed me to descend to their claustrophobic workplace filled with soot and fear and hunger.

I spoke to the wives of the miners to see if any of them knew Domitila Barrios de Chungara, who had coauthored a feminist manifesto with other miners' wives to protest the government's wage reductions and became an idol of mine after I'd read her work in my Women's Studies classes. The women, wearing their iconic bowler hats, laughed at me for appearing to take an interest in their lives. Gringuita, they called me, with affectionate contempt.

To me, these women were heroines. In Bolivia, miners were seen as the scum of the earth because most of them were indigenous. So imagine how the wives of the miners were looked upon. They were the least powerful in the food chain, which meant they had nothing to lose. When you have nothing to lose you're willing to take all kinds of risks. I saw this with my own eyes—how "powerless" indigenous women had resisted, waged their own strike, created change, and fought for basic justice in Bolivia and throughout Latin America. This was another manifestation of what American labor leader Dolores Huerta talked about: people power. The lesson here was that the most powerless people can sometimes be the ones who first motivate everyone else to join together for a cause. They start by believing in the power of their own voices.

Ruben met up with us in Peru and we traveled to a socialist village in the middle of Lake Titicaca where the men knitted clothes all day and the women herded the sheep. It was an egalitarian utopia in real life. We slept in people's homes made of wood and clay with dirt floors. That night I became sick to my stomach and had to use the bathroom, but there were none. Everyone was asleep at three o'clock in the morning on an island in the middle of a lake 12,500 feet above sea level, while I was looking for a place to squat far enough from the house, but not too far. This was my first communion with the majesty of the stars. At that moment, I felt like I understood why the ancestors read the stars and made up stories. The whole world was silent, but above there were millions of stars and they were talking to me.

After Bolivia, Peru, and Ecuador, I made my way to Mexico and then back to Chicago. I had been away long enough to miss the fall session at Barnard, so I decided I would live at home and work as a waitress to save up money before I returned to school the next year.

When I returned to New York in September 1982, I went back to doing my radio show. I hung out in the Latin American trovas and cafés all over Manhattan with Salvadoran revolutionaries, war refugees, and survivors of rape and torture. I had moved up to Washington Heights with my new best friend, Deyanira, a lesbian Afro-Dominican drummer who was also longing to move to Peru.

Our apartment became a safe space for raucous dance parties that went until 4:00 a.m. with a scrappy group of Latin American PhDs, college students from the radio station, activists from every sector, Puerto Rican feminist independentistas, Afro-Panamanian intellectuals, radical poets, live drumming, and the music of Rubén Blades blasting alongside Lionel Richie singing, "We're going to party, karamu / Fiesta, forever!"

When there weren't parties, there were meetings of all sorts happening at the house. We held meetings there for *Nueva Canción* at WKCR, which Deyanira was now hosting with me. The show had created its own community of fans who listened every week from Spanish Harlem and the Bronx to Connecticut and the upstate prisons. We had our own section in the music library and had amassed a collection of a couple hundred records. People were sending us their music to play for free.

Everything in our space was about being welcoming without judgment and it started with our roommate, who was Deyanira's seventy-five-year-old grandma. Biemba had grown up in a humble shack in Villa Mella, one of the poorest parts of Santo Domingo. She had raised Deyanira. Biemba was shorter than me, hunched over now, with dark brown skin, gray eyes, and sprouts of an uneven gray Afro here and there. She lived in her bata, always had arroz con pollo ready to heat up, and made café con leche out of something that looked like a thin old sock. She welcomed Deyanira's lovers as her own children and would join in at our parties for an hour here and there. I had never seen anything like this. Family that was non-homophobic and let you live your life in the open?

Our collective space was part of my attempt to foster an environment where I could embrace the woman I had become: Pan–Latin American, feminist, artist, political activist, radio show host, influencer, community creator, intellectual but also anti-intellectual, with a growing spiritual exploration into Santeria. During one of the many nights of women gathering for meetings at our apartment, I realized my thesis was right there staring me in the face. It would be about the women I was living with and learning from—Salvadoran refugees who were living their lives on their own terms and, more than ever, as a response to everything that was going on around them.

The Reagan presidency had been a farce portraying itself as the "shining city on a hill"; the president had been implicated in the criminal enterprise of selling cocaine from Colombia and pushing it into black and Latino barrios and then selling arms to Iran in an undercover deal to raise money for the Contras in Nicaragua. Reverend John Fife was on federal trial for supporting the sanctuary movement and giving sanctuary to undocumented refugees and immigrants fleeing violence. Salvadorans and Guatemalans were desperately asking for refugee status after escaping what some were calling a genocide and then being detained in the US. The government was going after activists again, as they had the Black Panthers and the Young Lords. And the AIDS epidemic was exploding along with the radical activism it had inspired. The country was on edge and divided.

I started my thesis by interviewing a series of Salvadoran refugee women I didn't know personally so the research wouldn't be subjective. I traveled to Long Island for my field research and documented the many obstacles these women faced as they arrived and tried to integrate into new society. I captured stories of women who survived prison in El Salvador, escaped their town after being lit on fire and didn't know whether their parents were still alive, or who were guerilla fighters who never gave up on the idea of revolution despite having to fight off unwanted advances from fellow guerillas. I wrote about the trauma of war and relocation to "the best country in the world," but it was the US intervention in their countries that made them end up here in the first place.

When I first met Teresa, her face haunted my thoughts for many days. She was like a quiet and enigmatic angel who had long, straight black hair and a beauty mark above her left eyebrow and almond-shaped eyes. I rarely saw her smile. When she first arrived in our friend group, there were murmurs to be aware of Teresa because she was in a fragile state. I didn't approach her for many months. One day we had a moment alone and she told me the reason she had come to the US was because she had been imprisoned and tortured in El Salvador for being a teacher's union activist. I was twenty-two and Teresa was twenty-eight. I was a kid trying to process how someone I knew, who was not much older, had been imprisoned for being a union organizer and was tortured and sexually assaulted there. The thing that had made her seem mysterious was actually her pain.

The newly appointed head of the Latin American studies department at Barnard, who was a conservative literary critic, failed to see the inherent value of my thesis. The chair of the political science department, Peter Juviler, read it instead and was so moved he gave me an A.

Meanwhile, I supported my radio show and activism by waiting tables. I had no idea what I wanted to do after college, mostly because the careers I thought about always seemed impractical. An international human rights lawyer? How would I make it through law school? I wasn't smart enough to read those thick books. A dancer or actress? I had given up on that long ago and needed to stop dreaming about it. Move to El Salvador and work in the rebel radio station? A nice thought, but it was more Che Guevara daydream than reality. An intellectual academic or professor? That's exactly what I did not want to do. I wanted to be with the people, on the ground, not in an ivory tower.

I had one other idea that I didn't talk about because I was convinced I was not smart enough or good enough. Empirically, I knew I had a voice. I actually used it every week on the radio and spoke to tens of thousands of people even if it felt like only one person was listening. I had created a name for myself in the city I came to conquer. I was respected as a young Latina leader and would soon be graduating magna cum laude from Barnard College. Everything pointed to me being a success. Why was I so worried?

The truth was that during school I had waited tables to pay for my living expenses and that made it hard to take internships because I needed my shifts to pay rent. Here I was at the end of college and I hadn't done one single internship. I was so embarrassed that I was afraid to go to the internship office. As a rebel, I had rejected the notion of having to dress up and compete for an internship. My insecurities held me back. The truth was that I couldn't afford to do an unpaid internship and I was too ashamed to reveal that. Now that I was graduating, I had to do an internship so I could add something to my résumé. I forced myself to go to the office.

My hands were trembling as I leafed through the huge internship folder with listings for ABC News, the *New York Times*, and *New York* magazine. All I kept saying was nope, nope, nope. I stopped on the clear plastic folder from National Public Radio. It was an internship named for Susan Stamberg, who was the anchor for the network's most important show, *All Things Considered*. The internship was based in DC, but a Barnard alum would provide free housing.

Nope, I could never get that, I said to myself and leafed past it.

After half an hour, I found two internships that I was excited about and thought I might have a shot at—the international Lawyers' Committee for Human Rights and the Institute for Policy Studies, which was a progressive think tank. Both were in DC, but did not come with housing.

I was sitting at the table looking a little overwhelmed when a woman who worked in the office came and sat with me. She was calm and patient and asked me what I liked about school. I talked to her about my thesis and work documenting the hunger strike. I told her about WKCR and the twenty-four-hour music festivals I had produced. I told her about the authors and musicians and other journalists I had interviewed, and she listened intently and with such curiosity.

"You're missing one application," she pointed out.

"What's that?" I asked.

"You must apply to NPR. You must."

"No! I'll never get it! That's impossible."

She looked into my eyes and said, "You are good enough. You're wonderful, but you just can't see it. I do."

She took a deep breath, looked straight into my eyes again, and said, "Apply."

So I did.

Chapter 6

Finding My Voice

NPR called me while I was working at WKCR. In my final move to prove to the radio guys and to myself that I was more than just a disc jockey, I had taken on the position of program director and was now helping to run and manage a full-fledged radio station in NYC. As a result, I practically lived at the station, which is why I put that number on my internship applications.

One of the jazz DJs, Phil Schaap, who was on the air, came into the studio where I was logging tapes and told me there was someone on the phone for me. I thought it was a regular business call or a listener complaint. Instead, it was Ted Clark, the mild-mannered executive producer of *All Things Considered*, calling to offer me the internship. Because I was in a soundproof studio, I started screaming and jumping for joy. Schaap—we called each other by our last names—applauded from behind the glass inside his studio across the room.

Maybe NPR was for me after all?

I'm not sure what more I needed to do to prove to myself that I was qualified. I had hosted a weekly, three-hour live show for five years, documented cultural events and covered news stories, produced twenty-four-hour music festivals, helped run the station, worked as a waitress, maintained a 4.0 average, and still I didn't feel worthy. Why did it look so much easier for the guys?

This internship at NPR would be a test to see if I could function outside of the bohemian bubble and free life I had fashioned for myself as a student activist. My friends were all counterculture disruptors and that's where I felt at home—with queer radicals and feminist revolutionaries of all races and my liberation theologist leftist Salvadoran refugee family from the Bronx, Los Chacón. Everyone was rooting for me and the NPR internship. I felt the weight of this success because it wasn't just for me.

My restaurant buddies were also a huge support. They all chipped in and covered my shifts for the next month at the new place I was working called Caramba, a three-story Tex-Mex restaurant on Ninety-Sixth Street and Broadway.

On January 2, 1985, I left Washington Heights at 7:00 a.m. in a purple livery cab that smelled like rum and Coke from the night before and caught an 8:00 a.m. Amtrak to DC. I made my way from the old DC train station to the Metro, which was so quiet and clean compared to NYC. There was carpeting in the subway, which I thought was crazy and uncivilized. I got out of the Metro in the nearby city of Arlington, where my alma mater host lived, and felt like I walked into a science fiction film on a Sunday afternoon. The city was all tall sleek buildings in empty downtown streets with no numbers and no street signs. I went around in circles feeling discombobulated and wondering whether this was a precursor for how things were going to go at NPR.

It appeared no one had actually ever walked to the luxury apartment building from the Metro since everyone there had cars. When the doorman saw me huffing up the driveway, he ran down to meet me.

"Barbara Colby," I said to him, a bit exasperated, repeating the name of my host, who had graduated from Barnard in 1942.

Mrs. Colby was a sweet older woman with dyed-blond hair curled in the style of Rose Marie from *The Dick Van Dyke Show*. She was proper and socially engaged in a way she might have been taught to be at a finishing school. I wondered how I would build a friendship with Mrs. Colby, which is how I realized she liked to be addressed. By her proper name.

After I dropped my bag off in the guest room of her tenth-floor duplex, I excused myself so I could get back on the train and figure out my commute for the next day, Monday, the first day of my internship. I had to be at NPR at 9:00 a.m. and I was not going to be late or lost.

Once I got back, I stepped into my host's expansive living room with floor-to-ceiling windows and a balcony overlooking the Potomac. The full moon was rising over the river with the Capitol lit up in the distance, shining like a white sun in the pitch-black night, the Lincoln Memorial slicing the darkness with a beam pointed skyward. It was breathtaking. Suddenly, I was filled with gratitude. If it hadn't been for a lady named Jane in the internship office, who believed in me more than I believed in myself, I wouldn't be here. I was living in DC for free for a month and starting an internship at NPR tomorrow! I felt like I was in a circle of privilege and gratitude that I could actually touch.

I turned around and joined Mrs. Colby in the kitchen, where she was making a simple oven-baked chicken breast, iceberg lettuce salad with a prepackaged Italian dressing, and instant "minute rice" that I had only ever seen in TV commercials (Mami would never have used it). Mrs. Colby poured herself a glass of white wine, or maybe it was her second by now, and she asked me to join her. The *PBS News Hour* was on in the background and then Mrs. Colby began to talk about the people on the TV like she knew them—the vice president, another cabinet member, the anchor of the show—and it slowly dawned on me that proper Mrs. Colby was no shrinking violet in this town.

She knew everyone, and I loved the way she talked about the men in the headlines with such ownership. Then we heard the TV reporters talk about the nuns who were murdered in El Salvador and there was silence. Was Mrs. Colby going to reveal that she supported the US military intervening down there? I braced for the worst.

"Those poor decent churchwomen didn't deserve to die this way. The soldiers, they knew better . . ." she said, tapering off. "How disrespectful to these women. That should have been enough to cut off all relations with their government. But no. They keep on sending money down to that murderous military!"

Then she continued. "They like to call themselves honorable men, but they are not. They are not honorable. Just like my ex-husband. You call that honorable? What he did to me?"

She shook her head and lifted the crystal wineglass to her lips as a tear emerged from the corner of her eye.

I tried to follow along, but her cross-fire comments were all very muddled. I was already tipsy with just one glass of wine. Maybe that's why, right then, I decided that I needed to start being a journalist and take myself seriously. No more waiting for approval. I straight-up asked, "If you don't mind Mrs. Colby, who are you? Who is your ex-husband?"

"My ex-husband left me for his young secretary," she said without skipping a beat. "He just wrote a book called *Honorable Men*. My ex-husband used to run the CIA. His name is William E. Colby."

I quivered for a second. Was I really in the apartment of the ex-wife of the former head of the CIA? Me, the one with Central American leftist books and the phone numbers and addresses of countless activists in my bedroom, just steps away?

Over the next month I spent a lot of time with Barbara. I had seen her name in news stories simply because she was the wife of the former head of the CIA. But now I was seeing another side of the story. It's obviously disarming to see anyone in their bathrobe, but for Mrs. Colby, it broke down her sense of privacy and she became more relaxed around me. She told me candidly how she felt after having spent her entire life being "the good wife," traveling around the world, and adjusting to his schedule and his life and his career. She was searching for happiness now in ways she had not been taught.

———————

On my first day at NPR I remember walking into the newsroom and seeing the whiteboard divided up into thirds, with each section representing thirty minutes of air time on *ATC* (*All Things Considered*), creating a visual for how the show would run. Each line listed the title of the piece, the last name of the reporter, and the length of the story.

NPR didn't look like the radical lefty radio network that some believed it was. It was mostly men running the meetings in button-down shirts, some with loose ties, and a lot of loafers and Top-Siders, a few running shoes. Women were present in the meetings, too, but they weren't running the shows. They were, however, producing many of the pieces that were carrying the shows through every night. In the end, these women seemed to be interested not in challenging issues from a woman's perspective, but rather, proving they were smarter than men at every turn—something I was familiar with. They didn't want to change the status quo. They wanted to be it.

I was assigned to follow Ellen Weiss, who was then the best production assistant on the show, known for her speed. She could cut a fifteen-minute interview down to four minutes in less than thirty minutes. I liked her. She was strong and determined. She walked around in tight pants and brown and white cowboy boots, the kind you can afford to buy when you have a job. I wanted a real job like that.

I wanted to be her and be part of a team of young journalists who were deciding together what stories mattered and then broadcasting them to the world. I liked the people who worked there and they were familiar to me because of my years in Hyde Park, Barnard, and Columbia. I knew, though, that I was different, but I understood them enough to explain my own reality to them. They seemed to like different things, quirky things. I knew "different." I had become an expert at being the other.

During morning meetings, I watched producers propose stories from *USA Today* or the *Washington Post* that I considered pretty predictable and bland, but I didn't raise my hand. I could feel the competition in the room, thick and oppressive like a storm cloud. People's ideas were batted down all the time. It felt very cliquey and it was uncomfortable to watch. The last thing I wanted to do was to speak up in the meeting. No one was asking me to, anyway.

After two weeks of shadowing Ellen and the other producers and feeling like I had the basics down, I started to worry that I needed to do something dramatic in the two weeks I had left. Since I wasn't speaking up in meetings, I was disappearing into the background. I could not let that happen.

This was my shot, but I didn't know where to shoot. There was no way I was going to be fast enough to get a piece on *ATC*. And if I didn't pitch my idea in the editorial meeting, it was never going to end up on that whiteboard.

Ronald Reagan was about to be sworn in as president for his second term and *ATC* was planning their coverage of the official event. I knew about the unofficial protests that were being organized. I was sitting on a story that no one else had brought up.

I took several deep breaths and told myself that I had a responsibility to make this internship worth it. *You didn't suffer through four years of classes at a top college not to be bold, right? You have to make this worth it—for you and your parents.* It was like the immigrant gene took over. I *had* to do this. I *had* to try.

The newscasts were produced in a separate part of the newsroom where they were anchored by Lori Waffenschmidt in the evenings. She and the daytime anchor, Carl Kasell, seemed like sweet, normal human beings, not like the high-strung, highly competitive men of *ATC.* Lori was a woman with power. She decided what would end up in her newscast. The other women, I realized, were working for men who had the final say. I decided that I needed to find the capacity to ask another woman for guidance, as I had learned from studying at a women's college. That was the least I could do for myself.

I told Lori about the anti-Reagan protest and asked if she would like me to report on it for their Reagan inauguration coverage. The organizers wanted to draw attention to the bombings in El Salvador under Reagan by protesting the celebration of his second term. Without thinking twice, she said yes. I went home to Mrs. Colby's luxurious duplex and told her I had my first official assignment. The former wife of the head of the CIA thought covering the protests against Reagan's inauguration was a great way to start my career at NPR.

I attended the protest, which other journalists had missed, and I came back with two short interviews, plus environmental sound from the protest. I grabbed a piece of three-ply carbon paper, slipped it into the electric typewriter, and like I had seen the production assistants do, I wrote a script that included the natural sound of the protest as well as a cut of tape from a protester.

I handed the script over to Lori, who treated me like a peer, not an intern, and she told me to record it. Her confidence in my ability to deliver the report made me feel like a fellow professional journalist. I recorded the piece and signed off by saying my name with an English pronunciation. My voice ended up on the air that evening during *ATC.*

Lori told me I did great, and then I told her about another protest; this time, conservative activists demonstrating against immigration reform at the INS headquarters. Reagan was disliked by the Latino left but he was also disliked by the conservative anti-immigrant academics and think tanks, who taunted him for granting "amnesty to the illegals."

Lori was thrilled to have fresh material for her newscast. Most of the senior reporters viewed filing one-minute news spots as the most tedious part of their jobs. For me, filing another news spot made me feel like I was well on my way to becoming a real reporter. Because of my activism and academic and cultural work, I knew about people and issues that no one inside of NPR had ever heard of. I made a decision to break with my past activism. As a reporter, those people became my sources. I began to realize that sources were one of the most important parts of being a good journalist, and I had a lot of them: just-about-to-break-through artists, activists who were spearheading policy change, educators who were advocating for more equity in the classroom, intellectuals from NYC to Uruguay, unsung human rights workers, frontline Central American organizations like CISPES, Casa Nicaragua, El Taller Latino Americano, NACLA, and refugees themselves.

People had heard that the quiet intern from Barnard had ended up voicing a spot for the newscast the night before and I had sounded as good as any other reporter on the air. The day I went into the studio to record my second news spot, I had a big decision to make: Who was I going to be?

By now, a lot of my life in NYC was lived in Spanish. I studied and read in Spanish. My friends from El Salvador all spoke Spanish. Our meetings and my own WKCR radio show was in Spanish.

So, was I going to say my name in English or Spanish? I knew whatever I chose was going to stick with me forever. I had to be me, and I also knew there was no way I was going to be able to compete unless I stood out. I was either going to fade into the background from trying too hard to fit in or I was going to shine as myself. I decided to pronounce my name in Spanish. That was my authentic self.

By the time I left the monthlong *ATC* internship, everyone knew my name and who I was. As an intern, I had my antenna up all the time. I understood I was on the inside of a powerful institution and that every moment I was there I could be learning something. *Networking* was the buzzword on everyone's lips, so I was trying to do it. I had heard how infamously hard it was to break into being an on-air reporter. No one at NPR would return your calls or say yes to any of your pitches. It sounded horrible, like exactly the kind of rejection I ran away from in acting.

During those long Metro rides to and from Arlington and DC, I convinced myself that if I had gotten on the air with two spots during my internship then I was smart enough to be able to pitch and file an entire piece. I decided to stop shooting myself down and instead start talking myself up.

As I neared the end of the internship, I thought about how to take on the challenge of pitching stories from New York and getting the East Coast editor to say yes to them. I asked one of the *ATC* staffers to introduce me to him. I was nice and coy and smart. I told the nerdy-looking editor I would be in touch. I'm sure he never could have imagined how elated I was that I had met him, that he knew my name and to expect my call.

A week after I got back from DC, I wrote up five different story ideas and sent them to the editor. I was more anxious while waiting for the editor's call than I had ever been while expecting a call from a lover. That's how much I wanted this.

I didn't hear back. Absolutely nothing. For a week—and a half. He did not return my calls.

After two weeks, I went to the NPR bureau in New York, which I had visited during my internship. There, I used an internal line to call the editor, who finally took the call. He sounded shocked to hear me on the other end of the line.

"Why are you calling me from there?" He sounded put off, as if I had tricked him somehow.

"I'm here working on my story pitches. The executive producer of *ATC* told me I could work out of here every now and then." I pulled on my immigrant girl chutzpah pants and asked him straight up about my five pitches. Would he like me to start working on any of them?

"Um, no. Thank you. Nice job, but we're not really looking for any of the things you wrote up. Thanks anyway. Bye."

Asshole, I said to myself about myself. *Te lo creíste. You told yourself you were good enough. You weren't.*

This was supposed to be my big break. I was crushed. All of those times that I forced myself to believe I could do it, talking myself up, puffing out my ego, were a waste of time. I was never going to make it as a journalist.

¿Pa' qué?

That night, I went out dancing with Deyanira until three in the morning at a party for the Committee in Solidarity with the People of El Salvador (CISPES) and Casa Nicaragua in a run-down loft in Chelsea off of Seventh Avenue. There was a live band playing salsa and a disco ball. It was a celebration of some sort. Bombs were literally being dropped on the family members of some of the people in the room, yet everyone also understood that all we had was this moment. My hair was long, loose, and curly down to my back. People here knew me as the WKCR radio host, but also as the girlfriend of one of the heavies of the movement. Most nights, I was a passionate dancer who could go from 10:00 p.m. till 4:00 a.m. with barely any rest. But tonight, after the East Coast editor's rejection, a cloud hung over my future and I was melancholy.

I was angry at everyone. Tired of waiting tables and having to look cute and be cuter to get better tips. Tired of Ronald Reagan in the White House. Tired of having a cara de pendeja.

The brooding was deep. Most days there were tears. It was too late to apply for law school. *All those years at college and you can't get more than a sixty-second news clip on NPR.* Tears. *You don't have a real job. What a total and complete loser and failure you are.* More tears.

It was real easy to slip back into that mindset. There I was, cradling my head in my hands, when Deyanira said, "Phone call, Malu!" That was the nickname my family used for me in Mexico—Malulis, or "Malu" for short. Ceci gave me the name and only my closest friends called me that.

On the other end of the line was a senior producer at NPR I had met during the internship after introducing myself to anyone who might be able to help me—my networking moment. I had sat down and studied the different departments, then asked Ted Clark to introduce me. I met the folks who worked the arts desk and the science desk, the people upstairs who produced the jazz and classical programs, and the fourth-floor unit, where a bearded guy with a big belly produced content for specialized audiences. His name was José McMurray and he was calling on my landline.

"Hey, Maria," he said, pronouncing my name in Spanish, "I wanted to know if you'd like to do a one-hour documentary for our Hispanic Heritage Month programming for my unit. Also, I'd love to connect you to two shows who want you to pitch them, but in Spanish. They heard your spots on *ATC* and they want you to file for them. Can I give them your number?"

Finally! The thing I had been waiting for! Someone seeing the value in my work. I was going to work on a small project for NPR, but the only person who wanted to work with me was the one other Latino at the network who produced "minority programs" on the fourth floor. He wasn't from the main newsroom on the second floor, where all of the editorial power was based. "Okay, it's gonna be like that, then," I said out loud to myself. It's like being a Latino actor who gets cast as the drug dealer or the maid. *That's some bullshit*, I thought as I shook my head. But then I smiled because at least now I was *in*.

I decided to deliver the best one-hour of radio I could, considering I had zero experience. The central character for my report would be a Puerto Rican small-business owner who had a flower shop in the Parkchester section of the Bronx. It was a story that challenged the many narratives created and maintained by the mainstream media that Puerto Rican women were takers and not doers or creators of wealth, that the Bronx was burning, that Latinos didn't have disposable income to spend on flowers, and that Latinas didn't run businesses. I wanted to break those myths. I had also now received multiple assignments after just one call each with *Enfoque Nacional* and *Panorama Hispano*.

I was a waitress by night, sometimes hiding from the same NPR correspondents I worked with during the day who came to eat at the famous Caramba restaurant. They had no idea I made ends meet by waiting tables, and I felt ashamed. The thought of them seeing me with my little waitress apron, tight black jeans, and T-shirt over a push-up bra was humiliating. I was proud of my work ethic and that I made enough money through waitressing to have an okay life. And yet, I didn't want them to see me. I knew that if they saw me waiting tables, they would file it away into some strange stereotype about Latinas. I was a freelance journalist now, with real assignments, and I needed my colleagues at NPR to take me seriously.

In early spring, it was quiet enough in the mornings in the Heights that the sparrows and the chickadees would wake me. Merengue would ooze out of open apartment windows, the rat-tat-tat staccato of Dominican Spanish drifting through the streets, the aroma of café con leche on every corner. From there, I would head all the way down to the NPR bureau, right across from the United Nations on First Avenue and Forty-Second Street, where there were mostly people in suits, bureaucrats, and businesspeople. I straddled two completely different worlds that were just three miles apart.

I decided to start showing up as often as I could to the NPR bureau so the people there could get used to seeing me around. No one except for the quirky Margot Adler—NPR's science correspondent who was known for being a Wiccan priestess—said much to me, so it was painfully uncomfortable to be there and feel like I was taking up space. My fellow freelancers, who were also contending with staff contributors, saw me as the competition; every minute I got on the radio with one of my stories meant less time on air for their stories. It was a dog-eat-dog environment. I had to ask where to sit every time I came into the office, sitting at a different person's empty desk each time. No one spoke to me. No one said hello unless I did first, and even then they looked at me like I was a stranger. At three o'clock, I would clean up my desk area at the bureau and head over to Ninety-Sixth Street to start my eight-hour shift at four p.m.

My first national news stories began to air in Spanish on *Enfoque Nacional*, which was produced out of KPBS in San Diego and was a mini *ATC* with reporters filing three- to four-minute news and feature pieces from all over the country. I was also filing for Vidal Guzmán, who anchored and produced a public radio show out of Madison, Wisconsin, called *Panorama Hispano*, a Spanish show dedicated to arts reporting.

The Spanish anchors and producers had all heard my name when I filed those two news spots at *ATC*. It took them a while, but eventually they found out who I was.

That risky move—stepping up to Lori Waffenschmidt and asking her if I could file for her—changed everything. In spite of some dude who had tried to cut off my wings early on, I was ready to take flight now. Since he wouldn't put me on the air, I had figured out my own way to get there. I'd work with people I didn't have to convince of my value—people who saw me.

"Hello, Maria? It's Scott Simon on the line. How are you?"

Was I dreaming? No, it was actually Scott Simon, a star reporter and international correspondent for NPR, calling *me*.

Years before, after my travels through South America, while living at home, longing for the Paraguayan, and working at a downtown Chicago restaurant, I had seen Scott Simon on the cover of the *Chicago Reader*, the most widely read, free, independent newspaper in Chicago. I learned that he was a hard-nosed Chicago boy who became an international correspondent for NPR and whose reporting on the war in El Salvador was some of the first on the radio to humanize the attention-grabbing headlines.

At that moment, I was in an emo crisis because the Paraguayan had ghosted me. I was in Chicago and living through another one of those depressive moments when I dared myself to pick up the phone and call the NPR bureau in Chicago. I asked for Scott Simon, and then, in a very serious tone, I told him that I anchored a show on WKCR in NYC about Latin America. Could I come and meet him? To which Scott said, "Sure."

We met for half an hour and I was sure he had quickly forgotten about me afterward, but he actually never did. He saw me again during my internship and recognized me, and came by to say hello. Cut to me standing in the kitchen while Biemba padded about making her sofrito for the chicken wings she was getting ready to cook, one of her staple meals. The kitchen smelled so Dominican; meanwhile, I had this very white dude from NPR on the phone. My life, mi vida.

"I heard great things about you from the *ATC* crew after your internship," Scott said. At that precise moment, my legs gave out.

Scott said that Jay Kernis, the man who had created *Morning Edition*, wanted to meet me. Jay had been tasked with creating a new show and Scott was going to be the anchor. Scott called to ask me to apply for the job of production assistant, and in a few days, I was on a train back to DC to interview for the job with Jay Kernis, one of the most important news executives at NPR.

Jay and I hit it off immediately. He was nothing like the uptight, high-strung men of *ATC*. Jay laughed a lot, was very stylish, and had famously fabulous hair. In fact, he told me we were going to break with NPR tradition and get the anchor to laugh on air with this new show. (Not everyone was happy about that.) Jay and I talked about everything—growing up, politics, travel, Mexico, books, theater— and then he said, "I love you! Please join us!"

He offered me the job right there on the spot.

"I have never met a Latina, Ivy Leaguer, radio producer, international traveler who loves theater, speaks two languages, and is so politically aware!" he exclaimed. "I doubt there are any more out there like you! Please say yes and be one of the founding staff of *Weekend Edition Saturday* with Scott Simon."

Of course there were more people like me out there, but Jay's comment, though to me clueless, was also a result of people like me being invisible, for the entirety of my life. Young, hungry, smart, and sophisticated Latinas were everywhere except for in the news media. I said yes to Jay and the job, and that marked the beginning of one of the most long-lasting professional relationships of my life, with Jay.

Scott Simon was a new breed of NPR anchor. He was sensitive, and told stories from the human side. He was a brilliant writer who laughed a lot and loved the arts and sports. Everything about our show was fresh and modern and different. Jay and Scott encouraged me to bring all of myself into the newsroom. The team loved my ideas and encouraged me. They saw me, included me, and bought me food, and they joked with me, not at me. In many ways, they were like my Hyde Park Jewish family, and that felt just right.

Most of the time.

I was valued because I was a good journalist with fresh story ideas and new perspectives on issues, and I was reliable and fast. I now understood that what made me a good journalist was the fact that I was different. It was incredible to be part of a team of human beings who recognized that I knew about things no one else was discussing and saw that as a plus. While interning at *ATC*, I had felt the pressure to conform. Now Jay and Scott wanted me to think big.

I spotted a short piece in one of the New York papers about a new drug that had just hit the streets called crack. My team green-lit the story. In fact, they were fascinated because no one else was brave enough to report from sketchy Times Square, where crack was flourishing. I spent days on the phone and was finally able to set up an interview with a guy named Hawk. He was a sex worker who used crack. A local grassroots organization that worked with the homeless had connected us.

He agreed to do the interview on a park bench in Bryant Park. Hawk was a gorgeous black man with light brown eyes and lips that looked like two halves of a luscious apricot. He moved like a woman, with slow shoulder motions and eyelash flutters. His voice was like thick honey. He was such a sweetheart, and Scott brought out his humanity, even after Hawk revealed that he was high on crack during the interview.

A drug addict, sex worker, and sometime homeless person had become more than just the labels pinned on him. He came through as human and smart on the national airwaves. People all over the network were calling Jay and Scott to congratulate them. Correspondent Nina Totenberg came by to meet me and personally congratulate me on a job well done.

I sat at home, alone on the floor of my apartment with a celebratory beer after all of the kudos. I appreciated the acknowledgment. My story had made a national impact because I had decided that the best way to understand crack was to be there, in the streets, unafraid, and Scott went there with me. On the other hand, my personal career was going to flourish in some ways because of another man's anguish. While I was very proud of making something invisible visible and telling a dramatic human story, I dwelled on the fact that I had just put a black man who was a drug addict on the air at NPR.

One day, as I was dropping off some cassette tapes at the network RC (record central, where everything was being recorded), I saw the long ends of someone's beautifully groomed dreadlocks as they were leaving through the other door. The two did not connect for me. Dreadlocks and NPR record central?

I made a little skip out the door and found myself standing right next to a tall, stunning African American woman with dreadlocks down to her bum. She was rocking an outfit in caramel colors with a matching suede skirt and cowboy boots. NPR was pretty white, so anytime I saw a person of color there, I noted it. I was the first and only Latina at the NPR news headquarters in DC.

"Hi! I'd love to meet you! Who are you?" I said, remembering that someone had told me I needed to meet a high-powered news executive named Sandra, who was black.

"I'm Sandra Rattley," she said, gazing down at me from her perch at five foot ten.

"Can I please invite you to lunch?"

Sandra formerly ran the entire National News Desk at NPR and now she was one of the senior leaders of the entire network. Despite her lofty credentials, she agreed to have lunch with me, a mere production assistant.

A week later over lunch, she told me her closest friends called her Sandy. I never asked her to be my official mentor, but we formed a sisterhood that day between the two of us. She was the first black woman editor at NPR and now in leadership. She felt she needed to be by my side since I was the first Latina, but we also just connected, spiritually.

That day at lunch, I asked Sandy how she did it, how she had not lost her patience from being one of the few women of color in the space and always having to translate our existence and give it validity.

"Take deep breaths and pick your battles," Sandy said, smiling tenderly and putting her hand on mine.

The truth is, I was awed by her statuesque beauty, the inner calm she exuded, the way she smelled like musk and glided through the stuffy NPR hallways—how she, too, saw me and promised she would be there for me.

We had an immediate profound and honest affection for each other, and we understood there was also a strategic alliance we needed to make. We didn't know it then, but our lives would be intertwined forever.

———

Sesquicentennial.

What kind of a word is that? I remember thinking. It kept rolling off of Jay's tongue as he repeated it excitedly. *Texas sesquicentennial!*

Jay had called me into his office to tell me they were so pleased with my work that they were assigning me to do a series of stories for the 150th anniversary of the founding of the state of Texas.

Everyone wanted Scott to go to a real-live Texas rodeo as part of the reporting on the sesquicentennial, but my mind was on a different story. I knew that if I gave Jay and Scott the rodeo piece they wanted, I would be able to get in two very radical ideas.

Instead of looking at one of the oldest Texas traditions (started, historians say, by Mexican vaqueros), I turned my attention toward some of the newest Texans. Corpus Christi had been a major relocation spot for thousands of Vietnamese refugees after the Vietnam War. They were the people I had grown up hearing called that horrible term, "boat people." These human beings seeking refuge had been turned into dehumanized objects. The news media used that term without any qualms. Now I had the power to meet them and finally hear their voices and let them speak for themselves. Jay, Scott, and the team loved the idea.

Then I told them I wanted to see where they were housing all of the Central American refugees who had come north to escape the war. Had the border of Texas become a new, welcoming port of entry like Ellis Island, or the opposite?

First we went to Houston, where we told the beautiful and dramatic story of a young, handsome Texas cowboy who wanted to win the rodeo championship but buckled at the last minute. The entire stadium let out a collective groan when he fell off his bull so fast and so close to its hoof.

Afterward, we got in my first-ever puddle jumper and flew from Houston to Harlingen. I sweated the entire time and cursed the decision to fly instead of drive, but we had so few days to traverse an entire state and report several stories.

At the immigration and naturalization processing center in Harlingen, the largest detention camp in the country, the scene in front of my eyes looked like a World War II refugee camp. There were men of various sizes, but all of them were gaunt, standing in the hot sun behind a barbed-wire fence in orange jumpsuits. Sometimes they were forced to stay out there for eight hours. I remember seeing their fingers wrapped around the fencing, their eyes squinting in the harsh sunlight, with looks of longing to be on the other side of that fence, to be free.

I thought about the people I knew who'd been on hunger strike when I was in college and how maybe some of those men could have been their fathers or uncles. They looked so dejected. They were not criminals. They were seeking asylum, asking for a safe place to escape the bombings and the death squads. Wasn't the United States the one place in the world where you could ask for asylum?

In another era, the American government had attempted to keep undocumented immigrants in custody—until the Supreme Court ruled it "needless confinement" in the 1900s. But our history has a tendency to repeat itself. When Cubans, Haitians, and Latin Americans started coming to the US in the 1980s and applying for asylum, detention, that needless confinement, reared its ugly head again.

At Harlingen, referred to as "el Corralón" or "the Corral" by locals, these men were locked up and held there until INS either deported them or permitted them to stay in the country. The youngest detainee was seventeen years old. Scott described the facilities starkly:

"Looks and sounds like a prison. Long squats and cinder-block walls, the rooms and hallways strangely dark in the incessant sun of South Texas because there are no windows. Iron gates are locked loudly into place over pitted cement floors."

This was the first immigrant detention camp I ever saw. It was 1986.

We ended our trip with a visit to Corpus Christi, where a local Vietnamese woman, a refugee and organizer, agreed to show us her community. Because of the influx of refugees, Corpus's shrimp business had grown exponentially. The Vietnamese were expert shrimp trawlers, but not everyone was happy about their arrival. One local fisherman told Scott that he felt the Vietnamese newcomers were given preferential treatment and not ticketed as often as he was.

"I love my country, I want to go back," our guide told us. "Here, I don't have to worry anything. I don't have to worry that I will be hungry. I don't have to worry that in nighttime the companies will come over and knock my door and put me in jail again forever. In here, I don't have to worry that way, but I'm *lonely.* I'm very lonely. Even if I have local friend, even if I speak English and communicate with the local people, but I'm lonely."

The woman was a proud American citizen now. In her tiny bedroom, she showed us a picture of her family back in Vietnam. The people who had once been reduced to unidentifiable masses on the covers of magazines now had names as she showed us each of her relatives. She cried about leaving them behind. She didn't understand why they hadn't been let in with her. She started crying and paused for a moment, then took several deep breaths and began singing "The Star-Spangled Banner."

This was the new face of patriotic Texas.

Very few people had seen that side of the immigration story until we put it on the radio, because most journalists were focused on the truly historic immigration reform that Ronald Reagan, a Republican president, was about to sign into law. Americans overwhelmingly supported the Immigration Reform and Control Act (IRCA), which combined increased immigration enforcement with the first large-scale legalization process for undocumented immigrants already residing in the US. Approximately 2.7 million people who had been living without papers and had no criminal background would be granted "amnesty" and processed for green cards. Activists fought over the word *amnesty* because they wanted to make sure people understood that the migrants were not lawbreakers. They were people who were intrinsically American, who would sacrifice everything to get themselves and their families a better life. Activists wanted the media to drop the word *amnesty* and call it *legalization.*

Signed in November 1986, IRCA marshaled in a new era of immigration form, the likes of which we had not seen since INA in 1965. The legislation was drafted based on the recommendations of a bipartisan Select Commission on Immigration and Refugee Policy (SCIRP), formed by Congress under President Carter, which proposed creating penalties for employers who hired undocumented immigrants, a small increase in the allowance for legal immigration, and a one-time legalization program for undocumented immigrants.

As a result, people could finally live in the US aboveboard, procure their documents, buy houses and cars, obtain driver's licenses, open more businesses, and send their kids to college. Equally important, people were now able to enter the economic mainstream of banking and start saving money.

The real story is that legalizing undocumented immigrants ended up helping, not hurting, the American economy. According to the Bureau of Labor Statistics, almost immediately after people regularized their status there was an overall 20 percent wage increase for undocumented workers. Statistics show these now-legalized immigrants started spending 200 percent more on their own education, including learning English and getting GEDs, and this ended up generating new investments in businesses and, as a result, more jobs.

This one law ended up helping the economy weather the recession, a beautiful and unprecedented act that solidified the history of America as a country of immigrants, a country that welcomes the other. It was also a highly political act. By now, the Republican Party had begun courting Latino voters and, as I was told by a Republican insider, they were going to secure Latino votes by proactively pushing through a massive immigration reform package. Ronald Reagan famously said, "Hispanics are already Republicans. They just don't know it yet."

IRCA was the brand-spanking-new shiny object that media and politicians were all in a tizzy about. On the one hand, the US government was holding up the success of IRCA, while on the other hand it was aiding military regimes terrorizing Salvadorans, Guatemalans, and Hondurans. Reagan's anti-communist military interventions in these countries over the past five years had ramped up to full scale with the development, funding, and arming of the Contras, US-supported and trained soldiers fighting against the legitimate Sandinista government in Nicaragua. Regardless of the obstacles presented by the Boland Amendment, which from 1982 through 1984 forbid all US military aid to fund the war against the Sandinistas, in total the US provided the Contras with $322 million of support.[1]

Reagan famously addressed the American public from the Oval Office in an attempt to garner support for the Contras, saying, "Central America is a region of great importance to the United States. And it is so close—San Salvador is closer to Houston than Houston is to Washington, DC. Central America is America, it is at our doorstep. And it has become the stage for a bold attempt by the Soviet Union, Cuba, and Nicaragua to install communism by force throughout the hemisphere." He continued: "What we see in El Salvador is an attempt to destabilize the entire region, and eventually move chaos and anarchy toward the American border."[2] The communists from Central America were the new boogeyman, in contrast to the nice Mexican immigrants we were legalizing.

Put bad immigrants behind the fences. Only the good ones get amnesty. A majority-white Congress and a majority-white and conservative Republican Party made this happen, and changed the lives of millions of immigrants forever. Many Mexican families living in the US at this time named their firstborns after Nancy and Ronald as a way to show their gratitude.

————————

Since I had tipped Jay off that there were other Latinas out there like me, within a few months, Cecilia was hired by *ATC* to work as a production assistant. Her job was a grind compared to mine. Her daily deadline caused her so much anxiety, but she excelled. Soon, Richard Gonzales was hired, and then Claudio Sanchez. In one year, there were four of us at the network.

I had learned so much from being in the field with Scott. He had a way of meeting people exactly where they were. I watched him get down on one knee to speak to a child and observed how he gently put his arm on Hawk's shoulder, or hugged the Vietnamese Texan woman. No other journalist I knew or had watched at work ever did this. Scott taught me how important the human touch was to create comfort and security.

Seeing Scott at work made me realize that I wanted to be him, which meant I didn't want to work with him any longer. He was my only reference point, so I decided I wanted to be the Latina Scott Simon. If he could do it, so could I. But I knew the only way I would ever be able to get on the air as a reporter telling my own stories was if I left NPR. A producer can't just get on the air as a reporter.

So I bought a used car, learned to drive, packed up my baby Honda Civic, and drove with David, one of my close friends from college, for five days across the country to San Diego. I had accepted a job as the new producer for *Enfoque Nacional*, a Spanish-language version of *ATC* that aired on some NPR stations. The show that gave me my start as a reporter in Spanish would now be under my direction.

Cecilia was deeply hurt that I was leaving her in DC, and no one at NPR could believe I was walking away from a job inside a network that was quickly becoming more competitive. I think people thought I had a big ego and that I was a bit ungrateful, but others knew it was a strategic decision. I knew what I wanted to be when I grew up: a correspondent for NPR based in NYC. Finally, a clear career goal.

Now that people knew me well inside the network, they told me to call them with my story pitches once I got to San Diego, where the show was produced. I could do *Enfoque Nacional* during the week, and then go out and file stories for NPR as a freelance reporter on the weekend.

One of the first stories I got on the air was my attempt to flip the narrative on immigration between Mexico and the US. I was surprised to find out that there was a sizable population of Americans who were living and working in Mexico without papers or permission—the American "illegal alien" living in Mexico.

I interviewed a man named Robert who said he chose to leave California for Tijuana because his quality of life was so much better and cheaper in Mexico. He loved seeing families everywhere and liked that people had a social life. San Diego, he said, was asleep by 9:00 p.m.

"Economics is not the only reason why people like Robert have decided to move south to Tijuana," I reported. "Mexico has always been seen as the perfect place for retirement by thousands of Americans. In fact, the largest number of Americans living outside the United States are living in Mexico." I discovered that sixty thousand Americans were living between Tijuana and Ensenada, Baja California, and many of them had immigrated without the appropriate papers.

I loved living a life on both sides of the border. I was American from nine to five and then I would cross the border to my apartment in Tijuana and be Mexican. But on the job in San Diego, I ran into trouble. My male coworkers were the biggest Latino machos. They made me feel less than and like a servant. I started wondering if I had made the right decision to leave NPR after all. I had felt sidelined there, but here there was in-your-face machismo every day.

It was right around this time of confusion, when I began feeling rudderless again in every way, that I received a phone call from a friend at NPR. She told me that the CBS Radio Network was looking for a seasonal fill-in to help the producers who would be gone on long summer vacations. I called up Norman Morris at CBS immediately and he flew me to NYC. I met him downstairs at a swanky restaurant on West Fifty-Sixth Street, and he offered me the job of summer fill-in network producer, doubling my weekly salary.

Now I had a network job, what my father had always wanted for me. My overnight shift at CBS News on West Fifty-Seventh Street was calling me, so I left my border life to go back to the familiar rhythm of New York City.

Chapter 7

—

You Can Take Care of Me a Little

One night I heard ranchera music playing on the street in Spanish Harlem. It was 2:30 a.m. on a Wednesday in July 1986. I knew right then and there that New York City was about to change forever.

I was in a car on my way to start the overnight shift at CBS News, where I clocked in at 3:00 a.m. I regularly worked on segments for *The Osgood File* or *First Line Report* with Judy Muller. I had three hours to prep material for the anchors who would walk in at 6:00 a.m. and write their scripts. Once that was done, I would put everything together for the 8:00 and 9:00 a.m. newscasts. Then after rebroadcasts and some paperwork, my workday would be done.

That night in July was one of those nights—a typical, boiling-hot summer night in New York City, so hot that even though the sun had been down for six hours, the black tar of the streets was still steaming. I was exhausted and struggling to wake up as the car slowly drove west down 116th Street, El Barrio's central avenue.

We passed a twenty-four-hour bodega on the corner of 116th Street and Third Avenue. The white lights shone over the boxes of fruit out front and the bustle inside the bodega made it appear like three in the afternoon, not three in the morning. I could see the store shelves stocked with all the colors of the rainbow in cans and candy bars and fruit drinks. And there, right outside the store, under the gleam of the urban moon, I saw a group of men sitting on empty milk crates, cleaning and boxing fruit and vegetables. Their bodies looked familiar to me—the way they were slumped but working at the same time, their hands moving quickly while their bodies stood still—and this reminded me of the men I grew up seeing when we went shopping in Pilsen.

Wait. *Are they Mexican?* I asked myself. *Mexican immigrants in New York City?*

Then I heard the sweet wail of the ranchera music coming from their boom box at full volume, echoing up and down 116th, a street that was usually ruled by salsa and, more and more, merengue at this hour. Who else would be playing ranchera? I asked the driver to pull over and I buzzed my window down all the way so that I could look at the scene in front of me with wonder.

¡Llegaron los mexicanos a Nuyol! And if there were three at that bodega, that meant there were more spread across the city. I didn't know it at the time, but I was witnessing the changing dynamics of Mexican migration patterns with my very own eyes. The economic crisis in Mexico during the 1980s—declining GDP, low wages, high unemployment—forced millions of Mexicans to look elsewhere for work.[1] At the same time, many formerly undocumented immigrants now had legal status, which gave them the flexibility to move around the US. Because so many Mexican immigrants were already working in places like California and the Southwest, especially after Reagan's legalization went through, newcomers had to venture farther out to cities like New York. It didn't take long for New Yorkers to realize the value of Mexican workers. They were willing to do the jobs no one else wanted for longer hours and less pay. Pretty soon Mexicans were in high demand and the immigration numbers during these years illustrate this demographic explosion. In 1980, there were less than 25,000 Mexicans living in New York City, and only a sliver of that population was foreign-born. By 1990, Mexicans numbered 56,000 strong with more than half of them migrating from outside the US.[2] (The 2010 census counted more than 319,000 Mexicans in New York City.)[3]

Could it be possible that my life in NYC was about to become more whole? While I had learned to love the Pan–Latin American part of myself, I also longed for Mexico. I longed for the humble familiarity of mexicanos and the biting satire of Chilangos. I missed El Dia de los Muertos, cilantro, avocados, and had to get my corn tortillas via US mail in a box from Chicago. I missed Chicanismo even though I didn't grow up with it (the movement was not based in Chicago); I wanted it around me now, that deep sense of pride in being descendants of mexicanos. I wanted people in New York to have a reference for mexicanos because we were invisible there. We didn't exist. Seeing these paisanos meant Mexico was on its way to the Big Apple.

Maybe I could be whole again on this side of the border. Maybe I put together the two things that I loved most—Mexico and NYC. Then I would know that I could stay in the US forever.

Men in my family in Mexico did not cry. Mi papá tampoco. Men on American television didn't cry, either. When Cronkite cried as he reported the assassination of President John F. Kennedy, everyone noticed. Even though he was the oldest and perhaps most stern of all the news anchors, he seemed more human because he had cried in front of us.

Toward the end of my summer contract at CBS, my boss, Norman, pulled me into his office and asked if I'd like to stay on past September. The assignment would be producing the famous Walter Cronkite end-of-the-year roundup called "And That's the Way It Was." I beamed. I had left El Barrio and moved back to my Washington Heights apartment with Deyanira and her grandma Biemba. That evening we broke out cold Dominican beers to celebrate my official reentry to New York City.

I was back for good. I stopped partying as I had over the summer. I started working out again. I wasn't thinking about anybody but me.

One day I came to work wearing what I thought was a beautiful outfit: beige leather pants, a tight tan turtleneck, and a beaded, wraparound necklace that I had bought from one of the African street vendors who had popped up in Harlem. Most of these vendors were Senegalese men who spoke French. Some were the sons of middle-class families, young adventurous men who wanted to leave the homeland and strike out on their own. Selling street wares was their version of waiting tables. I was rocking this look in the elevator, when out of nowhere a white female executive turned to me and said, "Wow, you look so tribal." And then she was gone.

I was one of the first Latinas to be hired in the news division at CBS. I had been through this before. By day, I crossed the border from the Heights into midtown at Columbus Circle, near where CBS was located, a twenty-minute subway ride. Once there, I went to work calling all of the top CBS News correspondents like Lesley Stahl and Bill Plante, setting up interviews with each of them so that I could collect their views on the most important stories of 1987. They had no idea I saw myself as an insecure and confused twenty-seven-year-old newbie journalist and fill-in producer. To them, I was a fellow CBS News producer who worked on the radio side. There was mutual respect among both departments. Their serious tone with me made me take myself more seriously as a journalist. If they took me seriously, then so should I.

But on Wednesday nights, I was back to doing my old radio show *Nueva Canción y Demás* at WKCR, till one in the morning. In my barrio, many of my Dominican neighbors had never left the forty-block radius of 145th to 181st Streets, had never been as far south as midtown. In the Heights, the only language spoken was Spanish; meanwhile, I worked at what was considered the national hallmark of English-language journalism. I would lie back on my mattress on the floor with its Mexican bedspread and think, *How did I end up at CBS News? How is it possible that I am writing copy for Walter Cronkite?*

It was the year of Oliver North, a decorated marine who revealed in his July 1987 testimony before Congress that he had previously lied to congressional investigators about his involvement in the Iran-Contra Affair—a plan that Reagan approved to sell arms to Iran, a known sponsor of terror, to the tune of millions of dollars in exchange for the release of hostages being held by Hezbollah. North had proposed using a portion of the proceeds from the weapons sales to fund the Contras in Nicaragua, who were fighting against the elected revolutionary Sandinista government there. The entire scheme was illegal, not to mention against the country's most basic values of law and transparency, but I was seeing a pattern. First Nixon and now Reagan? I thought we lived in the world's greatest democracy, but laws were being broken again in the White House? Americans were overwhelmingly against supporting the Contras.[4] The fact that North knowingly broke the law and then put forth a boldface lie to cover his tracks was an embarrassing low point in the country, second only to Watergate.

I suffered for days as I prepared to write Cronkite's end-of-the-year commentary. The other ninety-second segments I'd been assigned were easier to write because they were straight news wrap-ups of the year in business or science, for example. I paced my room overlooking Fort Washington Avenue and paused to stare at the street, terrified to write words for Cronkite, overwhelmed by my imposter syndrome.

Eventually, I forced myself to sit down with a pen and a long yellow legal pad, the kind that were everywhere at CBS, and began to sketch an outline for the commentary. *It's only ninety seconds long,* I told myself. *You have to do this. Just do a draft. Get something down on paper. You have no choice. Do it now!*

I looked at the outline and started writing. The first draft was long and filled with outrage. I immediately felt doubtful. Was I outraged about Oliver North because I was too close to Central America? I kept second-guessing myself, believing I had no right to be writing for Cronkite.

The more I thought about it—a network of secret criminals working in the White House and raising money to kill Central Americans in Nicaragua?—the more I realized my anger wasn't simply because I was a Latina, although that initially opened me up to seeing what was going on. I was angry because I lived in the United States of America, and I expected better.

I rewrote the script several times, finessing the rage, but keeping the undercurrent of disgust and dismay at our government. I was proud of my work, proud I had forced myself to believe in my own abilities. I took it to Norman, only to have him say, "There is no way Walter will read this!"

"This sounds like you wrote it," he continued. "But not a man like Walter. He won't read it!"

I had done a lot of work on this piece and had read it to several people, including Sandy. I was careful to make sure it was not an "angry Latina" commentary. It was an American journalist's commentary on the year 1987.

Norman wanted me to rewrite it, but Cronkite was coming in the next day. Walter came in for one day and one day only to do his recording. It would be impossible to come up with something new in time, given the fact that I had to prep everything for the recording session.

Surprising even myself, I said, "Let's take it down to the *Evening News* editor and have him look at it. Just don't tell him who wrote it."

I had heard Margot Adler, the NPR science correspondent, mention that Paul Fischer was nice. If Paul liked Margot, who was also a Wiccan priestess, I figured he might be cool. Norman knew my work and trusted my journalistic instincts. But in this instance, he didn't trust that I could separate myself from the story enough to write an "objective" commentary. I wasn't just fighting for this piece. I was fighting to believe in my own voice as a journalist.

I followed Norman, as if watching myself from above in an out-of-body experience. Before I knew it, I was in an elevator to the first floor and then I was walking behind Norman right into the famed "fishbowl" where the *Evening News* anchors sat surrounded by a half circle of glassed-in offices—hence the name *fishbowl*. Norman walked right up to Paul and handed him my commentary.

"Do you think Cronkite will read this for his end-of-the-year commentary?" he asked.

My legs went wobbly. I was in the fishbowl! I could see where Dan Rather was going to be sitting in just a few hours. For years, I had seen this set on TV and now I was here inside of it. I looked at Paul studying my work and felt nauseous immediately. I wanted to scream for joy and throw up at the same time. *Hold it together*, I kept telling myself. *Hold it together. Do* not *lose it right here in front of everyone.*

A second later Paul took out his red pen, circled one word, replaced another, handed it back casually to Norman, and said, "Yeah, he'll read this. It's good."

Norman looked at me, and I smiled. We said goodbye to Paul, whom I was never introduced to because he was such a busy and important man. Who was I, anyway? The next day Walter Cronkite came in with his assistant and read the fifteen scripts I had laid out for him.

"Nice job on the commentary," he told me as he put on his winter coat, his broad shoulders a little less broad at seventy-one years old. I stood there in awe. A news icon had just read my words. As his own.

Around this time, Jay Kernis, the man who gave me my first job in radio journalism and who had scolded and pleaded with me not to leave NPR, had become one of the people TV networks had poached from radio. NPR was finally seen as part of the mainstream media; it was no longer a fringe independent network the way conservatives had characterized it. Now they wanted their talents for TV.

Jay had been brought on with a new set of anchors to try to make CBS competitive in the morning time slot, which had been famously ruled by the *Today* show. Harry Smith and Kathleen Sullivan were at the helm of *CBS This Morning*. They were both seasoned anchors, but each had issues connecting with viewers. Harry was stiff yet seen as not serious enough and Kathleen was a beautiful brunette who was a bit icy on camera.

I was finishing my time with the radio team and, even though I had worked with every section of CBS radio, including the documentary and business report departments, there was no staff position for me. There was, however, an opening for a production assistant at the morning show, so Jay encouraged me to apply, and David Corvo hired me.

I made a great salary for a single woman in Manhattan. The economic security of a full-time gig at CBS was pretty enticing. Our days often started at 4:00 a.m. and our lunch hour came after the 10:00 a.m. meeting.

Life was pretty good except that I was working as a morning TV booker, which in the world of journalism was seen as the lowest form of the profession. I spent most of my time fighting with other bookers over who would get a guest first. Beating the competition by even a minute could mean everything, and I was always losing because we were third in the ratings. I wasn't being taken seriously by my colleagues and I was being ridiculed by the other morning-show bookers who had years of experience. They laughed at my attempts to compete in their sphere.

A low point came when I was dispatched to Winnetka, Illinois, a suburb near Chicago where there had been a shooting of three people, and back then that was huge news.[5] I had to compete with another show to get a survivor to speak to us. I was hoping to score the interview to please my bosses, who would gloat that we got them first. But my journalist heart was dying inside. After I'd spoken to the family in the middle of their grief and been so apologetic, they went with another network first. I was disgusted this mattered to anyone in a moment of tragedy.

I once got someone who had been shot by Border Patrol on the air. It was a huge get and no one else had the story nationally. But that was the only story I was proud of after six months of working there. My friends told me to stay. *Think about where you are and the audience you have access to. Think about your responsibility. Look how far you have gotten.* I was a success, but I didn't feel proud.

If I gave up on my dream of being an NPR reporter, maybe I could make it work at CBS News. I could focus on making a big journalistic impact at CBS at some point, slowly move up the ladder, and one day work in the fishbowl as a producer. I already knew I could never be on air. There were no on-air Latina correspondents at the networks, so why would I even think of that as an option?

I needed to stand out if I ever wanted to move up in the company, so I came up with the idea of having Kathleen Sullivan interview Fidel Castro. He had only given one interview and that was to Barbara Walters. I had sources who told me Fidel thought Kathleen was attractive. To be honest, this strategy felt grotesque: scoring "big" to prove myself; using a woman's beauty to help score the interview; pleasing my bosses in a way that felt unnatural.

When I asked what she thought of the idea, her response was

"What's the hook?" I offered an interview with one of the world's most enigmatic leaders who famously did not give interviews and, in return, I got asked for a hook? My journalist brain felt like it was shrinking to the size of a pea, but I'd become so dependent on all of the amenities that came with working in the mainstream media. A woman who was maybe seven years older than me told me to be careful of this place. "Know what you want to do. Otherwise you'll end up with golden handcuffs. You'll love the money so much you won't be able to leave what will begin to feel like a jail."

I was busy with work at CBS and at WKCR, each at opposite ends of the media spectrum. There was nothing like doing live radio in New York City at night in the 1980s. It was a wild time and people used to call into shows as a way to vent, almost like a rudimentary Twitter. Live, free-form radio was the radical, counterculture thing to do. WBAI, WFUV, and WKCR were seen as reigning supreme in this new medium. On my show, I didn't hold back. I was a secure working journalist and this allowed me to feel more rooted and stable as a grown woman, and that made me feel like I needed to give myself more credit for where I was. I fully expressed my voice on the air, making pointed critiques of the patriarchy or capitalism or imperialism—cultural or military. The show was seven years old and had a following. I was more relaxed, and I wasn't filing as a reporter for anyone. I saw myself as a corporate journalist by day and a cultural disrupter by night.

I was proud of who I was becoming: a tiny but strong Mexican-born journalist with an edge who called New York City home.

I was also a killer salsa and merengue dancer because my Dominican roommate had been hell-bent on making sure I didn't look like a Latina with no sense of rhythm. Many Sunday mornings we would work off our hangovers by dancing salsa and merengue until our sweat was salty and prolific.

Deyanira was working as a social worker in the foster care system and by this time we had both moved out of the Washington Heights apartment. It was getting more dangerous there, and I had already been held up at knifepoint. Her abuela had moved back to Villa Mella, Deyanira had moved in with her construction worker lover, and I traded in our uptown lease for a small one-bedroom on 107th Street near Amsterdam Avenue, where I felt much safer alone at night as a woman. I had tried to get away from the street dealing on the corners uptown in the Heights, but here it was, too, all along Amsterdam Avenue. I got used to the sight of emaciated people standing in line for crack at all hours on the sidewalk.

One night when I was dancing the night away at "Salsa Meets Jazz" in the famed Village Gate nightclub, Agustín, a Puerto Rican PhD student and activist who I had met at WKCR, came up to me and told me an important Dominican artist named Gérman Perez had seen me on the dance floor and thought I was beautiful. Did I want to meet him? Maybe interview him?

I walked over, and standing next to him was a tall, slim man with a short Afro, dark glasses even though it was nighttime, and full lips curved into an inviting smile.

"Este es el pintor Gérman Perez," Agustín said. "Él te quería conocer . . . ¿quizas lo quieres entrevistar?"

Gérman was gorgeous! I felt a slight electrical tremble tingle through my body when he gave me his hand and then bent down from his six-foot-two frame to lean in and give me a soft kiss on the cheek. He smelled like a Caribbean bakery and coconut. His voice was deep and mysterious. I was dying to see what his eyes looked like behind those glasses.

"Me dicen que eres periodista y me gustaria que vieras mi trabajo," Gérman said. "¿Me puedes dar tu telefono y yo me comunico?"

I wrote my home phone number on a napkin with a blue ballpoint pen. Now I had a real-live suitor, one I thought was gorgeous and intriguing. He was Dominican, born and raised, and not a US Latino, which meant he brought a Latin American sensibility to life. Gérman Perez, el pintor, era latinoamericano y caribeño, negro, Taíno, sensual.

Around this time, I quit CBS and ran away from the comfort of the golden handcuffs. The steady paycheck and retirement fund were not why I had become a journalist. I would not be able to achieve my mission in the mediocrity of morning television. There was so much happening in the world. Was I prepared to dig into the mainstream and fight my way up bit by bit? Or go at it alone?

I couldn't let go of my dream of becoming an on-air NPR reporter based in New York. If I really wanted it, for reals, I was going to have to fight for it and prove myself. I got a contract to file stories for a new national show called *Crossroads* for $500 a month, which would almost cover my $750 rent. As long as I had my rent covered, I would find a way to make it work because, really, who needs to eat?

But why did I give that gorgeous man my number? He was calling me every few days asking if I would go visit his studio and see his paintings. I finally summoned the nerve and called Gérman back.

A couple days later I walked up to 135th Street, north of Harlem, where there was merengue coming out of every open window and live geese tied to a fire escape. I heard the cooing of a rooster in the distance. There were dealers on the corner of Broadway, so I looked tough and pushed past them. I got to Gérman's tenement-style building, walked up the broken steps that smelled like urine to the fourth floor, and knocked on the door.

When he answered in a cutoff T-shirt with his huge, chiseled biceps and triceps in full view, it wasn't an electrical tingle but more like lightning running through my body. I tried to act nonchalant as we cheek-kissed, but my heart was blushing pink. The building might have been a scary tenement disaster, but Gérman had transformed his apartment into art deco pop. It was like his apartment had been airlifted straight from Santo Domingo—not only were there the pastel-colored walls, but he'd covered up the windows that looked out to an air shaft with large photos of kids fishing in the Caribbean.

He walked me into his main studio and I saw the most captivating painting: mystical Taíno Indians with palm trees growing out of their heads doing a moon and star dance in a circle. It made me want to be in it, dancing with them.

"You painted this?" I looked at him and said.

"Sí," he said as his eyes turned luscious and warm, drawing me in to him. More electrical sparks. I started to worry. I hadn't felt this gooey-sexy-romantic feeling for years. I wasn't supposed to be experiencing this sensation. The more I saw of his artwork, the more worried I became that with each piece of art I was slowly falling more in love with him.

Finally, he broke the silence and said he was going to fix himself something to eat—would I join him in the kitchen? *What? He cooks for himself, too?*

He sat down, and I felt so discombobulated, but he was perfectly at ease, a grown man comfortable in his own skin. After he finished eating, he asked me to come sit on his lap, since I had been sitting in a built-in wooden cupboard from the original 1900s tenement.

"No," I said, surprised. "Why would I do that?"

"¿Por qué no? Tú me caes bien. Y nada más es sentarte aquí un segundo. No es gran cosa," he insisted softly.

I wavered until the pull of his quiet beauty and strong arms was too much. I walked over and sat on his lap. I said nothing and neither did he. Gérman seemed content just to be there, but I was so aware of my internal electrical energy that I became terrified I might short-circuit and get stuck to this man. I jumped up as if someone had lit a match under me.

"I'm not sure what I'm doing here, but I really need to go," I said moving to the door. "Thank you for showing me your art," I yelled as I ran out of his apartment.

I couldn't give of myself and trust again in a man, so instead I jumped into the freelance world with gusto. Every pitch that was approved, every edit that went well, every connection I made in the business was a cause for celebration, which usually meant dancing alone in my underwear to Earth, Wind & Fire or Rubén Blades. All these little steps were confirmation that maybe I could make it as a journalist, that maybe my work had the capacity to distinguish itself.

To me, being a reporter meant seeing the humanity in everyone, especially people who are perceived as invisible, and then making it hyper-visible to others. The people and stories I wanted to do focused on the forgotten, the other, those who are thought of as different. At the same time, I aimed to evoke universal themes so that anyone, no matter who they were, could see themselves in my stories. That's how I learned to write a news story. Write it as if you were telling your mother what happened. Connect the heart of the story to someone else's heart.

I proudly wore a tough exterior, a combination of street and sophistication. I had my very own New York City Police press pass that hung around my neck like a trophy; it was bright lime green so that it would be visible to NYPD officers. I was becoming the kind of person I had only seen role-modeled in Mexico by my journalist friends Blanche Petrich and Guadalupe Pineda from *La Jornada*. They were independent women who knew in their guts that this journalism thing is a bug you can never shake. They worked their butts off as reporters but also had full lives, but not full-time live-in relationships. That was part of the challenge—finding a partner who would be okay with women putting a story first or being on the road all the time, often alone or traveling with other men. Neither of them had been able to. I mean, what kind of a man can deal with that?

What nobody told me about freelancing was that you end up working all the time. You always say yes to a job because you always need the money. There are no days off. Because there were hardly any Latina public radio freelancers out there, I began to see reporting on the community as another one of my superpowers. How did piragüas, Puerto Rican shaved ice, end up in Spanish Harlem? How does gentrification affect small, immigrant-owned businesses? What's the story behind the panpipe musicians who perform in New York City's busiest subway station? Who are New York's avant-garde Latinx artists? Why does the New York tristate area have only one multilingual radio station?

Still, none of my pitches were ever green-lit by NPR to air on any of the big tentpole shows like the weekday *All Things Considered* and *Morning Edition* programs with the biggest audiences. If it weren't for *Crossroads*, created and conceived by Latina journalist Elisabeth Perez-Luna and dedicated to telling stories about the "new" multicultural America, I might have given up on the world of independent producing. She loved all of my pitches, which allowed me to keep falling in love with journalism.

Ceci had left *All Things Considered* and was now working with Scott Simon on *Weekend Edition*, which was the darling of the network. They had the budget to travel anywhere, and she was doing her own groundbreaking work covering stories in Latin America with Scott. Ceci's skill at producing poignant moments made Scott come alive with tenderness and unfiltered curiosity. She made him sound amazing.

More and more, Ceci was modeling this other-life possibility that she and I had started to consider: What about becoming a foreign correspondent and traveling the world? We knew a lot of guys who were doing this—not so many women—but we could try. She had just come back from Cuba with Scott and her pieces were riveting. Producers have so much control over their work and Ceci was the best at it. She made me miss NPR, its reach and resources.

But the network was changing, and focused more and more on breaking news. The pieces were rarely longer than three minutes, when before a six- or seven-minute piece was the norm, and they were using less ambient sound to enrich the stories. NPR was being called the *New York Times* of radio, but old-timers longed for the days when the organization was scrappier, riskier, and more fun.

Competitors cropped up doing different kinds of independently produced audio. One of the first was a documentary series called *Soundprint* that featured, among others, the work of award-winning producers who had left NPR because of creative and editorial issues. *Soundprint* did hour-long audio documentaries—deep sonic dives into stories with highly produced elements that were, for the time, groundbreaking and a precursor to podcasts. Because the platform was run by a woman with a woman sound engineer at the helm, they gave many women a shot at producing. One day I got a call to join their ranks. It was like being asked to produce for National Geographic instead of the local news.

The assignment was to accompany acclaimed *Rolling Stone* magazine writer Peter Cohen to Medellín, Colombia, and go into the dark heart of Pablo Escobar–controlled territory to produce a companion *Soundprint* documentary for Cohen's magazine article. He would write both pieces, but I would be responsible for field reporting and producing the audio piece.

Finally, I had broken through. This was a major assignment for a major show, and I would get the chance to work with *Rolling Stone*. I started setting up the trip to Colombia. Ceci helped me to understand the specific challenges of international reporting and safety. She told me I'd need to think quickly and be congenial before I picked a fight with anyone. She knew me well.

Bombs were exploding in downtown Medellín, just like they would during episodes of *Narcos*, the Netflix TV show produced decades later. The feud between the Cali and Medellín Cartels, who were blowing up each other's businesses, meant you took your life in your hands anytime you went downtown. We spent most of our time in an area controlled by Escobar, just driving around to get a feel for the street vibe. Later in the day, we met sources in hotel rooms to interview them about their nine-to-five jobs as sicarios, a new word that meant "killer for hire on a motorcycle." We went to hospitals to interview ER doctors who saved the lives of gunshot-wound victims only to have armed killers come in and shoot them in the OR, and then threaten to kill the doctors and nurses. We were being watched by Escobar associates the entire time. I had no idea, but I later learned from his top killer, Popeye, that they decided not to harm us because it would have been more bad publicity than good for their reputation.

Medellín is one of the most beautiful cities in the world, known as La Ciudad de la Eterna Primavera, the City of Eternal Spring. It's also known for being one of the most polite cities in Latin America, where even the taxi drivers wear suits and ties and speak with the formal *usted*. The unease of our driver/fixer was the thing that set us all off. He was constantly sweating and fidgeting. He seemed deeply conflicted; he wanted the opportunity to prove that he could work with international journalists, but this line of work could also cost him his life.

Word on the street was that Escobar's people were not happy with our visit and our questions. I didn't believe it. The final straw came when we got back to Bogotá and someone had broken into Peter's hotel room. He left immediately, and I went to stay with friends to be safe. The last thing I did before heading to Cartagena to decompress was a ride-along with the Bogotá police as they took down a basuco or crack house. They wanted to put on a show for the American journalist. They busted into an abandoned building, running in with their guns drawn in full central-casting mode and pointed at people who weren't doing much of anything but wasting away. They didn't arrest a single dealer in that raid. I felt used and sick at the same time. One person hid in a pile of human sewage. The police made sure I saw that.

"Son animales," the officer said as he trained his flashlight on the man's terrified eyes and face covered in shit.

I flew back to the US and relocated for several weeks to Baltimore, where *Soundprint* was based. I started pulling and ordering tape and drafting an outline for Peter so he could get started on the writing. I had less than two weeks before I was headed into the studio to produce this monster. The most I had ever produced was eighteen minutes, and Scott wrote all of his scripts. I was now producing an hour with a writer who had never written for radio and it was my first international gig. If I proved I could do this, maybe international reporting was for me.

The days passed and the promises of a script came and went. I had three days to go. How was it possible that I, the cub producer, had to call a senior reporter to ask him about his script? I couldn't believe it. Worse, when I called him sounding a bit exasperated, he replied that he was busy working on the print piece and he simply could not write both.

"Plus," he said, "I've never written for radio."

This is exactly what I had been afraid of. Being left high and dry. Sandy had made plans to take me to dinner that same night, so I went into DC from Baltimore. She picked me up from the train in her impeccable Mazda sports car and I finally broke down into tears as I told her my script was due in three days and the dude had left me hanging.

"Malulis," Sandy said, as always with her voice like a honey throat lozenge—easy-listening, thick and soft, but no bullshit. "Honey, you're just going to have to write it. You can do this. I know you can do this."

My fear of writing was doing a number on me. First we went to a Chinese restaurant, and as we were ordering I had to run to the bathroom to throw up. We left and went to a Japanese place; I threw up as soon as we walked in. Finally, we ended up at a diner, and I was able to eat crackers and chicken soup. Then I threw up.

Sandy drove me back to Baltimore because I was in such bad

shape. She gave me an hour-long sermon about self-love. She purred to me about how, when she was starting off on air as a host, someone criticized her, and then she became self-conscious and lost her voice. She told me we can't let our fear take over and to look at how far I had come all by myself, to trust myself. She believed in me. She really did. And she was taking care of me right now. I was thankful she hadn't thrown me out on the street with all the crying, puking, and hysterics.

I hadn't realized I was in the middle of my first full-on panic attack. We didn't have the words for this kind of episode back then. I went to sleep, and when I woke up, I just focused on the work over the next two days. I tuned everything out, mostly the self-doubt. Instead, I heard Sandy's voice in my ear. I remembered the way I would encourage Ceci when she felt helpless with a script. I told myself I could do this.

And I was doing it. I was writing this complicated story as if I were telling it to my mother—everything that I saw, scene by scene. Peter read it and signed off, then asked if I would voice the piece instead of him because it was my writing. I would now have my first international byline. He didn't leave me hanging. He gave me a gift.

The piece for *Soundprint* was titled "Silver or Lead," "Plata o Plomo," and the producers loved it.

Not long after the piece aired, the phone rang again and this time it was the international desk at NPR asking if I would accompany Richard Gonzalez, the State Department correspondent, for a trip to Peru. They assigned me to report stories around drugs and violence and the radical fringe armed group Sendero Luminoso. I was becoming that person. This could be my new life!

In December 1989, the coordinated forces of several ideological bands of armed guerillas in El Salvador came together to declare the end of the war and their final offensive to take the capital of San Salvador.

They called it La Ofensiva del '89. As soon as it was clear that this protracted and slowly progressing leftist revolution had suddenly gone into overdrive, I got another call from NPR. They sent me down to San Salvador with Scott Simon and an engineer to produce several in-depth pieces from the front of this now full-out urban guerilla war.

At night, I could hear the bombs being dropped in Apopa, a city just outside of the capital, the place where my one-time Salvadoran college boyfriend still had family. The thuds were like powerful sound craters, creating punches muffled in cotton balls. Downstairs the international journalists would file their pieces by 6:00 p.m. and then the party would start: drinking, live music, waiters everywhere, people swimming in the pool while there was an actual war going on. Many of them had been there for so long they were numb.

I thought about the refugees and hunger strikers I had met in college. The situation in El Salvador had gotten worse and deadlier. The US-supported military wasn't playing fair. A hospital had been bombed, violating the basic rules of engagement. We went there and saw an eight-year-old girl who had been hit by shrapnel. The back of her thigh, hit while she was trying to run away, was missing a small, ice cream–sized scoop, something I had never imagined I would see. Scott hugged the little girl at one point and as always gave me a chance to ask any final questions, so I asked the girl about her mother.

"Está en EE.UU. Si puedes, mándale este mensaje," she said. "Yo quiero que venga a buscarme. Tengo miedo." ("She's in the USA. If you can, please send her this message. I want her to come get me. I'm scared.") Tears began to stream from my eyes and the little girl's.

Our eyes were fresh to all of this, but many of the other journalists had been covering this story for years. For them, this was a numbers story—how many bombs were dropped, how many guerillas died, how many soldiers were out, how many dollars were arriving, the names of the American advisers, the generals, etc. It was cold and unfeeling.

Right outside our hotel, half a dozen little boys wearing white clown makeup gathered daily in the middle of a busy intersection and attempted to entertain passersby for a few coins. They ate fire and did backflips during red lights. *Who are they? What's their story? Did anyone ever think of asking?*

I took Scott over to the boys and we sat with them on the side of the road. The boys were so sweet, yet they were alone to fend for themselves in the middle of a war. They were outside the hotel every single day because that is how they survived, and yet no one seemed to see them or care. They didn't have time for self-pity.

"How do you eat?" Scott asked them, and I translated.

"The way we get food is just by directing traffic . . . The little money that we make, we use it to buy food, and then we share it all," one of the boys answered. Right in front of us, through the haze from last night's bombs still rising from the mountains, was a huge modern McDonald's. Scott asked, "Have you had breakfast today?"

Before you knew it, we walked in with six boys dressed as clowns. Normally, they were not allowed inside because McDonald's was only for wealthy Salvadorans and these boys were considered street "trash." "The boys seemed to take some pleasure in the fact that today the guards could only watch them eat hamburgers," Scott narrated in the final piece.

"Yeah, a lot of the guards, like the ones who are here, sometimes even when we try to get here, they lock us up," another boy explained. "They put us away, like in stores and stuff, and don't let us out."

A boy named Carlos decided to save the rest of his hamburger for later, to show his mother. At one point, he dropped his voice and said: "My father was a guerilla. He was a guerilla, and all we know is that they found him. I think it was probably either the police or the armed forces. They probably tortured him and just left him to die."

We recorded them talking about their dreams as they ate. Of all the stories I produced from El Salvador, this is the one people liked most. It was a story that had been right in front of journalists' faces for years and yet for them and therefore the rest of us, these kids were invisible. Their stories didn't matter.

I made it back from El Salvador and what turned out to be a bloody but failed offensive in time to raise my right hand and take an oath to bear arms for America. I wish I could say that I became a citizen out of a sense of patriotic duty, but I didn't. I became a citizen out of fear. By now I had traveled to Cuba and Nicaragua, and I had been to Europe and multiple countries in South America. Every time I came in and out of Mexico, the place I traveled to the most, I felt more and more worried that one day US border agents would take my green card away and not let me back in. Just like that.

The old wooden courtroom in the court district of downtown Manhattan, where the naturalization ceremony took place, was huge and seated hundreds. There were people from everywhere in the world who were happy that they had finally made it to this point. For some it might have been years in the making. I had to leave my Mexican citizenship behind and return my Mexican passport in an act of humility and shame because at that time you still couldn't have dual citizenship. I was relieved it was done, but I had no idea that my citizenship would one day change how I understood my role in this country. Forever.

———————

A few days later I came down with the flu and a high fever and lay in bed with no one to take care of me. I was as close as I would ever come to being clinically depressed, but nobody called it that back then. The phone rang and the machine answered. I listened as the person began to leave a message. When I recognized the voice, I melted, but not because I had a fever of 101 degrees. It was Gérman telling me he was back in town and asking if I would like to meet up for dinner and dancing at "Salsa Meets Jazz," the first place we had ever laid eyes on each other. The last time I had seen him had been almost a year before.

My body jolted up as if by electrical impulse, attracted irresistibly to this man. I ran to the phone and picked it up. Just hearing his voice drew me to him, like a magnet. Like chicle.

"Hello? Gérman? You're back?"

"Yes, I just finished shooting this TV series around the world, but I made a big decision in my life. I sold all of the equipment from my production company and am dedicating myself completely to my art."

I melted some more. This man had ganas. He pulled the rug out from underneath his own feet because of his drive to paint and be an artist. This was the kind of man I wanted, one who knew who he was and didn't need to depend on a woman for anything except love.

He invited me to an upcoming dinner party at his place and then to join him and his friends later that night for dancing at the Village Gate. I said yes. He asked if he could come visit me and I told him I was sick in bed.

"Is there anyone with you?" he asked. I said no. "Then let me come and take care of you," he said, his rough Dominican accent now transformed into a poet's soft voice. No man had ever offered to do that for me. I said no thank you and hung up, terrified.

In an act of self-destruction and because of my inability to trust a man, I decided to not show up to Gérman's place. Later that night, I went with Deyanira to "Salsa Meets Jazz" at the Village Gate. Soon he showed up at the club and I did a double take. His black hair was now in a ponytail. He had pierced his ear and wore an off-white shirt and jeans, understated but sexy. His best friend, Isidro, came straight to the dance floor and was about to separate me and Deyanira in the middle of a dance, which meant he was about to get slugged.

Isidro put his hand on her shoulder, and when Deyanira saw him her face lit up. It turned out they were old schoolmates. They went off dancing and left me standing in the middle of the dance floor, not dancing and looking lost. That's when Gérman suddenly appeared in front of me, his hand outstretched, ready to pull me to him and start dancing salsa, as if he had been waiting to ask me forever.

I felt myself merge into him. With every pasito, my body conformed to his, my tiny frame fitting perfectly into his, my face at his chest level, my cheeks pressed into his linen shirt, his hand on my lower back, connecting me like a good dancer should, to his internal rhythm. We closed the Gate and walked down Bleecker to take the number 1 train home at two o'clock in the morning, holding hands as if we had always been a couple. I hadn't even kissed him.

At my apartment, I asked him up for tea and he sat on my sofa. Instead of making a move, Gérman simply laid his head on my lap. We stayed that way for a while—calm, breathing in sync. Then I couldn't stand it any longer and lowered my lips down to his; those lips I had imagined and thought about were now touching mine. My lips melted into his and my body followed.

That same night, unbeknownst to both of us, our mutual friend Ernest, from the Haitian band Tabou Combo, was shot and killed. Two nights had passed since our encounter, and when Gérman heard about the death and realized our connection to Ernest, he said to me once again, "Deja que te cuide un poco." Let me take care of you a little.

And that was that. The next day after I finished work, I rode my bike back to 135th and carried it up all four flights of stairs, the ones with broken marble and stinky garbage. I knocked on Gérman's door and when he opened I said, "Me puedes cuidar un poco." You can take care of me a little.

Chapter 8

A Taste of the Action

I experienced love so simply and full of trust with Gérman, the way I had before that night on the hilltop in Mexico, before someone I trusted to love me hurt me physically, emotionally, and spiritually. I could tell Gérman loved every part of me: my petite frame, my tiny, barely-there breasts, my small but shapely backside and thighs, my wild mermaid hair and funny-looking mismatched thumbs. This gorgeous man thought I was beautiful even though he was surrounded by the most stunning women in the world—Dominicanas.

He loved that I was a journalist as much as I loved his paintings. He understood that we were both storytellers, narrators of our generation, the ones who had something to say and were unafraid to do the hard work in a world where what you say matters. His work showed me what unbridled creativity and authentic artistic spirit looks like. I wanted to live in the worlds he imagined, full of ancient myths, stories, colors, and characters. And hope. Likewise, Gérman wanted to live in a world where the woman he loved, he told me with tears in his eyes, "challenged life to tell the truth."

Germán had to return suddenly to Santo Domingo to deal with family matters, so I joined him in the Dominican Republic a few weeks later. On one of our last days in there, we stopped by the open-air mercado in downtown Santo Domingo, where you can buy everything from a live chicken to bewitched candles blessed with perfume and glitter. The latter were for followers of Santeria or Yoruba, the Afro-Cuban spiritual tradition that has seven orishas, or deities, that represent nature. Yemaya is the ocean and the Mother Goddess of all things. At a little store Gérman bought some blue and white beads for Yemaya and, afterward, as I lay in a bright pink hammock in his apartment on the malecón, he wrapped them around my left ankle. He kissed me and told me he loved me, and though we never discussed it formally, we both intuitively understood that we had just become engaged. I flew back to NYC, but stayed in the clouds of my love.

WNYC, New York City's preeminent public radio station, called when I got back to New York and told me I had gotten the job as a reporter there. Having the big ovaries to "challenge life" was serving me well in my career and now it would be my voice on the air at a major public radio station. The producing I'd done in Colombia, Peru, and El Salvador had gotten me noticed. I would be on the air at WNYC almost every day, reporting about city politics, crime, education, housing, Wall Street, race relations, and the NYPD. Getting hired to work on a breaking-news show that demanded a quick turnaround time was a big deal and a new challenge. There were only four people in the newsroom: the morning anchor, the news director, another reporter, and me, the street reporter.

I spent many days in the Blue Room at City Hall putting the city's newly elected first black mayor, David Dinkins, on the spot and asking him about budget cuts and the poor from the front row of the press corps. Dinkins was known for biting back at reporters, but I could tell that on some level he liked seeing me out there, one of the few Latinas covering City Hall. Walking into that room full of seasoned city reporters as a cub reporter, a babe-in-arms journalist, was terrifying. I was always beating back the nervous churning of my stomach, full-on heart palpitations, and profuse sweating. My imposter syndrome was my daily companion.

Here and there I began to see fellow Latina journalists. Elaine Rivera, Rose Arce, Evelyn Hernandez, and Edna Negrón wrote for *Newsday*; Sandra Guzmán and Rossana Rosado were at *El Diario*; Blanca Rosa Vilchez reported for the Univision network; and Miriam Ayala for the local Spanish language station. Maria Newman along with Mireya Navarro were at the *New York Times*. We began to notice one another because we were all Latinas, yes, but also there was a way in which we moved in this world of reporting because of the communities we either came from or were reporting on. We revealed our humble badassery, Chingona-Afro-Taina-princess-guerrera-shit-mixed-with-humility only to some because to let down our warrior faces and to display our vulnerability to everyone might take away our superpower to survive. There were just enough of us that we had a mirror to hold up to ourselves. I was determined to learn from these Latina journalists. What I didn't realize was that they looked to me with the same respect and love as I did them. I was too insecure to see that at the time because the imposter thing can follow us everywhere like a pinche sombra.

George H. Walker Bush, Reagan's veep, won the presidential election in 1990. He was known for bumping into things, like his head on the Air Force One door multiple times, or his worst moment, throwing up in Prime Minister Kiichi Miyazawa's lap at an official state dinner in Japan. But he was more than just a klutz. In fact, these gaffes may have endeared him to the public because he was a Cold War hawk, an anti-communist, and a hard-liner who had previously led the CIA. For him, the enemy was everywhere potentially, from Moscow to Managua and in the millions of progressive, radical Americans the CIA suspected of being communist or socialist sympathizers.

On the issue of immigration, though, the Republican Party of Ronald Reagan's legacy sanctioned bringing more immigrants into the fold. This was partially an outgrowth of the party's Cold War agenda; it suited their strategic interests to allow immigrants fleeing Communist regimes in Vietnam, Nicaragua, China, and Cuba to land on American shores and proselytize the message of "freedom" to family and friends back in the old country. Meanwhile, immigrants from Mexico, some of them poor and working in the fields, some of them from the middle class, brought their conservative Catholic values with them. It's as if Republicans saw the writing on the wall and responded to demographic trends by supporting immigrants who could form a solid base of support for their party.

Bush Sr. claimed to love "Hispanics"—later, in his failed reelection campaign video, with his slight Texas drawl (though he was Connecticut-born), he promised that he had good reason to "help Hispanics everywhere," because he would also be "answering to [his] grandkids," the children of his son Jeb and his Mexican wife who were half Mexican.

In 1990, Bush built upon Reagan's IRCA legislation and expanded immigration reform even further. The Republicans wanted to own immigration reform. IMMACT 90, as the bill was referred to, admitted greater numbers of family-sponsored, employer-backed, and "diversity" immigrants into the country each year, raising the annual cap from 530,000 to 700,000 for the first two years, and then 675,000 after that. It also marked the beginning of Temporary Protected Status, which at the time especially benefited Salvadorans. IMMACT 90 was passed by an almost evenly split but still Democrat-led Congress and was truly bipartisan. Both parties went on the record with their support for allowing more immigrants to come to the US. Frankly, they humanized them and actually did something to make good on the Statue of Liberty's promise.

The bill marked a turning point in US immigration from the years of passing policy based on scarcity and quotas to control race and population. This was also a checkmate moment for the Democrats. Their rhetoric and imagery as a party was all about inclusion, but their policies around immigration, in fact, were regressive, in that moment and historically. At the end of the twentieth century, it would be the Republican Party, led by a former CIA director, that established an open-arms immigration policy, not the "liberal" Democrats.

Ronald Reagan had come in with a team that understood the demographics but also the needs of big business. They pushed through what the mainstream media would call the biggest and most progressive response to immigrants ever. Pro-immigrant-rights groups were deeply critical of the IRCA, saying that it left many out and that it was the beginning of criminalizing immigrants by giving them something called "amnesty." Immigrant rights activists didn't see this as amnesty at all but rather the responsible thing to do for people who had been working in our country for years or decades. IRCA solidified the you-have-to-give-us-border-security-or-nothing kind of narrative that doesn't correspond to the realities on the ground. Still, the Republicans had found a way to own the issue of immigration, while the Democrats didn't seem to make immigrants their priority.

Of course, though Republicans appeared to be smart about immigration in 1990, they were in part responsible for creating the mess we're in today. Through the Reagan war effort to stop communism from spreading in Central America, a decades-long campaign that included the US Marines stopping Sandino from leading a peasant revolt in Nicaragua in 1932, the Republican Party instigated problems they might never admit they helped to create.

Most people do not want to leave their homelands; desperate, increasingly dangerous circumstances are usually what push them to embark on perilous journeys to other countries like ours that say they accept those seeking asylum. So many immigrants say to one another, *We are here because they were there first.* The blame for interventions and imperialism and racism has been the purview of not one, but both parties for centuries.

Meanwhile, across the country, Latino and Latina activists were focused on gaining more influence over their local public media, whether it was radio or TV. They followed the radical tradition of people of color demanding inclusion and agency in telling their own stories in public media from Los Angeles to Washington, DC. Historically, journalists of color have understood that independent, public, and community-centered media is essential to our survival. Black American communities have been pioneers—from Frederick Douglass's abolitionist paper, the *North Star*, to Ida B. Wells's tremendous work as editor and co-owner of the *Memphis Free Speech*, to Mamie Till's courageous use of the *Chicago Defender* to amplify the injustice of her son's murder.

Members of Congress who had heard from constituents let the Corporation for Public Broadcasting (CPB) know that they were unhappy with the lack of progress in public media. Latinos were almost 9 percent of the population, and yet no new Latino reporters or editors had been hired at NPR since I had worked there as a production assistant in 1985. Richard Gonzales and Claudio Sanchez were still the only Latino reporters at NPR. (The network had to take this criticism seriously.) So, CPB helped fund a couple of positions at NPR—one for an editor who specialized in Latino issues on the national desk and another for a yearlong reporting position. Just as I was making it to my one-year anniversary at WNYC, I was asked to join NPR as a general assignment reporter in the New York bureau. My special focus would be to cover Latinx communities. I had finally gotten my dream job five years after I first walked away from NPR as a production assistant and everyone told me I was crazy.

Had it not been for the long line of women who had come before me and pushed those doors open, I wouldn't have been offered that job. Maria Emilia Martin and Flo Hernandez-Ramos were among the women who had paved the way, and decades before there was Ida B. Wells. Just like my friends from WKCR who had told me how Latino students fought for those three-hour time slots, I understood that I was part of a legacy of journalists of color who had fought their way to survive as American journalists.

As Sandy would say to me, I didn't have time to play. I was in the big leagues now. I would have to learn how to transform my insecurities and imposter phobias into hard work and long hours and new strategies to drown out the voices of doubt in my head. Most important, I would face the biggest personal and professional challenge of my life yet. Now that I was a national journalist, how was I going to define myself?

———

Berta, my mom, rarely came to visit me in New York City, but on the phone she could hear in my voice that something was different about the new man in my life, so she traveled to meet him. I hadn't said anything to anyone about our private engagement because Gérman and I had decided early on that, contrary to our previous relationships, we were not going to bring other people into this one. We planned to share nothing with outsiders, which marked the beginning of our clan.

It was a total surprise to Mom when Gérman went to pick her up at LaGuardia Airport with a little sign that spelled out her name.

Bumping along the pothole-covered NYC streets, Gérman told her in the back of the Yellow Cab that he was planning to marry her daughter and he hoped that would be okay with her. My mom kind of fell in love right there and then with my Afro-Taíno prince, same as I had. He showed respeto.

We held our wedding ceremony on July 20, 1991. It was 105 degrees outside, and my wedding party of about twenty people was supposed to be picked up by souped-up, lowrider Volkswagens and taken to the shore in Mount Vernon, about twenty-five minutes north of Manhattan. Sandy was wearing her African headdress. Dad was wearing his white guayabera, as were my brothers Raúl and Jorge, and Bertha Elena's husband, Dennis, and their son, Scott. Mom was wearing a multicolored, hand-embroidered huipil, as was my sister, Bertha Elena, and her daughter, Christen. Deyanira and Ismael, another Dominican friend, played their drums. We had white doves in boxes ready to be released and everyone else was carrying candles. We were a sight to see on the hottest day in New York in over a decade. We waited for an hour, but the cars never showed up.

We had an entire wedding party dressed and ready with no place to go. Instead, we walked a few blocks east and made a procession to the Great Hill on 106th Street in Central Park. The people there, who were more used to seeing crack addicts and sex workers, watched in awe and pulled out their Instamatic cameras to take pictures of our wild-looking procession.

Are they protesters or artists or lovers? they wondered.

We arranged our friends into a circle and assigned one pair of godparents for each element—earth, water, wind, fire. Each set of godparents gave us their blessing—lighting candles, planting a seed, touching our foreheads with moon-blessed holy water, releasing two white doves—as we declared our love for each other.

Mom and Dad entered the circle to put a silk-and-lace lasso around

Gérman and me, an old Mexican tradition, and as Dad "handed me off" to my new partner, the tears began to fall from his eyes. I could see that Dad did love Gérman, and he loved me, too. He knew that we were adults now. He had to stop worrying.

My tío Gordo, who attended the ceremony, later asked me, "Where was God? You never mentioned Jesus Christ during the whole ceremony."

"But, tío," I said, "open your eyes. God was everywhere in the park with us today."

———

Neither Gérman nor I saw the value in spending all our money on a party when we got married. For our wedding, we used paper tablecloths and only served finger food and limited liquor in the basement of a church on Tenth Street and Avenue A. It was the most authentically rascuache boda you could imagine, but we had a live Cuban band and people danced till one in the morning. Sure, some of our gifts got ripped off and some street people made their way in, but it was still a grand party while it lasted.

With the money we didn't spend on a fancy wedding, Gérman found a newly renovated building on 106th Street and Columbus Avenue, a block with several abandoned buildings around it. We put our money toward the top floor of a five-story walk-up and got the roof rights. It was the perfect size for us, with an extra bedroom, miniature though it was, and most important, affordable because it was a city-backed urban renewal project.

The city was achingly divided while Gérman and I were in our idyllic nesting period, making the new apartment our home. I watched Gérman knock down walls and paint them blue and yellow and orange. He moved his studio to our apartment to save money and I saw him work on his paintings every day. Our apartment looked like a loft with twelve-foot walls of exposed brick, so his paintings became even bigger and more intense than before.

Gérman's happiness bloomed in his paintings; he created one new series after another. The *Diablitos* series featured cute little devil migrants in yolas, the little boats used to leave the Dominican Republic when you have no money. Gérman exhibited at the Museum of Modern Art in Santo Domingo and people were buying up his work. It was the first time in his life, he told me, that he felt loved and supported in his art and life.

I had always imagined designing a bohemian space where people from all different backgrounds could party together. I wanted to go back to my college days of all-night parties in Washington Heights with Deyanira, but instead do it in our loft and rooftop. It would also force people to come into a neighborhood they usually avoided—our street's nickname was Crack Alley—and see another side of Manhattan. One night Scott Simon and Juan Luis Guerra both showed up for a party at our place. Neither one of them knew who the other was and I kind of loved that.

I did well in my breaking-news reporting and my editors loved that my stories revealed the human side of the headlines, while so many other stories focused on the numbers injured or arrested and police budgets, etc. I was doing reporting they felt helped set the network apart.

Work, however, was beginning to interrupt what should have been more nesting. Although Gérman understood that I had to cover breaking news—there was no avoiding it, as I was a newbie national reporter—it was disrupting our time together. Me having to be on deck to report at any time as a way of continuing to prove myself was exhausting.

Gérman called himself a feminist and worked at being one, too, so he tried not to make demands of me. I struggled with the feminist in me. Sometimes I felt like I was being a bitchy American woman who expected all of her needs to be fulfilled by one man and focused exclusively on her career and the nine-to-five bullshit. I came home late, I didn't make dinner, and sometimes I would keep on working. Even though he never said anything, I wondered if Gérman would like another woman more. A woman who would put him first. I didn't understand why I couldn't be that Mexican woman who walks in the world selflessly, giving affection, always upbeat and caring, an attentive partner to everyone, and never asking for anything, like I saw in my mom.

Gérman never made these demands of me. His stoicism was remarkable, but that's because he came from a family where he didn't get to have emotional expectations. I was the one with issues. I was having an internal battle between the Latina feminist and the loving, affectionate Latina, like my mom, who epitomized selflessness, but it was too much. Was I hesitant to be more giving because I was running away from becoming una mujer tradicional?

My insecurities were still there. I did therapy every two weeks with Andaye, my therapist, to try to get to the source of my insecurities that followed me like a needy puppy. But these relationship thoughts swirled in an anxious hurricane in my head. There was another question that kept coming up, too: Why didn't I enjoy sex as much as I thought I should? Why is sex just not that important in my life? Why is desire sometimes difficult for me? I loved my husband and he was incredibly sexy. What was wrong with me?

———

Another breaking-news assignment sent me back to Cuba. I stood on the Cojimar beach and interviewed a man who was about to make a life-or-death decision. The little beach was famous because Ernest Hemingway had once lived there, but now it was overrun with people; it had become a community dock for everyone who wanted to leave Fidel Castro's Cuba.

A circle had formed around us as I held my microphone up close to the man's face. He wiped away the tears that filled his eyes and talked about his decision to leave his beloved Cuba behind forever. I had watched him building his balsa, the makeshift contraption that he would use to leave—it was more than a raft but less than a boat. He didn't know how to swim. Then, in another moment of surrealness, he made a pass at me and said if I asked him to stay behind with me, he would. Only in Cuba . . . !

Fidel Castro had opened up his country to departures, which had previously been illegal, after hundreds of people, who felt choked by Castro's authoritarian rule, had spontaneously started to leave by building their own balsas. Often, these were no more than a couple of inner tubes tied together. The scene was surreal. Italian documentary filmmakers were there capturing Bertolucci-like shots with their cameras. Barbara Walters walked by in a white linen outfit carrying a gold-chained Chanel bag. Children were crying, saying goodbye to grandparents, trembling as they walked into the water, not because it was cold but because they didn't know how to swim and they were getting onto a raft with dreams of a new country.

As a college student I believed that Cuba was a genuine attempt at creating a just and educated society with El Nuevo Hombre. But on this trip, the man who served my breakfast in Havana told me, "No, chica, eso del nuevo hombre se acabó hace mucho tiempo." That hopeful vision of Cuba from my youth died when I heard a ten-year-old girl say she wanted to be either a foreigner or a jinetera (which translates to "horse jockey" but means a sex worker) when she grew up. The island of protest music and rum had become sadly corrupted with people drunk on their own power and the party machinery. How was it that the richest people in the country were Communists?

One of the most terrifying stories I ever reported on happened in Havana. Government disinformation in Cuba was so extensive that in the early 1990s, many Cubans were convinced that Fidel was spending all of his time trying to find a cure for AIDS. People actually believed this because it was reported by the state media. Cuba's policy on AIDS mandated that anyone who was infected be moved to a special community. Many said this was ostracism or forced quarantine, but many others, especially the infected people, were thankful the government had assumed their care. They lived in air-conditioned sanatoriums that provided meals and housing, all free. Once you were inside, the government left you alone. If you were gay, for example, you could finally be out of the closet and the police could do nothing to you.

The Communist Party was also cracking down on what they called "anti-social activities" during this time, such as practicing Santeria, Yoruba, or Palo Santo, being Catholic or Protestant or Jewish, identifying as gay or trans or lesbian, or simply being a skateboarder and rock and roll fan. The Cuban police were known to arrest teenagers whose only crime was skateboarding. For them and their families, life under communism was a constant hell. They were just rockeros who liked loud Led Zeppelin (like me), got tattoos, and wore all black, but they were treated like frontline enemies of the state.

They were also teenagers and gullible. When these kids heard about Fidel's commitment to finding a cure for AIDS within five years and the sanatoriums where you could live freely without the police breathing down your back, they came up with an idea to get the most out of an oppressive government that made them feel hopelessly boxed in. They found someone they knew who had AIDS, drew some of their blood, and then injected themselves. They gave themselves AIDS so they could live in the "hooked up" sanatoriums until Fidel had the cure. The girlfriend of the rockero I interviewed, Niurka, told me she was afraid of needles. So she got purposefully infected by having unprotected sex with her boyfriend Papo. She is still alive, though Papo died six months after I met him.

As the Cuban psychologist I interviewed said to me with utter disdain, "Teenagers in your country shoot themselves. This is what some Cuban kids do. No better or worse than you." It was horrible, but she had a point.

The feeling toward immigrants in America around this time was filled with contradictions. In many ways, the continued influx of people and refugees, first from the CIA-sponsored dirty wars in Argentina and Chile and then Central America, Nicaragua, El Salvador, and Guatemala, was a direct result of US policy and its role in destabilizing the entire region. The US had trained and funded the contras (contrarrevolucionarios) and helped stoke a war where before there was none. Salvadorans and Guatemalans were leaving because their countries were now flooded with military hardware, spies, mercenaries, and the very active remnants of right-wing death squads, all under the watchful eye of the US.

Without fanfare or any kind of major political fight in Congress, protections were extended to refugees from Cuba and others in the Nicaraguan Adjustment and Central American Relief Act (NACARA). This gave permanent resident status to refugees from Nicaragua, Cuba, El Salvador, Guatemala, and nationals of former Soviet bloc countries who had been in the US for at least five consecutive years before 1995.

Immigrants, refugees, people displaced by natural disasters like earthquakes and hurricanes, and undocumented people were given a place to be. They didn't have to stand in line outside or sleep on the concrete in Mexico. These people were not perceived to be lawbreakers or a threat. They were refugees and they knew of a place that welcomed them and let them in and let them be. That place was called the United States.

But it didn't last long.

―――――――

On February 26, 1993, a Ryder truck packed with explosives and parked in the garage beneath the World Trade Center detonated shortly after noon. Six people were killed in the blast and more than one thousand were injured, resulting in the evacuation of fifty thousand people. It was a terrorist attack perpetrated by seven men; their leader claimed the bombing was meant to avenge Israel's oppression of Palestinians, which had been backed by US aid. After this attack, security began checking every vehicle that drove into the WTC parking lot—that was the most obvious change. But a significant, less obvious shift in how we view national security also took place as a result of the bombing. Because the terrorists were also immigrants, some of whom had entered the country as asylum seekers, terrorism was now irrevocably linked to immigration.[1]

Headlines like "Lenient Visa Rules Permit Terrorists to Enter US," which appeared in the *Washington Post*, began to question immigration and refugee policy; asylum seekers were framed as potential attackers, or at the very least exploiters of a "liberal" system, people who could not be presumed innocent.[2] One Brooklyn resident wrote a letter to the editor of the *Times*, warning, "Now that the United States has entered middle age, it is time for us to acknowledge our inability to continue to absorb an endless stream of immigrants. . . . The World Trade Center bombing highlights another reason not to tolerate a lax immigration system: the unchecked entry of dangerous individuals harboring deadly anti-American agendas."[3]

Suspicious, refugees, Arab, Muslims, immigrants, terrorists—these were the kinds of words used in the coverage. In 1995, after those involved in the bombing were tried, the *New York Times* ran a piece that announced the verdict simply as "10 Militant Muslims Guilty of Terrorist Conspiracy."[4]

In June 1993, several months following the bombing, a boat called the *Golden Venture* carrying 286 Chinese nationals seeking to enter the US ran aground off the shore in Queens.[5] New Yorkers woke up to images of people pulling themselves out of the freezing water along the shores of Rockaway Beach at dawn. The conditions on the ship were horrible; the passengers had been traveling for 120 days in a small, crowded, windowless space, and were given insufficient food. Ten of the migrants who jumped from the grounded ship into the water died, either from drowning or hypothermia.[6]

A new narrative crystallized in response to these events. Foreigners from all over the world with unknown intentions were "gaming the system" to get into the country any way they could. Refugees could no longer be trusted. People who had committed no crime other than arriving in the US without a visa were now seen and treated as criminals. It was Democratic president Bill Clinton who ordered that the survivors of the *Golden Venture* be detained in prisons while they awaited their asylum hearings; some were detained for close to four years.[7] The detention of immigrants was not yet common practice at this time; in fact, the total capacity across the nation's immigrant detention camps in 1994 was only seven thousand.

Why didn't people stand up and say they didn't deserve to be in prison? They were innocent. Why didn't anyone say anything? Could it be the tone of the headlines? "Smuggled to New York." "Chinese Aboard Are Seized for Illegal Entry."[8] "The Golden Venture, Plus 100,000."[9]

What, in fact, got little coverage were the people who were showing up for these migrants, the real American patriots. A group of citizens in York, Pennsylvania, where 154 Chinese men from the *Golden Venture* were held at the county jail while they awaited their asylum hearings, became these immigrants' most passionate supporters. Their dedicated coalition included a local lawyer, a Vietnam vet, factory workers, teachers, and churchgoers who came together to hold rallies, file lawsuits, lobby Congress, and speak to media on behalf of the detained immigrants. They even helped to raise money for the men by selling the resourceful artwork they created behind bars: intricate sculptures made from nothing but toilet paper, legal pads, glue, and water.[10]

But the media narrative set by the white men who ran and still run our newsrooms had changed. Restricting the flow of foreigners and refugees into the US—the so-called barbarians at our gates—was now a national security issue. Immigration would never be seen in the same light again.

When I worked for Scott Simon I used to watch how physically close he got to the people he was interviewing, the way he would look into their eyes and, on many occasions, touch them. He broke down all the barriers between him and them; by the end of the interview, people loosened up and spoke to Scott as if he really were a confidant and friend. I was still learning how to navigate my relationships with sources. I had heard rumblings at NPR—some folks said I got too close to stories.

"I know all about you and your agenda," one of my editors, a nice middle-aged white guy said to me.

"Agenda?" I said. "What are you talking about?"

"Oh, Maria, c'mon. You and your Latino agenda."

I was infuriated.

"I guess that means you have a white-male agenda then," I shot back.

"Oh c'mon! It's not the same thing," he said.

"Really?"

This made me think about whether or not I had an agenda after all. I spent several days thinking about what that word meant to me in the context of my power as a journalist. Then I realized I did have an agenda. I wanted to make people feel.

I wanted them to experience some sort of deep emotion when they listened to one of my pieces. I wanted the people they met in my stories to be unforgettable. I wanted people to see and hear themselves in the characters they met in my reporting. I wanted them to feel what I felt when I met people—that we are all connected as humans, that when our paths cross you can see your suffering in mine and I can see a bit of hope in yours.

I've always thought of Mami in these moments. The way she spoke to la señora del mercado or the priest or the vecina, a judge or a cop in the same way, with respect but also with a sense of self, of ego. Ego in the sense that it takes someone with a sense of their own power to be the person who believes they can talk to anyone anywhere about anything. That was my mom. But you can't talk to people unless you show humility, unless you see them where they are, unless you have honey on your tongue and everywhere else, too. Talking to people of all different stripes as a reporter requires the same delicate dance between ego and humility.

Maria Emilia Martin's dream of creating a public radio program to cover Latinos was coming true. She, Mandalit del Barco, Gérman, and I were all in a DC hotel room giggling like kids even though we were dressed in our spruced-up best. We had been told that our Cinco de Mayo launch party that night for *Latino USA* was being talked about as the hottest party in the city. I was wearing something black and shimmery; Maria had done her hair up and was wearing a colorful huipil; Mandalit played up her wild curly locks; and Gérman was dressed in black and wearing a purple African kufi and his dark glasses. Tonight was a singular moment in our lives—the evening we were going to meet the president of the United States, who would do the official welcome to *Latino USA*, a new NPR-distributed show. Maria Martin had been tasked with creating it and Gil Cárdenas from the Center for Mexican American Studies at the University of Texas would house it in Austin.

Latino USA would be a forward-thinking voice that was journalistically sound and had the integrity of NPR behind it. The show was devised to respond definitively to the lack of Latino voices and stories on public radio and serve as a platform for stories that didn't find a home on other shows across the public radio network. It was about educating the public through journalism and humanizing a critical "minority." The show was funded by the Ford Foundation and the Corporation for Public Broadcasting. Maria Martin had made the decision to name me the anchor. NPR agreed to distribute it and loan me out every week so I could read the scripts Maria would send to me via fax from Texas.

Bill Clinton had just won the 1992 election with 61 percent of Latino voters.[11] He connected with Latinos on a certain level but also fashioned himself as a hard-liner on unauthorized immigration. A couple of years later, while running for reelection, Clinton's campaign boasted in an ad that his administration had deported 160,000 "illegal" immigrants and doubled the number of border agents working for Border Patrol. The ad also criticized Republican opponent Bob Dole for voting against a law that would reimburse California for the cost of jailing immigrants.[12] Latino voters loved him despite his immigrant policies, which was a clear sign to me of the increasing complexity of the Latino and Latina voter, the fastest-growing group of new voters.

Clinton's youthfulness set him apart from Reagan and Bush, and people were taken by this. He was attractive, played the saxophone, went jogging, and ate fast food at McDonald's like the rest of America. It was that evening at the launch of *Latino USA* that Clinton famously said, "I'm an NPR junkie," and became even more endearing to yuppies.

This statement and his presence at the event was a huge deal. Now it was official: our hip new president listened to NPR, the tiny little network on the left-hand dial of the radio. We were so proud of Maria Martin for pulling it off. Finally, NPR would have to respect the high-level convening capacity of its Latino journalists and take a show called *Latino USA* seriously. The next day, however, when the official NPR press release came out with the Clinton quote, it barely mentioned *Latino USA* until the last paragraph.

While *Time* and *Newsweek* had covers that celebrated the decade of the Latino and the Hispanic, and Bill Clinton was being celebrated for eating burritos and enchiladas, the new president was also cracking down on immigration.[13] He increased resources toward immigration raids, immigrant detention, deportation, and beefing up border security, effectively beginning the militarization of the region. He created massive security programs on the border with military-like names such as Operation Hold the Line and Operation Gatekeeper, which placed hundreds of Border Patrol officers along popular entry points as blockades.[14] Clinton was committed to giving the impression that his administration was not run by a bunch of bleeding-heart liberals, but middle-of-the-road Democrats who would be tough on crime. It's what white America wanted to hear—he was going to be tough on crime and lock 'em up and that undocumented immigrants were expendable. Anyway, those immigrants couldn't vote.

On *Latino USA* we reported weekly on these developments. We took our role very seriously since we were the only weekly national news program dedicated to reporting on Latinos. Even while politicians were drafting this anti-immigrant policy and codifying it into law, Latinos were also, in many respects, being courted as a growing cultural, economic, and political force. A record number of Latinos and Latinas were named to high-level government positions: Federico Peña to secretary of transportation, Henry Cisneros to secretary of Housing and Urban Development, Norma Cantú to the position of assistant secretary for civil rights within the Department of Education, and Ellen Ochoa became the first Latina to go to space aboard the space shuttle *Discovery*.[15] It was 1994—the year of Selena, the Mexican American singer from Corpus Christi, Texas, who sang in Spanish and catapulted Tejano music, a male-dominated genre, to the top of the charts. Her album *Amor Prohibido* was released and became one of the best-selling Latin albums in the country. That same year Mexico, Canada, and the US cut a deal to ensure free trade between the three countries and signed the NAFTA agreement.

Still, the contradictions under Bill Clinton's administration were everywhere; he was often referred to as the first "black" president—because of his perceived cultural savvy—and yet he signed off on the horrible Violent Crime Control and Law Enforcement Act, often referred to as the 1994 crime bill. This legislation intensified the school-to-prison pipeline that swallowed up so many black children and teens. It mandated tougher federal prison sentences and set aside funds to build more prisons and hire one hundred thousand more police, and encouraged law enforcement to pursue drug-related arrests.[16] Clinton was also seen among some as a "feminist" president, but sexual misconduct and a rape allegation had long followed him.

The country was a living contradiction as well. It was the end of the socially repressive and hawkish days of Reagan and Bush Sr. and a more open and "liberal" era ushered in. But everything was divided. The suburbs were exploding, but kids in NYC schools were shooting each other with illegal guns brought up from the South and now they had metal detectors in high schools. The economy was growing, but poverty was entrenched. Innocent black and brown men and women, like Anthony Baez, who died in a choke hold, and Abner Louima, who was sodomized, were being killed and assaulted by the NYPD.

California, like the rest of the country, was its own unique contradiction. It was the state with the fastest-growing diverse population but also a rapidly progressing reactionary movement against those population changes. California was also home to Hollywood, surfing, Deadheads, and pot farms, but it was run by a conservative Republican governor named Pete Wilson. His major issues were tightening the state's budget, deregulating industries like energy to increase investment, and reducing state funding for public assistance, which he justified with the popular language of the time—indictments of "irresponsibility" and "promiscuity."[17] He also wanted to throw immigrants out of his state by making it almost impossible for them to survive there.

In 1994, a measure known as Prop 187 was introduced to California's November ballot and Pete Wilson became its biggest champion. It was an outwardly hostile law aimed at undocumented immigrants, designed in the legacy of the Chinese Exclusion Act. All across the country, people were talking about this radical new law in California that would make it illegal for immigrants without documents to receive any public benefits like nonemergency health care or education, and that required all state employees to report suspected undocumented immigrants to the INS.[18] [19]

Undocumented Latino and Asian immigrants in California were all of a sudden living in fear: "Anti-Alien Sentiment Spreading in Wake of California's Measure."[20] Immigrants across the country began to worry their state could be next. The national conversation was dominated by a restrictive law that from the onset portrayed immigrants as takers and freeloaders without looking at the actual data.

The law passed in the general election on November 8, 1994, with support from 59 percent of voters,[21] but it was immediately challenged in the courts. On November 11, a temporary injunction prevented it from being implemented, and then was followed by a permanent injunction, so the law never went into effect. Requests from the state of California to have the injunction dismissed were denied.[22] Some say it was this law that created a generation of Latinx activists and helped, ultimately, to turn the state a deep blue.

———

Many months after "Manhood Behind Bars"—my story about a man named Suave and going to prison as a rite of passage—ran on *All*

Things Considered, my phone rang one morning around 11:00 a.m. I was sitting in my office prepping for an interview. It was Ethel Kennedy calling to tell me I had won the Robert F. Kennedy Human Rights Award for Journalism for my piece. The story was considered groundbreaking and humane at the same time.

I had met Suave in 1993 when I gave a speech at Graterford State Correctional Institution, a maximum security prison in Pennsylvania. He had been sentenced to life in prison without parole for his role in the murder of a fifteen-year-old. In a sea of faded-brown scrubs, Suave, who was twenty-seven, and had been in prison since he was seventeen and would be there for the rest of his life, asked me what he could do.

I said he could be the voice of the voiceless and be my source. Those few words changed his life and we began to communicate via letters and phone calls. I interviewed him about why going to prison was seen as "earning your stripes" in the street, not something to be afraid of.

I went to pick up the award in DC and attended the fancy awards ceremony, all the while feeling like I was that thing in the headlines. An alien! Here I was rubbing shoulders with the Kennedys! How could I not feel like an outsider? I was standing shoulder to shoulder with the family that my family used to watch on TV and see photos of in *Time* magazine.

While I was celebrating my award in DC, taking nighttime photos from the roof deck with my cheesy Instamatic camera, the white dome of the Capitol lit up like a half-moon of pure-white light, Bill Clinton, the Democrats, and the Republicans were enacting more regressive and punitive immigration laws.

No one was protesting against immigrants. There weren't cable TV shows ranting about them. There weren't anti-immigrant marches. The economy was booming. Seemingly unprompted, Bill Clinton signed the Illegal Immigration Reform and Immigrant Responsibility Act (IIRIRA) in 1996. This legislation began to militarize the border and build parts of the border wall. The bill aimed to prevent undocumented immigrants from claiming government and social benefits, and it criminalized immigrants based on their status. It created special kinds of crime categories called "aggravated felonies," which allowed for immigrants without green cards and even those with them to be held in detention facilities, introduced application deadlines for asylum filing, initiated expedited removal proceedings, made it nearly impossible for undocumented immigrants to apply for naturalization, and turned unauthorized reentry to the United States into a felony. This last one was particularly hateful since many of the returning people were getting caught coming back to see their kids. These changes essentially criminalized immigrants for their migration alone, and undermined the idea of due process.[23] Undocumented immigration was now officially being criminalized.

During his 1996 State of the Union Address, Bill Clinton proudly shared his plans to expand immigration enforcement: "There are some areas that the federal government should not leave and should address and address strongly. One of these areas is the problem of illegal immigration. After years of neglect, this administration has taken a strong stand to stiffen the protection of our borders."[24]

Did he have any idea of the hell he was creating? Did he foresee what was coming and was okay with it? Did he never imagine what would follow?

Or did he enjoy throwing immigrants under the bus, yet again, while no one seemed to be watching or paying attention?

Or did he think, *Well, they're just immigrants. Who really cares anyway? And they don't deserve anything anyways, those "illegal" people?*

No one was up in arms. And the people who were, all of the Latinx activists and academics and lawyers and historians and journalists, were all told to calm down, as we were sounding alarm bells.

Chapter 9

Working Mother

One early spring night, I looked at the full moon over our tiny cottage in Connecticut that we had named Boca Chica and felt a shiver in my belly. I knew that, finally, I was pregnant. Weeks later, the same ugly gray ultrasound machine that twice before had not detected a heartbeat discovered a little star beating to a perfect rhythm in the middle of my belly.

A few months later, however, I developed placenta previa, a dangerous situation where the placenta blocks the exit path of the baby. I could die of a hemorrhage if my baby tried to come out. As a result, my son's birth was the opposite of spontaneous. We decided the day and time he would arrive in this world via cesarean section.

Raúl was born January 2, 1996. He was named after my father, who was named after his father. Papi cried when my husband handed him our minutes-old baby to hold. Finally, I was that Mexican daughter who honored her father by naming her firstborn after him.

We decided to speak Spanish exclusively to Raúl Ariel, whose full

name is Raúl Ariel Jesús de Todos los Santos Perez Hinojosa. I wanted
to make something I used to hate—my long, very Spanish name—
something our son would come to love. For his naming ceremony,
which we devised instead of a christening, since neither Gérman nor
I were practicing Catholics anymore, we moved what was supposed to
be an outdoor service into our apartment while Hurricane Bertha tore
through the East Coast and plowed into Manhattan. My mom tried
to decipher the symbolism of this all, since the hurricane coinciden-
tally shared her name.

Raúl was the center of our life now. I was off from work and Gérman was staying true to his promise to be the best dad possible in
response to his own father's neglect and outright violence, so he took
care of the baby a lot. Gérman would carry Raúl in his snuggly and
play the djembe; I would take Raúl to the playground in Central Park
like a real New Yorker.

All of the parenting books I read extolled the benefits of nursing
your baby, but I loved it for another reason: nursing Raúl Ariel was the
one thing that forced me to stop and slow down. I could do nothing
but focus on my baby and, to me, that was a benefit. It was nature
making me stop. He and I would have these intimate meditative sessions in public because I was a fearless public breastfeeder. He would
stare into my eyes and I into his, and nothing existed except for my
body feeding his. We were connected in the most loving and vulnerable way that two human beings can be. It was all about the eyes—
Raúl Ariel never looked away. This ritual nurtured and grounded me
several times a day.

In Mexico se dice que los bebés traen muchos regalos, it is said that
babies come bearing many gifts. For me, Raúl Ariel brought abundance. One day the phone rang and this time it was not the wife of a
Kennedy calling, but a senior talent scout for CNN asking if I would
have lunch with him. CNN asked if I would do a trial piece of report-

ing for them, so I offered to do a story that I had done for NPR before my maternity leave.

So many innocent people were getting caught in the crosshairs of deadly street gun battles between drug dealers or crews in the Bronx that memorial walls were popping up everywhere. Graffiti artists were painting immense portraits of the fallen by using spray cans to render their faces in vibrant colors with intricate details on old concrete. The murals were as moving as any kind of high art. The last wall they had painted was of a toddler on the side of his home.

Because of its visual nature, the story was a perfect piece for TV. The artists, who belonged to the Tats Cru, were three friendly and funny Puerto Rican guys. They had transformed themselves into community artists by documenting moments of tragedy for the public's collective memory. Tats Cru was getting recognized for their art. Soon after I reported on them, Coca-Cola commissioned a wall from them, and they were on their way to Tokyo.

This tryout TV report captured the kind of journalism I wanted to do at CNN—street- and community-based, POC-centered, long-form storytelling. If I was going to leave NPR it had to be to do this, not just chase breaking news.

The executives loved what they saw, but when CNN asked if I would fly down to Atlanta to meet with them, I was overwhelmed with anxiety. I was convinced I was going to fail, but what I didn't recognize was that they were the ones who had called me. I wasn't looking for a new job. They were looking to make a new hire and they wanted me.

I could not see my own value and worth. Gérman was the one who told me I needed to learn how to eat my fear. He had survived the invasion of forty-two thousand US Marines on his island, the Dominican Republic, in 1965, when he was just nine years old.[1] He said fear is in your mouth, you can taste it, but if you just swallow it, it's gone. There is no aftertaste. The fear is gone with a gulp and it lets you break with it, make it invisible.

There was a war going on outside his tiny Santo Domingo home because the US had arrived to support the military junta that had overthrown Dominican president Juan Bosch, the first freely elected head of state in thirty years. Gérman, his abuelita, and his mom were stuck inside a closet during the day; at night they slept underneath the bed to avoid stray bullets.

The situation got so bad that they had to eat Gérman's pet chicken, which he refused to participate in. How could they eat his beloved pet? From that day forward he declared himself a vegetarian, to the ridicule of his family.

In prepping for my job interview, Gérman helped build up the woman in me who had been off the job for five months and was feeling rusty.

"Ask them why you should leave NPR," he said.

"That sounds really ballsy," I said hesitantly.

"Because it is," he answered. "They want you because you are good. Own it, Malu. Own it finally."

I went down to Atlanta in the first work suit I had ever bought and ate my fear. I asked all of the senior people I interviewed with why I should leave NPR to join them; in other words, what made CNN so special? Every one of them seemed shocked and then surprised, happily, that I had the chutzpah to ask powerful people that kind of a question and with a self-assured attitude.

They offered me the job, and I negotiated a four-day workweek and a salary increase.

After I broke the news at NPR, I overheard a colleague comment on my flashy TV job at CNN and say, "That Maria always had that air about her. That air of entitlement." Others dismissed the move as CNN making an affirmative action hire. Many people were happy for me, but many others remained dismissive of my work. Because I left radio for TV, the less-sophisticated medium, I was now also a traitor to our craft.

The day I walked into the New York bureau of CNN, I felt as though everyone looked at me like I was some sort of alien. At that time, CNN was an old-school, tight-knit news institution full of no-frills journalists. My hire was said to be part of an initiative to reinvent CNN, so my new colleagues looked at me with distrust and even disdain. Was I a part of CNN's makeover? It was pretty clear that I was a different kind of correspondent. My first pieces were about four to five minutes long and covered topics like young black men and their skyrocketing suicide rates, a circus with all black performers who had set up shop in an abandoned lot in Harlem, and the increasing power of Latino voters.

People sneered at my stories behind my back, but I learned to grow an even thicker skin. NPR was a piece of cake compared to this. I was used to working alone and now everywhere I went I was with a crew that almost always included two men—a cameraman and a soundman. Often my producer was a man, too. If I didn't get the jokes at NPR, here at CNN I had to pretend to be deaf so the jokes couldn't touch me. I overheard some of the guys cracking up about me being the new "Bronx Bureau chief"; another time they asked if I was hired for CNN en Español. I figured it was typical hazing and that I just had to get used to the bro-heavy environment. There was something about it that I liked, though. I was working with people from different class backgrounds. Not everyone around me had a college degree; not everyone lived on the Upper West Side or in Westchester or had a subscription to the *New Yorker*.

If the crews didn't, most of the executives did, though, and there were days when I would come home and cry to Gérman, who would say, "None of the men who are making your life hell now will matter to you in five years. They are not important in your life long term."

Still, I cried out of frustration. The hoops I had to jump through just kept getting higher. Didn't anyone see that I was only five feet tall? I couldn't keep jumping so high.

One of the forward-thinking editors in Atlanta wanted me to explore long-form storytelling and said yes to my pitch for a piece on something known in NYC as Las Casitas. These houses were replicas of the colorful wooden cottages found in small towns across Puerto Rico. Imagine walking down a trash-strewn street in Spanish Harlem or the Bronx, seeing a wall of nondescript public housing towers, and then in an empty lot just a block away discovering a little pink or blue or green house with a Caribbean-style garden, open for all in the community to enjoy.

It was a story I had done years before with Scott Simon, but it was even better for TV since it showed a different side of Latinos and Puerto Ricans. They were creators of their own stories by claiming the space and filling it with art and storytelling and collective public music, rumbas. This was such a Puerto Rican thing to do, but it was a story that rarely got told in any mainstream arena, which is exactly why I wanted to tell it.

My cameraman made a comment under his breath while we were shooting that it was a silly story and a sign of the substandard work that new recruits like me were bringing into CNN, a bona fide news network. He couldn't see that telling the true narrative of a community from the ground up, with respect and the capacity to listen to a different kind of community leader, was news—that we were in fact breaking news by telling this story.

Others at the bureau seemed to agree with him. Although Atlanta had assigned the story, the New York bureau did not schedule it to go on the air. It sat on the shelf for weeks until I asked Atlanta to air it. I was learning the basics of office politics in TV news. Get your story on the air in the best possible time slot, and get them to re-air the piece all across the network, every hour, and if possible on CNN International, which gave correspondents access to a worldwide audience on cable.

Soon I found out that the changes at CNN everyone was whispering about were coming true. Within just a few months of starting there, CNN was sold to Time Warner, as part of its $7.5 billion merger with CNN parent company Turner Broadcasting System. The network many journalists dismissed as the Chicken Noodle Network was now playing at the highest level of the cutthroat and competitive media market.

At home, Gérman and I were happily breaking with the traditional family structure. Gérman was the one who would carry Raúl Ariel around in a snuggly or back carrier. The guys playing dominoes on 106th Street would tease him in Spanish about being the man of the house. *No man of the house carries his baby on his back.*

To which Gérman responded simply by raising his fist in the air and shouting, "Fuck you!" That was the only answer jerks like them deserved, he told me later, laughing. Raúl was fast asleep, his head resting against my husband's back, his arms dangling from the blue backpack carrier, oblivious.

Gérman was painting every day now on bigger canvases and busy working on getting solo shows. Sometimes he would let Raúl hold a paintbrush and add some strokes. Raúl gazed into the paintings as if he could see a whole world speaking to him through the colors of the Caribbean. Gérman actually added sand to the paint sometimes to give the paintings texture.

So that Gérman could focus on his work as much as I was, we hired a part-time nanny named Gabby, a recent community college graduate who always carried around a thick novel with her everywhere she went. She was a Mexican New Yorker with a streak of purple hair and wore clunky platform boots. My kind of nanny.

One day when I came home from work, Raúl Ariel didn't want to leave Gabby's arms and refused to let her leave without throwing a tearful tantrum. Did he love his nanny more than me? What about that time he called me Ma-Pa instead of Mama? Did he love his father more than me? Maybe it had to do with my reaction to normal toddler crying and whining, which made me get all sweaty and anxious? I was a bad mother. Worse, a bad Mexican mother.

I continued to wrestle with my new role at CNN and how to strike the right balance as an ambitious working mother. Gérman's career as a painter was also flourishing. Raúl spent a week with my parents as I hopped an overnight flight from JFK to Rio de Janeiro. In less than twenty-four hours, Gérman was opening his first solo show at the famed Centro Cultural Correios, at that time a seventy-year-old renovated central post office in downtown Rio.

There was a lot of happiness and joy in our lives, but not a lot of sex, with our firstborn taking up so much emotional space. As usual, the enigma of why I didn't seem to miss it all that much nagged at me. It didn't seem normal. I thought about writing an anonymous letter to one of the sex columnists, or maybe to E. Jean Carroll at *Elle* magazine. I was ashamed.

The trip to sexy Rio was a chance to reconnect with our passion— this time not only with Oshun, the goddess of sensuality, but since we would be near the ocean, the mother of all orishas, Yemaya. I packed my bag only with clothes I knew Gérman would like: flowing skirts, off-the-shoulder peasant blouses, halter tops, lots of scarves, my gold hoops, delicious and pretty underwear.

I wasn't surprised when the hotel room turned out to be pretty dumpy with a view of an air shaft, because that's the entire Rio vibe— a facade. Anyway, Rio was never about spending your days and nights inside a tiny dark hotel room in Botafogo. It was about being outside, walking along the black and white cement tiles that looked like waves on the sidewalks of Copacabana and Ipanema beaches, getting a suco de fruta at one of the huge corner cafés and juice bars where they also sell tiny shots of caffeine or huge plastic cups of cold fresh strawberry and mango juice, and gazing upon all the amazing-looking Cariocas who make their beauty seem effortless. Mind you, Rio is one of the plastic surgery capitals of the world. But still, the people are striking.

One afternoon, the natural sex drug that is Rio overtook my husband and me. As I knew with my son, when we lay exhausted and sweaty in each other's arms at the end, I was pretty sure I was pregnant.

Before coming down and losing myself in pleasure, I had been so preoccupied with proving myself at CNN that I'd come up with a story idea I could shoot while I was in Brazil. I took a cameraman with me to Minas Gerais to meet the oldest living woman, who was 126 at the time. She had been born into slavery, and as a result, her birth had only been recorded by the church, not the city's official registry, because she had not been considered a full human being. As a result, *Guinness World Records* would not recognize her or add her to the official world record. Through this report, people around the world learned about her. She stood hunched over at just over four feet. She showed me the lesions on her back from when she was whipped, running her hands over the bulging century-old scars.

Back in NYC, the little plus sign on the pregnancy test turned blue and I screamed for joy so loudly that Raúl Ariel started crying and asking, "¿Qué le pasa a mamá?"

A month later, the ultrasound machine that I once feared confirmed there was a heartbeat. After two abortions (both in college while using contraception), two miscarriages with my husband, and now two pregnancies, I was proof that women don't need to feel guilt or shame because of their past decisions or health issues.

I was so thankful that lust and passion and Oshun had found their way into my heart and that my head had enough sense to understand that sometimes you have to give in to your senses and be led by them y la naturaleza, which is what the deity represents.

The thought of work, however, immediately filled me with trepidation. I would have to change how I was doing things if I didn't want to lose this baby in the very delicate first trimester. I couldn't stand on the top of microwave trucks and do live shots like I had before; I couldn't get by on four hours of sleep and do breaking news for ten hours on my feet. Not for the first trimester.

How could I tell my new bosses at my still-new job that I was pregnant? I was elated and at the same time overcome with a foreboding sense of shame. People already thought I was an affirmative action hire and an NPR long-form diva. What would they think once they heard I was pregnant again? Everyone was going to hate me. I didn't have anyone at CNN who was looking out for me. I had no dedicated producer and I was beginning to flounder. In TV, if you don't have a plan to get yourself on the air consistently, you don't have a career.

I was going to be on air while I was pregnant. I hadn't even thought about that. How was I going to look? Blanca Rosa Vilchez, one of my girlfriends from LIPS (which stands for Latinas in Power, Sort Of— an organization of extraordinary women that had been my lifeline through the years), once told me this horrifying reality: the network executive who makes decisions about whether to keep you on the air or off has a wall of TVs playing and they are all silent, so his decision will be based not on what you are saying but on how you look. You are just one of the faces on the twelve TV sets he is watching simultaneously. The message was clear: You gotta look fly all the time. And young.

I set up a meeting with Nancy, the managing editor of the New York bureau, and had to hold back tears when I walked in. How could I have gone and gotten pregnant when I was just starting a new job? Clearly I had chosen passion over pragmatism and my weakness was showing in the form of a tiny belly.

I took a breath and said, "I got pregnant in Brazil. . . . I'm so sorry." I winced after I said the words, unsure why I had shared such intimate information.

"Sorry?!" she said as her face lit up. "You have nothing to be sorry about! Congratulations, Maria! That is so wonderful for you! Congratulations!"

Nancy's reaction gave me the space to fall in love with my pregnancy. I knew that if I ever became a boss lady, I would react the same way every time an employee told me they were pregnant.

In some ways, the pregnancy made the crews I worked with take better care of me, which was weird, but I took it gladly. I came to love CNN and my coworkers, and after the months of hazing, they also came to love me. I appreciated the family vibe they had created for me and I became just as concerned as my colleagues about how this family-run network was about to change—and drastically. Time Warner's McKinsey guys had already arrived and were walking around the bureau like they owned the place. The little network that could was now part of a major media company. There was no turning back on what Ted Turner would later call the worst decision he ever made in his life. Everyone at CNN was beginning to feel like we were all on shaky ground.

———

Years before, when Ceci and I traveled to Brazil together, we went drinking down the hilltop of Corcovado, through all of the bars winding through barrio Santa Catarina. We ended up at a bar in Lapa, the red-light district, and at 4:00 a.m. I was drinking a cold beer in a beer garden. A tall, voluptuous woman with impressive arched eyebrows and perfect red lips sat next to me. When I asked her name she said, "Yurema." ZZZHHuu-reh-mah. I knew then I wanted that name for my daughter. Only many years later did I realize that the Yurema from that night was a trans woman and that the name Yurema is for an aphrodisiac plant and goddess.

I gave birth to this little revolucionaria on Cinco de Mayo of 1998. Yurema would snuggle to my breast and gladly fall asleep like that every night I was home. How could I deprive my baby girl of this exquisite mommy-daughter moment? She would lock her tiny mouth on my skin and not let go, playing with my ears, my nose, my forehead and cheeks as if she needed to have each of her fingertips touch every inch of my face to confirm I wasn't going any place. It was an expression of this little human being's deepest trust. She wasn't afraid or even needy, just filled with love. Like those silly Teletubbies with suns shining out of their onesies, Yurema was pure light, feminine, strong, and loving.

I went back to anchoring *Latino USA* one month after her birth because it only required one half day a week. I had to get out of the house as soon as possible because I still had to finish my second book, this one on motherhood. When I ran into the then-president of Barnard, Judith Shapiro, I was so desperate to find a place where I could nurse and write at the same time that I went out on a limb and asked if she would let me use an empty dorm room over the summer. Miraculously, she said yes. I was almost immediately back at work, trying to finish writing my memoir *Raising Raúl*. Every day I went to work in a Barnard dorm room, where my independent life had begun, with my baby girl by my side.

After my six-month maternity leave, I was back at CNN trying to figure out how to survive the new network president, Rick Kaplan, who was so famous he had been profiled by glossy magazines. The way old-time CNNers saw it, hiring Rick Kaplan away from ABC News was the clearest message that things were not going to stay the same. Kaplan was known for cleaning house, molding newscasters into stars, and injecting glamour, big personalities, and influence into the world of news.

I asked as many people as I could for intel on Kaplan so I could be prepared when I met him. Many I spoke to thought Kaplan might actually be great for my career because he loved character-based reporting and that was my forte. He was also very unpredictable, they said. The most important thing was to never get on his bad side. I figured I could at least do that. He was going to be based in Atlanta, and I was in NYC. My reporting was solid, but I was not a sophisticated TV network correspondent. I was an unpolished reporter with the Chicken Noodle Network.

The stress at CNN followed me home. To Gérman, my complaints were a never-ending list of men's names who were making my life as a journalist hell. Sometimes I could see him zone out as I unloaded tales of office drama at the end of a long day. CNN was no longer a mom-and-pop cable network. People saw the shiny, made-up faces of the correspondents on TV, but in reality, I started every day at work asking if anyone had been fired overnight. It was a baby media monster in the making.

Nursing Yurema was also beginning to feel painful; she didn't want to let go of me. This thing that was supposed to slow me down, calm me, and connect me to my daughter was instead leaving me frustrated and anxious. I had nursed Raúl until he was sixteen months old, but the pressure to be able to travel at a moment's notice was taking precedence over the actual health of my child. One year would have to be enough for my baby girl, because as the only member of the family who got a biweekly check, I could not lose this job.

I thought I was going to be fired any day. But what I couldn't see was that my husband was the one who wanted to fire CNN from my life.

———

I attended the annual conference for the National Association of Hispanic Journalists (NAHJ), where Mexico's president, Vicente Fox, was slated to speak. His appearance at NAHJ was seen as a coup that demonstrated the increasing power and prestige of Latino journalists. Fox spoke to several hundred engaged Latino professionals that afternoon, pledging to move forward with massive immigration reform with the newly elected George W. Bush. Following in the footsteps of Ronald Reagan, Mexico would be made a partner in making immigration an issue of concession and collaboration instead of controversy and chaos between the two countries. It felt like a moment when Latino journalists were again flexing their muscles and getting a response. It was the first visit from a sitting president to the conference.

When President George W. Bush took office, he and President Fox became fast friends. They seemed to have a kind of instant geo-cultural kinship: they both embraced cowboy-esque values of independence and conservatism. They met three times during Bush's first few months in office, and Fox and his wife were the first state dinner guests the Bushes entertained at the White House on September 5, 2001.[2] The two presidents talked about plans that would give legal status to more than 3 million undocumented Mexicans in the US; they also hoped to extend guest worker programs in the US.[3]

The analysts and academics and activists were skeptical about this very conservative Mexican president and a Republican president making a deal on immigration. What were their real interests behind this immigration reform? Access to cheap labor for wealthy Republican business owners? Or was it something else entirely?

Chapter 10

The End of the World Will Be Televised

As the mother of two young children, I had gotten into a pattern of waking up early. I had to tiptoe out and leave our front door unlocked so it wouldn't slam. That way I could squeeze in my workout and still be back in time to walk Raúl to school. Today, this perfectly warm but not too hot September morning, three-and-a-half-year-old Yurema would be starting her first day at a new pre-K in the basement of the historic St. John the Divine.

Yurema, my little baby, wasn't getting to connect with me the way I had with Raúl, where we had almost a full year and a half of uninterrupted time together before I had to go back to work. I was on my book tour when Yurema was just over a year old. I made up for that by waking up at 5:45 a.m. to get to the gym by 6:00 and back by 7:00, when Gérman and the kids were just getting up. They were usually watching Elmo and eating Cheerios or a full mango, one of their favorite things to eat, surrounded by bursts of color and art everywhere in the apartment, huge paintings on every single wall.

On Election Day for the mayor of NYC, a Tuesday in September,

I had been assigned to the Bloomberg headquarters. This was a big deal because it meant I would be with the potential winner, Michael Bloomberg, the controversial billionaire who wanted to be mayor. I was happy because this assignment meant I still had cred in the bureau. I was in my happy ego place as I walked home from the gym just after 8:45 a.m. I had decided to work out later than usual since I was going in at a later time to cover the election results.

I switched to the FM radio on my well-worn cassette/FM radio Walkman so I could check in on the beginning of Election Day in NYC. I stopped on the Spanish language salsa station with *El Vacilon de la Mañana*—the original shock radio—and there was a distressed woman on the phone saying that a plane had just crashed into the World Trade Center. The anchors were laughing at her attempt to prank them, as if something as crazy as that could never happen. She held the phone up and screamed, "Can you hear the sirens? I'm serious!"

Damn it! My day just got ruined, I thought. *How could someone be so stupid as to pilot their plane into the tallest tower in the city?* It was probably some rich kid playing with their father's plane.

I ran back the two blocks to my house from Broadway to Columbus and when I opened the front door, Gérman said, "They've already called. The bosses said to get down to WTC however you can. The crew will meet you down there and Rose is already on the air and on her way there, too."

I jumped into the shower, and as I was drying myself off, I caught a glimpse of the TV. That's when I realized this was not a two-seater plane. This was huge.

I got as far downtown as Twenty-Third Street on the East Side when the trains stopped running. By now even people underground had heard there had been another plane crash. Strangers looked at one another in the subway car in quiet anguish. We were under attack. But we were just New Yorkers. Why us?

As soon as I got aboveground, I desperately searched for a pay phone since the cell towers were knocked out. The line was so long and everyone looked desperately anxious. I politely said I was a CNN correspondent and that I would only take thirty seconds, and to my surprise (which later would become the norm of strangers helping one another) these distressed people let me jump the line.

I was told to make my way to St. Vincent's Hospital on Thirteenth Street and that my crew would meet me there. For now I would work without a producer because Rose was already at the WTC. I hung up and stepped onto Fifth Avenue, and that's when I finally saw it myself: both towers in flames. My chest started moving up and down as if my body were a wave machine. I couldn't control it. My breathing quickened. The scene in front of me felt like it was from a movie. *This can't be real, but I know I'm alive and I just said goodbye to my husband and kids.*

New Yorkers had come down from their apartments and stumbled onto the sidewalks where their fellow New Yorkers, who may have been in the towers, were now running north past them as fast as they could—the horror was stuck on their faces like a mask, and they were not stopping to look back. In that mass of people, I saw one of my LIPS friends, Neyda, who worked downtown. She was one of those people with the look of terror in their eyes, a look I don't recall ever seeing in the eyes of anyone I knew, not this kind of desperate terror.

———————

The attacks on the WTC changed my life in ways that covering a story never had before. I had been to war zones, but they were always faraway places that I would travel to report on and then come home. Now my home had become a war zone. On a regular basis, I went to Ground Zero or to the Ground Zero of pain in the homes of people who had lost someone on 9/11. Afterward, I caught the subway home to my community miles away from downtown; everyone there was busy trying to make life seem normal—not for the adults, but for the little New Yorkers who were kids like mine. Normal meant pretending not to be terrified for them.

Downtown there were soldiers in riot gear with machine guns at the ready, firefighters walking around the rubble and crying, destruction everywhere. The attack meant many things, but it was certain that the conversation on immigration was going to go backward.

All of the collective work on our end—me at CNN and on *Latino USA*, and other journalists, too—to humanize the stories about immigrants and refugees with complexity and care had been for nothing. Lowkey, always simmering, anti-immigrant blood began to boil up again.

I found myself identifying deeply with people through their pain. This had nothing to do with me being a Latina or an immigrant or a woman. I opened my heart and let the people who had lost someone come right inside. Most were people with whom I shared nothing in common, who in fact could not be more different than me: parents of Wall Street bankers, the Long Island families of firefighters, young widows who weren't even thirty years old, an African American Mississippi transplant who answered 911 calls that day and listened to people say their last words to her. They all came into the core of my heart. The shock I had experienced made me softer, less judgmental, and it allowed me to connect with my subjects on a deeper level, which came through in my writing and reporting. And in seeing myself in them and finding hope in our common humanity, on the streets, in the subways, buying a cup of coffee and suddenly locking eyes with mourning strangers.

Twenty-four hours after the attacks, the posters went up. Pictures of people in their happiest moments, smiling passport photos, and pictures of strangers with their adored pets, hugging their kids—these intimate photos started to appear everywhere in the city. In some ways, the posters were a real-time response to George W. Bush trying to paint the attack in nationalistic tones. New Yorkers were saying, *This is who we are. These are our loved ones. Look at them. Look at us. We are you: immigrant, gay, straight, Jewish, Catholic, queer, Muslim, Hasidic.* The posters and photos all shared one word: MISSING. Missing, or desaparecido, a word that people had come to know from the missing of Argentina and Chile during the dictatorships in both countries.

I knew there had to be undocumented people among the missing and the dead. I called Asociación Tepeyac and they gave me the number of a woman whose husband worked at Windows on the World, a touristy, high-end restaurant on the 107th floor of the World Trade Center that was once hailed "The Most Spectacular Restaurant in the World" by *New York* magazine.[1]

On September 13, I met with Julia Hernandez and her kids. We showed up at her cramped one-bedroom apartment in the Bronx. "We were just getting ready to move," she told me. Her four kids were in tears and had been crying on and off for two full days. All they knew was that Papá was desaparecido. Missing.

Antonio Melendez was a prep cook from Puebla, Mexico. He and his common-law wife had decided to make the big move to NYC, where he had a friend who had a job waiting for him at the tallest building in the world. Antonio couldn't believe it (a restaurant one hundred floors up!), but he did live by this credo: No dejes que te lo cuenten; hazlo tu mismo. Live life for yourself and tell your own stories.

Antonio moved to NYC and saw that it was true. There was a building with a kitchen in the clouds and he soon became one of the favorite prep cooks. Julia followed him to the US and they had more kids. Life was good for Antonio and Julia in the Bronx: their baby boy was just going to turn one; they had two girls in the middle; their oldest son was nine; and they were about to move, finally, to a three-bedroom apartment.

But now Papá was gone. Rose and I, the cameraman, and a sound tech all ended up in tears, something I never thought I would witness, but being with Julia Hernandez and her kids hit us all hard. The three-minute piece Rose and I produced made people cry all over the country. Viewers sent Julia cards from all over, calling her a patriot.

Still, she was alone and undocumented. She wasn't even sure if it would be safe for her to apply for 9/11 aid and reveal her status. Her husband was an invisible hero, and she was an invisible widow of a man now called an American patriot.

As a country under attack, the basic protections of our democracy were suddenly in question. Everything was a potential threat. Then-mayor Rudy Giuliani wanted to suspend the mayoral elections indefinitely or for several months. President Bush declared a national emergency, stating the country was in a state of war and that meant his administration could take drastic actions that bypassed formal checks and balances. The Patriot Act was passed by Congress. There was talk about martial law.

On *Latino USA*, we spoke to a military expert who said that because of the declaration of war, the War on Terror, undocumented people could enlist and be processed for expedited green cards. The national emergency meant that undocumented people already serving in the military would be given amnesty and granted citizenship. In fact, it turns out it's the law. The Military Selective Service Act, first passed in 1948, says that in times of war any man age eighteen and older, whether they have permission to be in the US or not, can be called up to serve if a draft is reinstated.[2] "Almost all men age 18–25 who are US citizens or are immigrants living in the US are required to be registered with Selective Service. US law calls for citizens to register within 30 days of turning 18 and immigrants to register within 30 days of arriving in the US."[3]

The US has known since its inception that there would always be undocumented soldiers in the American military. It's like a sick joke. Why aren't undocumented people applauded for their service to a country that isn't even theirs? Instead, they are shamed and invisible as they bear arms.

It was one more thing to be sad about. Managing motherhood and being a wife during all of this became a daily challenge. I was all faux joyful at home. Whatever horrible thing I had seen in my reporting that day (a woman burned over 70 percent of her body, a father weeping for his daughter, a firefighter in emotional shock) went into a dark part of my brain, and when the images tried to reemerge, I pushed them right back down, like a Whac-A-Mole.

Sometimes my sadness was too much even for Gérman.

"Most people escape death and they are happy. You escape death and instead of being happy you ask, why didn't I die? It's been months!" he said, exasperated.

I started to get physically ill because of it, and the stress, anxiety, and guilt. Emotionally, I was numb. Crying was easy, but that was about it. I had no joy, but I did have terrible cramps whenever I ate. The gut doctor told me I needed to go on IBS meds, and that was the last straw. This tragedy was not going to make me sick for the rest of my life.

Our naturopath pediatrician connected me to a specialized MD acupuncturist who said he would treat me with needles along with a total detox cleanse. "But I can't treat your sadness," he said matter-of-factly. If I wanted to mend the emotional trauma and PTSD, he suggested I see Fiona, the Reiki healer who came to his office one day a month. "Get on her months-long waiting list soonest," he told me.

Three months later I was on a table lying back with my eyes closed and a tiny blond-haired woman, smaller than even me, performed my first-ever Reiki healing session in silence. I almost fell asleep, but remained calm and breathed slowly.

After close to an hour, when Fiona was done, she told me, "You are carrying many spirits and much grief. You are enveloped in sorrow. We got through some of it today, but you have layers of this, so come back as soon as you can. You're going to be okay. But there is much weight on your soul."

I went to pay but was told Fiona did this work for free. I remembered that my acupuncturist had said something about Fiona being married to a kind man who helped a lot of people in Harlem and had a distinct name. I recalled a *60 Minutes* piece I had seen about Stanley Druckenmiller and how he funded the Harlem Children's Zone. I looked him up and he was a former banker who was now a multimillionaire and his wife, my healer, was a Reiki master and power philanthropist in her own right.

————

There was the buildup to a military assault and then there was the assault at home. In the post-9/11 haze of threats, real and imagined, President Bush and Congress passed the draconian Homeland Security Act in 2002 as a way of coping with the dangerous new world we found ourselves in. The bill created the Department of Homeland Security, which moved immigration issues from the Department of Justice to the Department of Homeland Security. Immigration was now a security issue and laws had to be "enforced." There had never been an agency to look after "the homeland" because the homeland had always been declared safe by multiple presidents in their State of the Union speeches. Keeping the "homeland" safe was now directly tied to keeping others out.

We were in a state of war against an idea—terror—with color-coded threat levels that flashed on TV screens 24/7. The Department of Homeland Security and the battles over how many freedoms we were prepared to give up was a real actual conversation in Congress. Senate Majority Leader Tom Daschle originally supported the Patriot Act like most members of Congress directly after 9/11, but by February 2002, he began to question the effectiveness of the US's anti-terrorism policies. Representative Tom Davis, a Republican from Virginia, latched onto Daschle's expression of doubt and criticized him, claiming his "divisive comments have the effect of giving aid and comfort to our enemies by allowing them to exploit divisions in our country."[4]

The DHS's mission was officially to "prevent terrorism and enhance security; secure and manage US borders; enforce and administer US immigration laws; safeguard and secure cyberspace; and ensure resilience to disasters." This led, in 2003, to what some might have seen as simply a bureaucratic reorganization of government. But in fact, this shift changed everything in terms of how immigration is categorized and discussed in America. The INS, or Immigration and Naturalization Service, transformed into Immigration and Customs Enforcement, or ICE.[5] How our government manages immigration flipped from serving people we are happy to welcome to this country to, instead, enforcing laws that would exclude, surveil, discriminate against, and punish a specific group of people simply because they were not born in the US. It went from "Service" to "Enforcement" and, without having to work too hard at it, anti-immigrant think tanks and conservative groups had won a major battle in that moment. Hardly anyone took notice.

The ethos of how we understood immigrants changed drastically; we no longer embraced the welcoming sentiment of the Emma Lazarus poem and instead were told to see immigrants as outside threats.

One of ICE's first campaigns was titled Operation Endgame, and its goal was to achieve a 100 percent deportation rate of all "removable aliens." Clearly, this wasn't just rhetoric. In immigrant neighborhoods, the low-level fear of immigration agents ratcheted up and now people were talking about being afraid to leave their homes. But ICE had no infrastructure yet. With just over 2,700 officers, and compared to the resources the agency has now—20,000 officers and a $7.1 billion budget in 2018—it was then a fledgling organization.[6] [7] [8]

In March 2003, Bush declared war on Iraq and ordered 200,000 armed forces to disarm the country and depose its leader, Saddam Hussein. People took to the streets of NYC at nine o'clock that same night, running along Second Avenue toward the UN. These were frantic, angry people who knew that the almost three thousand New Yorkers who died on 9/11 would pale in comparison to what was about to happen in Iraq.

The government called their military strategy "Shock and Awe," and so did all of the news media, obliviously or willingly engaging in the use of propaganda in a time of war. There were no longer two sides to the story, and the network I worked for had called its side with a graphic of the American flag waving in the wind that now opened all of the Iraq War coverage. To question any of that meant your patriotism could be questioned as well.

Within the massive AOL Time Warner, CNN was a tiny fish in a huge corporate ocean. I was a teeny part of a small fish, and yet, I still needed to find a way to survive. But I had to ask myself: Was I doing good journalism? Was I helping or hurting? Was I humbly representing and teaching or was I feeding the beast of my ego? Or the beast of American mainstream media? Or the beast of CNN and its survival?

When the US invaded Iraq on March 19, 2003, it marked the beginning of what would amount to 460,000 deaths.[9] Many of the people who died had no ties to terrorist groups whatsoever.

CNN had already churned through four or five new presidents since I had begun working there, so every year or so all of the correspondents would have to do the dog-and-pony show for the new executive on the job. Our jobs depended on this. If they liked what they saw, you were in better shape than if they didn't. I had been on both sides of that equation. Now the small group of reporters based at the NY bureau were actively competing against one another for slots on prime-time shows. The chummy family feel of CNN had disappeared, but the war was a surefire way to get viewers. Eyeballs mattered.

Chapter 11

Confrontations

L ou Dobbs, who had been at CNN from its inception and re-joined the network in 2001 to anchor his program *Lou Dobbs Tonight*, was a reflection of the typical network anchor and executive. Even though Dobbs had a bad temper and was known to berate and boss his staff around; even though his ratings were just so-so; even though he had left CNN at the height of his career to launch Space .com, in 2001 they hired him back as a prime-time anchor of *Money-line*, the financial evening news show that became *Lou Dobbs Tonight* in 2003. He was mediocre and everyone knew it.

One year following the national mourning that had unified the country, a new graphic was created for Dobbs's show. A bold and clunky red, white, and blue–inspired graphic with a 1980s feel to it would appear on the screen. In it, several men were depicted climbing over a wall—the first physical barriers had been constructed in 1990, and then a fourteen-mile border wall was approved by Clinton's administration in 1996, but the development of this secondary fence stalled.[1] Every night on prime time the graphic introduced a segment on his show called "Broken Borders," dedicated to reporting about the horrible things immigrants did. Every. Single. Night.

He claimed that immigrants, especially those who are undocumented, depressed the wages of American workers by billions of dollars and were a burden on the economy, that they brought communicable diseases like tuberculosis and leprosy, and that they committed higher rates of crime, representing "a third of our prison population."[2] It didn't seem to matter that these points were false—either flatly untrue or misleading. Mexicans had become the enemy. They were so much closer than al-Qaeda and they were everywhere.

That singular moment of hope, that tangible moment of confluence when two leaders, Bush and Fox, could have passed comprehensive immigration reform legislation, had been dashed immediately by the events of 9/11 and forgone.

The Patriot Act authorized the NSA to begin surveilling citizens without any check or oversight on what they were doing—except for dogged journalists who stayed on the story like a dog snarling on a bone for days. The government demanded that James Risen, a reporter for the *New York Times* who had been reporting on the CIA and the War on Terror, reveal his sources because they had leaked information on national security. A two-time Pulitzer Prize winner, Risen spent years fighting this dispute and took it all the way to the Supreme Court.[3]

The news media teaches us to racially profile and target people based on national origin. It's like history just keeps getting repeated because we've been through this before. During World War II, American citizens of Japanese descent were imprisoned in the so-called Japanese Internment. What an improper name; they were not Japanese and they were not interned. They were innocent American citizens of Japanese ancestry who were imprisoned in camps and were told it was for their own good by their own racist elected leaders.

Raúl and Berta in
Tampico, 1953

Passport photo, taken in Mexico
before I first arrived to the United
States. *Top row, from left to right*:
Bertha Elena and Mom. *Bottom
row, from left to right*: Raúl, Jorge,
and me as a baby, just weeks
before the immigration agent
tried to separate me from my
mother, 1962.

Me and Mom in 1964
on the South Side of
Chicago *(Courtesy of
Berta Hinojosa)*

Mexican consular certificate proving that I, eleven, am Mexican. The last date validated in 1977 would be a month to the day before my rape in Mexico.

BELOW: Showing off my outfit during my disco phase in 1976. Check out the cobija. *(Courtesy of Berta Hinojosa)*

Me and my then boyfriend, Gene Fama, during our punk phase, 1979. That's the crazy kitchen wallpaper. *(Courtesy of Berta Hinojosa)*

Dressed in black for prom in 1979. It was all secondhand style except for the shoes. *(Courtesy of Berta Hinojosa)*

Ceci and I in our second year of friendship visiting Manzanillo, Mexico, in 1981. This was our all-time favorite photograph. *(Courtesy of Raúl Hinojosa)*

My funky style as I said goodbye to Washington, DC, driving cross-country to San Diego, 1986 *(Photograph by Cecilia Vaisman)*

I made it into the *Los Angeles Times* when I moved to San Diego to produce *Enfoque Nacional* at KPBS Radio, 1986 *("KPBS Latino News Show Gets New Boss" by Hilliard Harper is reprinted with permission of the* Los Angeles Times; *photo of Maria Hinojosa courtesy of David McNew)*

DAVID McNEW

KPBS LATINO NEWS SHOW GETS NEW BOSS

By HILLIARD HARPER,
San Diego County Arts Writer

SAN DIEGO—Born in Mexico City, raised in Chicago and educated in New York, Maria Hinojosa brings a sharp news sense, along with a cosmopolitan background, to her job as the new producer of National Public Radio's "Enfoque Nacional."

The only NPR program to emanate from San Diego, "Enfoque Nacional" is produced each week at the KPBS (89.5 FM) studios and beamed by satellite to about 80 radio stations around the country. The 30-minute news program, in Spanish, focuses on national issues of concern to Latinos. Its name translates as "National Focus."

Hinojosa, 25, is still amazed at being tapped to produce "Enfoque," which made a big impression on her as a teen-ager. She first heard the program over a Chicago radio station while she was a high school senior.

"I was glad to hear non-commercial Latino news, seriously and professionally done—not 'And here comes the latest news from Mexico City!'" Hinojosa said, mimicking a juiced-up Latino disc jockey. "Hearing about Latinos nationally in Texas and California and the issues—I'll never forget it. I never thought I would be working here."

Hinojosa gives an impression of endless energy held under tight control. She came to San Diego last month, fresh from a year's stint in Washington as a field producer on NPR's "Weekend Edition." There she earned a reputation as a producer with a nose for the important story and the skill to make it a human story as well.

Working with "Weekend" host Scott Simon, Hinojosa chose and produced the kind of touching and incisive news features that have become "Week-

Producer Maria Hinojosa at the KPBS radio studio in San Diego.

end's" trademark. Among them: a segment on a 22-year-old New York City "crack" addict named Hawk; a series about detainees in a holding facility for illegal immigrants in Harlingen, Tex., and a profile of the Vietnamese community that is struggling to adapt to life in Corpus Christi, Tex.

At "Enfoque," which airs locally at 9:30 p.m. Thursdays and is repeated at the same time Fridays, moves from producing segments to producing the entire 30-minute program.

One of three NPR programs produced in Spanish, "Enfoque" was born in 1979. It is the brainchild of three men: Jose Mireles, Hector Molina and Jose McMurray, who once lobbied to produce programs in Spanish.

"We saw a need for a bilingual program and the

NPR to take a leadership role," said McMurray, now NPR's producer of bilingual programs. "We have such a growing Spanish-speaking population in the United States, and the Latinos—surveys have shown—are the people who listen to the radio the most."

Of the 14 million to 15 million people in the United States who speak Spanish—20 million if Puerto Rico is included, McMurray said. "We listen to radio a lot. When we get information in Spanish, we tend to believe it more."

Designed to inform the Spanish-speaking population in the United States of matters that affect them,

My wedding photo with Gérman on the Great Hill in Central Park, 1991. *He's the one wearing white!* *(Courtesy of Raúl Hinojosa)*

Meeting Celia Cruz and her husband, Pedro Knight, at Columbia University, 1994

On the stoop of our apartment on 106th Street, 1995. That's my cassette recorder next to me and my microphone in my hand. *(Courtesy of Gérman Perez)*

This was days after 9/11. I was working. *(Courtesy of CNN)*

BELOW: Supreme Court Justice Sonia Sotomayor and me backstage at El Museo del Barrio before our interview in front of a live audience, 2013. *Latino USA* former editor Nadia Reiman recorded the event. Sonia was rocking the purple. *(Courtesy of Latino USA)*

Reporting in New Orleans weeks after Hurricane Katrina, 2005. We were shielding this man's identity because he was undocumented and working to rebuild the city. *(Courtesy of William Brangham)*

Walking through the Willacy Detention Center, 2011. This was for my *Frontline* investigation "Lost in Detention." It was the first time cameras were allowed inside. *(Courtesy of Catherine Rentz)*

I'm a Christmas card lady for real, 2018 *(Courtesy of Bienvenida Beltre)*

HOLIDAY ❄ WISHES

WITH LOTS OF LOVE Y MUCHA PAZ PARA 2019. LOS PEREZ-HINOJOSA
Walter, Raul, Maria, German y Yurema

BELOW: With my Futuro team, 2019

Taking on Steve Cortes when he used the term *illegal* as a noun in a moment that went viral shortly afterward, 2016 *(Courtesy of MSNBC)*

Four-year-old Bobby, who is able to see just a bit of the world if he makes a big effort, 2019. His healing, love, and laughter inspire me. *(Courtesy of Virginia Child)*

The government was surveilling its own citizens, the FBI was telling men from certain countries to report and "register" themselves, and cable TV news was now flashing images of a different kind of people to hate—Latino immigrants. My hair was on fire, though the journalists I saw every day didn't feel that way. They didn't feel targeted. I searched for the story that no one else was telling: the young Muslims, Middle Easterners, and Arab Americans who, instead of registering with the FBI and almost certainly being detained or deported and losing everything, were packing up their bags and catching midnight buses to the Canadian border to ask for asylum.

We convinced CNN to let us film this story. I went to Plattsburgh in upstate New York and Rose went to the Port Authority bus station near Times Square at midnight. Sure enough, Rose spotted a nervous young couple carrying two pieces of rolling luggage, like they had packed in a hurry. She shot some B-roll of them getting on the bus and then introduced herself and asked if we could meet them in Plattsburgh before they crossed into Canada. They said nothing, acting as if they didn't speak a word of English. They looked scared. If a journalist had spotted them, then who else had?

That morning, when it was still dark at six o'clock, my crew and I waited at the bus station for a couple looking like the one Rose had described. We saw lots of brown folks getting off amid the white Upstate New Yorkers and students. For some reason the couple we were looking for was not coming out. I realized later they were delaying, hoping we would go away. Finally, they came down the front steps of the bus, but before I could get to them, they jumped inside a cab and took off super fast on the almost frozen road. Before they sped off, I had managed to yell out that we were journalists from CNN, that we meant no harm. We got back in our car and I drove so the cameraman could shoot video from the highway as we followed.

These people were running for their lives to escape being taken in by the federal police, held in a camp, chained, and forcibly deported, but sure, they'll make time to stop and talk to a TV reporter and her crew in the middle of the highway that straddles no-man's-land—neither US nor Canadian territory. It was right there where the cab made a sudden stop in the middle of the empty highway, not even on the shoulder. The couple got out, grabbed their suitcases, and sprinted north through zero-degree freezing wind to the promised land of Canada. This image was seared into my memory—you wouldn't believe it unless you saw it with your own eyes. Our cameraman was only able to get a few shots. They were running so fast, I had no idea where to park our car, so I pulled into the island in the middle of the highway not too far from the Canadian border. We were CNN. We would be okay.

What a miscalculation.

My cameraman ran out behind the couple as they raced toward the checkpoint at the Canadian border. The sound tech and I sat in our car with the blinkers on, when all of a sudden I saw a Border Patrol agent walking toward us with such force and determination. I got so scared I put my hands on the wheel and started to focus on deep breathing. He banged on the window and said, "Give me your passports, RIGHT NOW." Slowly, I lowered the window and handed them over. And then he walked away.

After several long minutes, during which the three of us sat in the car not saying a word and not moving one centimeter, the agent stormed back and thrust the passports at me.

"You need to move on and get out of the middle of the road. Pull a U-turn or go north," he roared. "What were you thinking, making a move like that? This is crazy. Don't ever do that again. Move on!"

I shrank in my seat. We settled back in the car and started shooting as we crossed the border into Canada to film that part of the story and to see if maybe we could find the couple. Of course, the Canadians spotted us and sent us over to their press office. They told us they were going to confiscate our tape. It was all a bureaucratic mess and it required fast thinking on all of our parts, including our cameraman, who took out what he had filmed and inserted a blank tape to give to them.

After being harassed on both sides of the border, we made it to the Montreal YMCA that had become a catchall for new arrivals, some of whom already had family living in Canada and some who knew no one there. Our loss, their gain, was how I saw this exodus, since many of the people fleeing were students or businessmen or the sons and daughters of professionals who were now taking all of their talents and skills they had acquired in the US and moving to Canada. Their memory of the US would always be tainted by the fear that prompted them to run away from the free-est country in the world.

The day after our story aired on CNN and all over the world, Canada officially shut down its borders to refugees from the United States. People would no longer be allowed to apply for asylum from inside of Canada. After all of that reporting, our story ended up making the policy worse for human beings. Not better. It was a low point in my career. I was doing the opposite of what a good journalist was supposed to do.

I was sitting at my desk planning out calls for our next story when a desk assistant came to get me.

"They want you in the newsroom now," she explained. "And they said you should get your go-bag ready. You'll be leaving as soon as you see this video they need you to watch."

Damn it. Another overnight story. Another disappointing phone call to Gérman that I wouldn't be around for at least a day, maybe two. My kids would be upset. More guilt. *C'mon, Hinojosa*, I told myself, *suck it up*. As I walked to the newsroom, I repeated these words in my head: *Your job means you travel and your family knows that. Stop feeling guilty.*

In the newsroom, a small group of the senior producers and assignment editors were gathered around a computer with dark expressions. "An al-Qaeda video has just been released of a young American man named Nicholas Evan Berg who's from a small town in Pennsylvania. He's a Jewish guy who went to volunteer, but he was kidnapped," Chris Kokenes, our always calm assignment editor, said. My eyebrows furrowed into a knot.

"You're going to be leading the coverage on this story from in front of his family's home. A live truck is already on its way to get a spot."

"Okay! So what is really going on?" I asked, confused. "Why am I here and not running to the car?"

"Sit down," Chris said. "You have to watch this because it's a part of the story. They are going to cut off his head."

What? NO! I can't! I was screaming inside of my head. *NOOOOOOOO.*

I knew there was no way around this. It wasn't as if I could stand up and walk out on the entire senior editorial team of the NY bureau. I was literally surrounded.

"Okay, go," I said. I watched till I couldn't anymore, which was just after Nick finished struggling and the knife was brought to his neck. I closed my eyes and heard the gasps. I was screaming on the inside, but I didn't move one inch. All I needed to know was that Nick Berg struggled to stay alive until his last breath was taken from him.

By the time we got to Nick's parents' home in suburban Pennsylvania, there were already a dozen satellite trucks and journalists there doing live coverage. My stomach churned at the sight: live trucks for two blocks with loud generators on all night; strangers suddenly living in front of your house; people laughing and congregating, eating, putting on makeup while a family is in mourning.

As a lead reporter on a major international breaking-news story, I was going to be here for days, if not a full week. I had just seen something so horrific I wanted to immediately forget it. I had witnessed how the will to live is something we carry deep inside each of us, and I thought about how Nick wanted to get away, fight or flight till the end. Somehow in his will I found something to believe in. His will to help.

He went to Iraq a confused and starry-eyed technical wiz who wanted to help the country with reconstruction. But his name was Nick Berg. He was Jewish. Al-Qaeda thought he was a spy. And also, he was Jewish. So they killed him. The first beheading of the digital front of the war. The video went viral, before we had a name for that, immediately.

I was on the air every hour, sometimes two or three times in an hour to do different networks like Headline News, CNN Español, and CNN International. I was surrounded by the competition, and the entire network, the entire world was watching. If I could break something on this story, if I could get an exclusive, it would be huge for me. Ugh. For me.

I knew that Nick's dad was progressive. The only interview he had given was to Amy Goodman at *Democracy Now*.[4] I thought maybe he might know my work and appreciate it if I reached out. It had happened in the past during 9/11; some people knew who I was, appreciated my style of reporting, and were thankful to speak to me. Maybe Nick's dad might want that?

In my competitive zeal to prove myself, I did something that took me back to my morning TV booker self. It was the worst kind of in-your-face journalism. In the middle of live shots, I got this surge of competitive blood in my system that propelled me to break protocol and walk onto the family property. No one had done this. I walked around to the back door, which was propped open, and could see through the screen door to the family kitchen. Trembling, I said,

"Hello? My name is Maria Hinojosa and I'm with CNN. I'm so sorry about Nick. Is there any chance—"

The back door slammed in my face and I almost fell backward on the stairs. I ran away from the house as fast as I could and went straight into the trailer, where I pushed back on the tear ducts of each eye, because I could not cry, not now. I was about to go on the air and I had to look good because I was a pro.

I knew how to talk to the anchors without memorizing my script; I had a soft yet serious presence on the air; I was proving to all of the executives and every single show producer that I could do this, that after five years of constant auditioning for the role of a breaking-news TV journalist, I could say that I was one. I had covered 9/11, the *Columbia* shuttle explosion, and now this.

When I finally got home after a week on assignment, Gérman was waiting for me with a bath drawn. He hugged and kissed me tenderly. He was proud of me. No matter how much he criticized CNN, when he saw me doing work he felt proud of, he let me know.

My TV network was happy, my bureau and bosses were happy, my husband was happy, even my kids were happy. I was back in time for the Double Dutch Park Party I had organized at my kids' progressive grammar school. It was a private school, and so I had wanted to create an organic way for the families of color to connect and for white families to join in to build a sense of community.

As we jumped double Dutch and listened to old-school R&B on the boom box, my heart went back to those days during recess in the schoolyard in Chicago, when jumping rope gave me a way to feel proud of myself. I was good at it and loved it. Jumping rope, I was no longer the little Mexican girl outsider. For me, jumping rope in the schoolyard was quintessentially American and I could double Dutch with the best. We were double Dutch sisters.

These memories from decades ago made me smile in Morningside Park in Harlem that afternoon. But the memories from the week before were still fresh—the beheading, the campout, the funeral procession—and were like sandbags weighing me down with sadness.

I was concerned not only about the death of a young man, but also with how I was acting as a journalist, the decisions I was making, and more important, why and to please whom? What was playing the game at CNN taking from my own soul? I felt like a part of my journalist self was dying a little bit every day.

It wasn't enough now to do the solid reporting that I had just proven I could do and had the stamina for. No, the network wanted us to get "involved" in the story. MSNBC reporters, a top CNN competitor, were doing a new style of point-of-view shots and "going on a journey" live shots. CNN executives wanted us to do that as well. A lot of executives are just great copycatters.

When a newly hired correspondent allowed himself to get tasered on camera, the executives were thrilled! I was horrified. He was a fellow Latino. So *this* is what I would have to do? The message from the higher-ups was: bring things up a notch and think of ways to get more involved in the reporting to get more eyeballs. By getting ourselves tasered?

The correspondents felt humiliated. Gérman wasn't happy.

"The next thing that's going to happen is that they're going to force you to do something silly on-air and you will lose all of your credibility," he argued. "Do you want to let this network make a fool out of you?"

People were starting to laugh at CNN, specifically on late-night TV. Which means they could very well be laughing at me. My fellow Latino and Latina journalists weren't laughing; they, along with academics, activists, and even regular TV viewers, were angry at CNN for giving Lou Dobbs a nightly platform. Several activists said the words coming out of Dobbs's mouth were not journalism but hate speech.

After Rose, my producer, wrote a letter from the Latino CNN employees, the senior executives agreed to meet with us. When I told them that Lou Dobbs was going to spark boycotts—not of Dobbs, but of the entire network—they looked at me and hissed that that would never, ever happen.

At the end of the meeting, I walked up to the president of CNN US and told him that at the very least we should be allowed to tell another side of the story, a side based in fact. I asked him if I could do an hour-long piece through the CNN documentary unit. He gave me a look, almost as if to say, *Okay, but if I give you this, will you leave me alone?* and then he said, "Yes. I can make that happen."

———————

The first time I visited Atlanta was for the Unity 1994 conference that was organized as a collaboration of the four major associations for journalists of color.[5] It gathered thousands of American journalists, all of them of color or queer—Latino, Asian, Native American, black, and the gay journalists association. I had been asked by the NAHJ to develop a radio training program, and John, a former Queens crew member who had been a subject of my reporting, had applied for and received a spot to attend the training workshop for budding journalists. He was assigned to do a story trying to locate "el barrio" in Atlanta. Most people had no idea what he was talking about. "Barrio?" the crowd answered back in a thick southern accent.

But that was back in 1994. Because I had been traveling to Atlanta for CNN since 1997, I'd been paying attention to how things were changing. I am that Mexican immigrant who is always looking for others like me everywhere, searching for visibility in others.

Ever since that night years before when I heard ranchera music blasting from a corner bodega in Harlem and correctly predicted the arrival of Mexican immigrants in New York City, I had my eyes peeled for other sightings across the country. I understood that Latinos were going to start spreading out across the country and beyond big cities. A lot of people were surprised to hear about the decades-long presence of Latinos in the Midwest, but I knew because I was one of them. So I was aware of these Latinx communities that were perceived to be invisible. As a journalist, my job is to keep my eyes open, always watching for trends.

I had been watching Atlanta change for a decade. Every year I saw more signs in Spanish and more Latinos. First in restaurant kitchens. Then I saw grocery stores pop up and started hearing about mexicanos moving to Georgia to work in the chicken and carpeting plants. I spotted Latinos in their cars, women with babies, men driving with landscaping and roofing equipment. There was a quiet boom of Latinos and Latinas in Georgia and no one was talking about it on a national level. This was what I was going to make a documentary about—undocumented immigrants in Atlanta.

Unfortunately, the documentary unit at CNN was an exclusive club and Rose was not allowed in. Instead, the EP assigned me the newest and least experienced producer on his team.

Kimberly and I could not have been more different. She was petite, wore higher heels than me, and had long, straight blond hair and big eyes with false eyelashes. She was a southern belle in tight jeans.

We both understood what had happened here. The EP had been forced by the president to work with me. It wasn't his choice that I join his exclusive club. I was forced on him because of internal politics, and he resented being told what to do. So he assigned the least valuable person on his team to my project.

But Kimberly and I fell in love with each other as journalists. We called ourselves "Ebony and Ivory." We knew we were typecast to fail—the blonde and the Mexican—so we decided to make the best documentary and prove them all wrong.

We did a lot of groundwork, but we couldn't find anyone willing to go on camera and tell their story of being undocumented in the American South. Immigrants were afraid.

Then one day we went into a little dive of a taco place, scouting for people to talk to, and I started chatting with the waitress, who was beautiful, smart, and personable. Rosa had two kids in Mexico and was undocumented. She had come to the US a year before because she wanted to find a way to give her children a better education and life. There was no one left in her small village except for women, children, and viejitos. Everyone else had already left for El Norte. All she wanted was to bring her kids here, too, so that they could be reunited.

Rosa wanted to be the best mom she could be, and for her that meant leaving home and making money. She understood the risk of being on camera, but she also knew she had done nothing wrong.

"I want people to understand that it's people like me who are their neighbors who are coming here. We are not criminals and we are not a threat. I want them to see me. I love this country."

There were two other main characters in the documentary. One was a white man who was married to a Korean immigrant, had a daughter, and was now, suddenly, an anti-immigrant activist. Another was D. A. King, a former marine and so-called activist who enjoyed going up to immigrants and asking them for their immigration papers. It seemed to me like he was having fun while using an easy form of intimidation.

Rosa made a plan to have her kids travel to the US. We asked if we could meet them in Mexico beforehand. We met Rosa's eleven-year-old son and twelve-year-old daughter in their small village of a few hundred people inland in Veracruz. They were incredibly sad and had what looked like permanent frowns on their faces. For over a year, Rosa had been calling and sending gifts, but she hadn't come home and or sent for the kids. They were filled with longing and despair, but maybe more than anything, consumed by anger at their mother for leaving them.

Several weeks later we finally received the call we had been waiting for. Rosa's kids would be on the border in a few days with their grandparents, who had been instructed to hand off the children to a smuggler who would cross them all the way to Houston, where Rosa would be waiting.

Rosa had told us we could wait for the kids in Houston with her. At the last minute she changed her mind and said she would allow us to witness her children being crossed. Kimberly and I were screaming when we got off the phone. This was reporter gold!

A week later we met the kids and grandparents in Matamoros, Mexico. The kids were scared. All they knew was that soon they were going to be with Mama. We tried to calm them. They were excited to see me and Kimberly and our crew because by now we were familiar faces.

The next night we assembled in a supermarket parking lot to meet one of the two women transporting the kids. The woman was probably about fifty years old and Mexican; she looked more like any middle-aged woman than a member of a criminal smuggling enterprise. I was surprised. Smugglers are some of the hardest people for journalists to meet. As a precaution, we were introduced to her as an American couple who knew the kids and would be following from several cars behind just to make sure they got to the other side safely.

A minute later, the children said a quick goodbye to their grandparents. They were barely given enough time for a hug. This was not a moment to get emotional was how I read the smuggler's attitude. She had been through this before.

She quickly got the kids into her van and then she took off. We followed until she stopped on the side of the road, took the kids out, and put them in another car with a younger Mexican woman, who already had another two or three kids in the car. Off they went. And off we went.

I drove so my cameraman could shoot as much as possible without being seen by the police or the second smuggler, who didn't even know we were following her. She pulled up to the checkpoint to enter the United States.

I replayed the words of the older smuggler in my head. "This woman has never been stopped," she had said in the parking lot. "She has an incredible record. She is a mom herself. All of the kids I have given her always make it to the other side."

She's never been stopped. I kept on repeating this to myself as I watched her, two cars ahead of me. Then, instead of being waved through, I saw the agent send her and all of the kids in the car, including Rosa's two children, who had never left their pueblo until now, over to the Border Patrol building. They had not made it through.

We showed up at the Brownsville Border Patrol Station at 11:15 p.m., about twenty minutes after they had been sent to secondary inspection. If the Latino Border Patrol agent could have screamed at us, he would have. He was just about to close the office for the night and now he had a woman and five kids detained and there was a CNN reporter, producer, and two guys with cameras in their hands. His night had been ruined.

"I know why you're here," he said to me. "I know who you are."

"If you know who I am, then you know my reporting, and right now all I want to know is what is going to happen to those children you just detained. That's all we want to know and we'll leave."

He threatened to have us removed because we were on federal property and his office was now closed. We went back to Mexico, where a devastated and distraught abuela had already received a call that the children would be sent back to Matamoros that night to child services, probably a quick turnaround because of our presence. At 3:30 a.m., as we were going to sleep, we got a call and ran out again to film them meeting up with the kids back in Mexico.

The next morning, when we called our senior editors in Atlanta to debrief, we were ordered to come back home. Our EP said enough was enough and that he was concerned for our safety. The next day, a local Brownsville TV station's website ran a headline saying something to the effect of "CNN Pays Smuggler to Transport Kids." The report said

I had paid the smuggler $5,000 to take the kids across the border for a story I was doing. We moved into quick-response mode. The CNN lawyers immediately got in touch with the Brownsville station (which was an affiliate of CNN!) and read them the riot act. How dare they publish those allegations without even speaking to anyone at CNN first. The story was up for less than ninety minutes before they took it down, but the damage had been done.

Then I got a call. The president of CNN was on the line. After a few niceties, he asked me if I had done it.

"I have to ask. Did you pay the smuggler?"

"Of course not!" I responded in shock. "I would never do something like that. I'm a journalist."

Pause. Silence.

"And if you don't believe me, I will send you my credit card and bank account statements so you can see that there is no place to squeeze out an extra five thousand dollars."

I had to defend myself to CNN. I was humiliated.

My summer intern at CNN that year was a Nicaraguan American Mormon from Salt Lake City. She made dozens of calls to immigration organizations across the country to let them know that my documentary, *Immigrant Nation, Divided Country*, would be airing and encouraged them to watch.

The documentary was dramatic television. One of the employers featured in it, who owned a family restaurant and hotel, said the government would have to come through him if they wanted to take his Mexican immigrant workers. Another character, an undocumented mother, was dying of cancer. Meanwhile, D. A. King, an anti-immigration activist, was accused of being a member of a hate group and another character's marriage broke up because of his anti-immigrant activism. Rosa had gone down to Mexico and found another way to get the children into the US. Now they were all together again and happy in Atlanta.

The footage was raw and gritty and showed all sides of the immigration story unfolding in an unlikely place—Georgia. I was proud of the work even though I had to battle my EP the entire way. He told me that DHS had recommended I address the allegation of paying the smuggler in the documentary. I resisted. Was the government threatening me? Ultimately, I added the line to the finished documentary, but under protest. This piece would either make me or break me, is what I had told Gérman.

When it ran, *Immigrant Nation* had the second-highest audience engagement for any CNN documentary at that time. A month later, the day before Thanksgiving, Kimberly called me. Immigration agents had shown up at Rosa's boyfriend's house and taken her and the kids. The government had gone after my sources, plain and simple. The old rule of not targeting undocumented immigrants who speak to the media had been broken. When I screamed as loud as I could to the senior executives, letting them know what a travesty this was for ethics in American journalism, I was told to be silent. Told to never speak of this to anyone. Ever.

Rosa and her boyfriend blamed me, hated me, and told me to stay away from them.

In the end, I was right. The documentary had broken me.

After all this, Gérman couldn't understand why I would want to stay at a place that treated me this way. I was a woman in her forties. I was afraid of being tainted goods, of not being able to find a new job.

CNN was the enemy now. Every time I had to work late or travel, the news was met with a snarl from my husband. I used to tell him about all of the office politics and mostly he would just listen and nod, but there was none of that anymore.

I was struggling to survive and treading water in the sinkhole that was CNN. Even the stars of the network had fallen. Aaron Brown was out. Anderson Cooper was in. I had been around since 1997. I was considered way old-school and in a few months my contract was coming up. I had no mentor, no protector.

Even when I came up with unique angles on stories I got turned down. I pitched ideas to all the producers so I could get on the air and it was hard. People didn't think the ideas I was bringing to the table were special anymore. Still, I didn't stop. I kept on looking for the underside of stories, the untold, the thing staring you right in the eyes and yet nobody else sees it.

Out of frustration and, frankly, in a desperate attempt to save my job and prove my relevance to the network, I sat down and wrote up three pages of story ideas. I wrote investigative pitches, music pitches, urban pitches, all different kinds of story ideas so no one could say I was limited in my scope. I even had a pitch about sports. It was a last-ditch effort before I had to renegotiate my contract. I had already been told that they only wanted to renew me for one year. A sure sign that I was on the outs.

Out of the three pages of story ideas, the new news president picked the one I had put down as sort of a joke. Mia Navarro, a LIPSter friend of mine from the *New York Times*, had done a story in Texas about women from the Bible Belt who sell sex toys at Tupperware parties. We had found a couple in South Carolina who were prepared to let us come and film the wife at her sex toy sales party with a bunch of Jesus-loving women who passed around ten-inch dildos as if they were passing chocolate chip cookies. The boss said he wanted it on the air for the many eyeballs it would bring. This is what my work as a journalist had been reduced to.

Chapter 12

Citizen Journalist

Gérman took off the dark glasses that he wore every day of the year. He looked me in the eye and told me he believed CNN had sucked out my soul. I pulled back and returned with an angry *"What?"* But inside I thought about my silent addiction to being on TV and wondered if he could see that I was jonesing.

"You've gone from being a hippie to being a diva. It's been a total transformation. You don't wear the long dangling earrings on TV anymore and you're straightening your hair now at the Dominican salons. You even had a relaxer put on your hair? You used to wear your African jewelry and now you look like a corporate woman," he said, frustrated that I couldn't see what he saw: his wife, the fighter, was now fighting to fit in.

I didn't fit in anymore at a network whose new mission was "to get eyeballs."

I was fuming with anger toward Gérman. He didn't have a right to push me to leave my job because he didn't like what he saw on the network or the style of hair and clothes I wore in order to survive. All the little and big things in our marriage had accumulated and caught up with us. A Gérman se le habia colmado el plato. For my husband it was his last straw.

He talked to my therapist, Andaye, who was a good mutual friend of ours. We had first seen her before we got married when Gérman wanted me to understand the notion that he, as my partner in life, was my priority—not my friends or my job. At the same time, he made me his number one priority. Relationships are two-way streets. But my feminist self inherently resented that notion. Andaye was eventually able to get me to see that in a couple you actually do have to put each other first. My partner had to be my priority, and it needed to come from love, not forced commitment or resentment.

I continued to resist the idea of a man telling me what to do. I resisted having any kind of relationship that looked like my mom and dad's in the sense that my dad could not function without my mom, who did everything for him, including cooking every meal and choosing his daily wardrobe. I couldn't see that my self-sufficient husband didn't want a relationship like my parents'. He cooked for himself and the kids and his closet was more organized than mine.

No, what he wanted me to see was that this network was changing my essence, the core of who I was as a person and who I was as a journalist. I could never see that because as soon as Gérman criticized CNN, I felt I had to defend it. I was terrified that if I began to hate CNN as much as my husband did, I wouldn't survive.

When Gérman saw Andaye, he told her he planned to give me an ultimatum: either leave CNN or he and the kids would move to Punta Cana. Life was safe and secure down there and a new school had just opened up.

"She can come visit us anytime she wants," Gérman said in all seriousness to Andaye.

I remember thinking, *You can only hate what you love*, because I was hating everything right then, my husband and my life. How could he do this?

You can't have it all, I said to myself. Women, fellow Latinas, held me up as an example of someone who could and did have it all. Yet I was on the verge of losing my husband and kids and my job all at the same time. I felt like I was losing my mind, too.

"Hello, Maria?"

"Yes?" I answered, after my cell phone rang.

"It's John Siceloff," he explained. "I am the EP of *NOW* on PBS with Bill Moyers. David Brancaccio from PRI is now the anchor of the show that Moyers created. We'd love to talk to you about joining our team of long-form investigative TV. We're a smaller version of *60 Minutes*."

Oh my god. If I get this job I might still be able to save my marriage and keep my family intact. It might even get me one step closer to 60 Minutes.

I had met Bill Moyers when another one of his teams had thought about me as his possible coanchor a year before. When I met him, I turned into that twelve-year-old girl who had watched him sit at the anchor desk at CBS News and read scathing commentary that was neither from the left nor the right but rather from a point of view of justice. *NOW* was part of Moyers's legacy and had been created as a response to 9/11, a show that would present hard-hitting investigative reporting on a weekly basis. It was journalism with a mission made for public television, an institution that proclaimed itself dedicated to giving voice to the most underrepresented in the country and doing so without commercial interest or gain.

My two worlds—the years I had spent in public media as a reporter for NPR and my tenure on television at CNN—were coming together organically. It felt like my career choices finally made sense, and, unbeknownst to me, had led me to this moment.

I interviewed with the senior team at *NOW*, which was a small independent production company that had less than twenty-five staff employees, many who were former network producers or from ABC, where Siceloff had worked as an EP. One week later they sent me an offer. I'd be taking a substantial pay cut and would go back to working five days a week instead of four, but I would be doing important work. And they agreed to give me the title of senior correspondent.

CNN was still dangling the carrot of a one-year contract and a small bump in salary. I struggled with the idea of breaking away. What if this time things got better? What if the new executives coming in liked me and I missed my big opportunity?

I was scared of change. I also didn't want to be seen as a failure. The first Latina correspondent needed to walk out with her shoulders back and her fingers snapping because I would be the one who had made the decision to leave. Not them.

I was torn.

When I told Gérman about my decision he hugged me so tightly that I realized I had forgotten what that felt like. He was elated and showed it by taking off his dark glasses, looking at me with his hazel green eyes, and kissing me lightly. I said goodbye and, as per usual, I got on a plane, this time to Austin, Texas, to attend the yearly NAHJ conference.

As I walked through the massive convention center, where I would be speaking on several panels (I was considered a high-profile, "successful" journo no matter how I saw myself), my fellow Latinx journalists congratulated me for my work at CNN, especially my documentary, *Immigrant Nation*, which had run just a few months prior. They thanked me for finally humanizing immigrants on a network that was known for attacking them every single night, sin falla. Young journalists came up to me and hugged me because of *Latino USA*, telling me they loved the show so much and that it made them see themselves in the world and feel hopeful. They gave me kudos for my book, *Raising Raúl*, and asked me how I was able to "have it all." *What a great relationship you have with Gérman—thank you for making it so public.* They didn't know how close I had been to losing it all just a day or two prior. Oh, and they would have never guessed that my bank account was about to be overdrawn.

I had made the decision, as frightened as I was, to leave the place that I had come to love and cherish; that had taught me the adrenaline rush of live TV; where I had lived through tragedies with coworkers; that had brought all different kinds of people together to make journalism (not just the elite); where the camera guys (and two women), the editors, and producers were from different class backgrounds, a form of diversity I appreciated.

But I was ready to say goodbye to the monster it had become for me and my family. I wanted to be the one to announce my decision to the staff first and then make it public, but in a final corporate jab, CNN's PR department sent out a companywide email and an accompanying press release announcing my departure without even letting me know beforehand. The announcement was subtly worded to make it seem as though leaving was not my decision. The goodbyes started to pour in— Wolf Blitzer, Miles O'Brien, Soledad O'Brien, and dozens of others.

————————

The step down from the corporate world into public media was so pronounced that it was as if the "news gods" were rubbing it in my face. I had gotten used to having a shiny office at the brand-new Time Warner Center, at the time the building with the highest market listing in Manhattan.[1]

My new office was located in what many often considered the ugliest building in New York City, a massive quarter of a block built right above the train tracks on Thirty-Third Street and Tenth Avenue.[2] This area was a no-man's-land in Manhattan, but for me it was the pot of gold at the end of the rainbow. My new job would change everything.

We celebrated with a picnic in the park, one of Yurema's favorite things to do in the summer. On the Tuesday after Labor Day, I went to my new office and Katrina hit New Orleans and Gulfport. As we watched some of the initial footage, I thought about how CNN would have sent me out that same day. Now I was antsy to go. I had to calm my need to get on a plane immediately any time there was breaking news. It was only after the images of people stuck in the Superdome broke, in early September, that they decided to send me down with a producer. *NOW* didn't have a travel department to book the flights and find us rooms. We booked ourselves a flight to Memphis and then rented a van and drove down through Mississippi. We stocked up on everything we needed: lots of water, dried food and canned stuff, waterproof gear, a tarp, and sleeping bags for the four of us—me and my crew, three middle-aged white guys.

We stopped in Greenwood, midway down Mississippi, because Brian, our producer, wanted us to get one last good night of sleep before we began several days of reporting in who knew what kind of conditions. Like many news producers, he was a bit quirky. He had found a beautiful boutique hotel decorated with ornate furniture and antiques in a modern setting. It was all very over-the-top and surreal. He took the entire crew to eat at an old restaurant from the days when each table had a private room with a curtain so that nobody could see who was having dinner with whom. No black people had been allowed in to eat at this secret place.

I went to sleep in a comfy bed with sheets that had a thread count of several hundred, but I barely closed my eyes because I was so distraught at what I had seen at dinner. Wealthy people living the life, celebrating birthdays and drinking out of fine crystal while only four hours away, people were hungry and thirsty and many had no place to sleep.

We left in the pitch-black of a hot summer night at four in the morning. I slept in the van till the sun was shining in my eyes and the drool on my chin had hardened. I was mortified—but then I turned my head to look out the window and saw long lines of cars trying to get gas. The lines went so far back I had to imagine it would take a day of just waiting out there in the sun to get service. I remembered the gas shortage in the seventies and here it was in front of me again. An advanced country brought to its knees.

The highway signs had blown off and a roof was missing here or there. We kept driving till we got to Gulfport right on the Gulf of Mexico and the spot where Katrina had hit land, as if this little city had a target on its back just like the WTC.

I didn't know what to compare what I was seeing to since it was my first time there. On 9/11, Lower Manhattan had been covered in debris—mountains of steel, concrete, and paper from the thousands of offices. In Gulfport, it was shreds of wood everywhere.

I found myself standing in the middle of another ground zero, but this one wasn't a terrorist attack or a shuttle explosion. I had dealt with the other two tragedies; however, a natural disaster like this was something I had never seen with my own eyes. I was walking on the rubble not of financial towers but of tourist ships and horse carriages and hotels and casinos.

We did interviews all day and went into the poorest parts of the city, where we saw the most vulnerable and forgotten in this country, people who didn't have a car or money to put gas in the car they did have. These were the same people who didn't have a stocked kitchen because they lived day-to-day. They had special-needs kids like other

Americans, but because they were black and poor they didn't appear in the network TV version of America that likes to see stories with "pretty"—usually meaning white and wealthy—people in them.

I interviewed Patricia Clayton, a local resident who was staying at her brother-in-law's house and doing her best to care for her autistic son in the hurricane's aftermath. She asked me to please make sure her hair looked right because she knew she was going to be on TV. My producer didn't want me to take the time to get a mirror so she could comb her hair, but I did my best to acknowledge what she was asking for and needed so that she could look at me and tell me her truth in that moment. Tears fell as she carefully touched her pressed hair.

"It ain't about me no more. It's about him," Patricia said of her son, who was clapping along to "If You're Happy and You Know It, Clap Your Hands" to pass the time while they waited for relief aid. "I'm going to tell you the truth. There should be more help than this."[3]

People told us that no one had come to help. One of the Red Cross trucks wouldn't even stop; it just drove through the streets throwing pizzas out the back door. They were too afraid to stop because it was a black neighborhood, the neighbors told me.

No one was reporting on the immigrant workers, many of whom had been recruited from Mexico and beyond and who were arriving every day to help rebuild the city. I had seen it with my own eyes. We went back to New Orleans to do a story on the abuse of workers in the corporate cleanup business.

Several weeks after Katrina, we followed one of the buses transporting migrant workers to and from cleanup sites. We had heard about these backwoods work encampments tied to BE&K, a company that had been contracted by Halliburton, which was once run by Vice President Dick Cheney.

At the camp, there was an armed guard and a moat with alligators surrounding the rows upon rows of shipping containers that housed

the men in three-tier bunk beds. Those were the workers' accommo-
dations. Imagine a packed sleeping compartment on a train, forty-two
men to a trailer. They got that plus three baloney sandwiches a day
and a measly wage.

I met a man from Nicaragua named Pablo who had been recruited
to work in El Norte. He'd left his wife and kids behind because the
bank was threatening to repossess his land; the only thing he carried
with him from home was a beat-up Bible. On his first job he spent a
week roofing, but the contractor disappeared on payday and he and
thirteen other workers never got paid.

"We couldn't do anything. We feel defenseless. We can't act because . . . yes, it's true, we are undocumented," Pablo told me. "We
didn't get paid. But what can you do? Complain about bad luck, and
that's it."[4]

The story of Latinos and Latinas arriving to help rebuild New Orleans became too big to ignore. President Bush had even lifted regula-
tions requiring employers to confirm the immigration status of hired
workers, as well as a number of other labor laws, like minimum wage.
Then, at a forum with local business leaders, New Orleans mayor Ray
Nagin said, "How do I make sure New Orleans is not overrun with
Mexican workers?"[5] His comments were swiftly denounced by both
African American and Latino advocacy organizations, though they
were representative of the tensions at the time.[6]

We discovered that there was a complex backstory to these workers and their persistent and perennial presence in the South. They
also weren't the first Spanish-speaking people to arrive there: Spaniard
colonist explorers first encountered the coast of what is now New Orleans in 1542, and then about two hundred years later, France ceded
control of Louisiana to Spain until 1800.[7] Starting in the 1920s, Nola
was the place where wealthy Mexicans sent their kids to study. For the
rich in Yucatán, New Orleans was closer than Mexico City and it lent

more cachet at parties in Mérida to say that your child was in boarding school in New Orleans than in El DF.

Guest workers, like the ones I saw that morning in Gulfport, have existed for centuries, if not since the beginning of time. Whether this labor has been forced, as with slavery, or contracted via immigrant populations, it has been the driving force behind this country and its capitalist economy. But you don't see it in the mainstream history books.

We learn about the founding fathers, the "brave" westward movement to achieve Manifest Destiny, and skyscrapers built by white men, when in fact the First Transcontinental Railroad was built on the backs of immigrants: Chinese and Irish workers. The former made up 90 percent of Central Pacific's workforce on the western leg of the railroad, earning half the wages of their Irish counterparts, and were often subjected to beatings by white foremen.[8]

Throughout the 1930s, and especially in 1931, the Hoover administration instituted a program they euphemistically called the Great Repatriation, a mass forced exodus of 1.8 million people of Mexican descent, about 60 percent of whom were actually US citizens.[9]

It was not a repatriation at all. It should have been called the Great Deportation. The federal government, as well as local agencies and businesses across the country, rounded up hundreds of thousands of people in unexpected raids in public parks, homes, and workplaces, and sent them to Mexico.[10]

Be careful what you wish for. During World War II, so many young men and women were called up to serve that the US economy stalled because it needed more workers. The Bracero Program started in 1942, conceived as a temporary solution to a labor shortage—compounded by healthy Japanese American men who were forcibly relocated to concentration camps. The United States and Mexican governments agreed to an arrangement in which Mexicans, eventually

4.6 million of them, would legally come to the US to work through short-term, mostly agricultural labor contracts.[11] It was sold as a perfect solution. Basically, Mexicans would be allowed to come to the US on work visas and work at certain factories and farms. They could go home, where they would supposedly receive that withheld 10 percent of wages—but most did not—or re-up. There was never a promise that this would be anything more than Mexico giving the US their most productive workers, letting the US use up their labor, paying them just okay, and then sending them back after they were squeezed of productivity with no pension or health care. *Isn't that a great deal for the both of us?*

The Mexican government, frankly, being a very poor and self-hating negotiator, didn't mind throwing these migrants under the bus. They allowed worker exploitation to happen because they, too, were racist. They didn't consider brown-skinned workers to be real Mexicans anyway. Only the light-skinned Mexicans got to decide who was or was not of value.

Braceros kept on coming until 1964, when the apparent exploitation and labor violations inherent in the program became untenable, especially during the civil rights era, when people were paying closer attention to these kinds of injustices.[12] Under the program, 4.6 million labor contracts were signed.[13] The braceros helped to keep the US economy afloat and advance agricultural productivity during those years. Yet there is almost no record or acknowledgment of their contribution today. A seven-year lawsuit, settled in 2008, finally got some bracero workers, or their direct descendants, their due benefits to the tune of $3,500 each, awarded by the Mexican government as back pay for the wages it withheld from workers between 1942 and 1946.[14]

Somewhere along the line, Tom Lea Sr., the mayor of El Paso, began a campaign in 1916 to disinfect the immigrants coming across the border daily, labeling Mexicans as dirty. He demanded that the federal government install a fumigation facility, which opened in 1917 and required that Mexicans be checked for bugs and disease. Full cavity searches, in addition to gasoline baths and other toxic "delousing," were conducted on all Mexicans crossing for forty years.[15] Immigration agents in Texas were told to look over Mexican bodies and root out the ones that were undesirable.

In the year 2005, the conversation among both white and black people in New Orleans was about what these new Spanish-speaking arrivals meant for the city. Were they "desirable"? Would locals welcome the people who came to their aid when the government didn't? Or were they going to judge and ostracize them? In 2010, the census recorded 91,922 Latinos in Nola, a 57 percent increase from only ten years before.

Every time I returned to New York from New Orleans, images replayed in my head. The larger-than-life Chinese American sheriff, Harry Lee, who took us around on his boat, the motor humming as he talked in a boisterous voice about the bodies floating in the water that first night when the levees broke. On CNN and MSNBC and in the *New York Times*, senior media executives were complaining publicly and expressing anger that Bush's administration was lying so blatantly to journalists. In my brain there was a loop of Bush flying over Nola and looking out the window of Air Force One with concern for the people of New Orleans and Gulfport without stopping.

Whenever I met up with journalists of color, we did the eye roll. *Oh, the network executives finally understand that the government lies? How long will they continue to care about a city that is majority people of color, majority black? Another phase?*

I had gone back to that ritual of arriving at my front door at home and rubbing the sadness and trauma off my body and then shaking it off my hands before I walked in. All the voices and stories from the day had to be wiped away.

I didn't talk about what I was seeing, because if I did, I wouldn't be able to stop. I couldn't believe that here we were in New York with everything at our fingertips, while there were people in our country who were dying from dehydration because the government couldn't seem to get them help. I was holding it all in and putting it someplace else when I was home. The rest of the time, I was thinking about how the crisis was all about racism and race, yet it was discussed in a cursory way. White reporters were shocked to see blatant racism. That, too, was part of the problem.

Gérman was back to being angry, first at W for being so obvious in his disdain for the poor, who in this case were black, and then at me. The pitch for the new job had been that I wouldn't have to travel as much, and here I was, back on the road even more days than before. We had to shoot four days for a twenty-minute piece. I would come back depleted only to have to do it again in two weeks. At CNN, more often than not, it was one night away at a time. The new job that was supposed to make everything better was making it all worse.

I was back to doing critical journalism. Though I was exhausted, I loved it with every bone in my body. My husband? Not so much.

———————

In 2005, most of us had "moved on" from the tragedy of 9/11. If you were Muslim or from the Middle East in the United States, life was still far from normal. There was a real longing for the old days when Arab American stereotypes mostly implied smart and hardworking. In the 1960s, a survey had recorded Arab Americans as the immigrant group seen as most trustworthy. They were forced to register with the government. But now the entire country seemed to turn away when their rights were being violated.

After 9/11, Islamophobia and fear of Arab Americans led to a 1,600 percent increase in documented hate crimes, and why not?[16]

If the government was asking immigrant men and boys to self-report to the DHS, weren't they already suspected criminals? As a result of the National Security Entry-Exit Registration System, NSEERS, also known as the "Muslim Registry" (a precursor to the Muslim Ban), 138,000 men from 151 countries registered with the government.[17] If you didn't register, you could be charged criminally or civilly. Out of those who registered, 13,700 men were placed into deportation hearings. This was the largest group of people identified for deportation since the focus on Mexicans and to a lesser degree Central Americans.

The concept of deportation, which is now officially referred to as "removal," dates back to the Alien Friends Act enacted in 1798 under President John Adams. The law gave the president the power to deport noncitizens who were deemed "dangerous to the peace and safety of the United States." Deportation was conceived of as a political tool; President Adams wanted to deport people who were critical of his administration, primarily Irish and French immigrants. However, no one was actually deported under this law and it expired in 1800. The idea of deportation didn't appear again until 1891—ninety years later—when a new law passed authorizing the deportation of any "alien who entered in violation of immigration laws."[18]

As a result, our government has records of deportations stretching back to 1892. That year, 2,801 people were removed from the country and deportations have been on a slow but steady rise since then. At the height of the backlash against immigrants in 1924, 36,693 people were deported. In 2014, under President Barack Obama, "removals" clocked in at 414,481.[19] Any smart businessman would look at that trend, see hockey-stick growth, and think about taking advantage of the "captive" market.

And so, at some point in the nineties, the lightbulb turns on and a seismic shift takes place—a massive earthquake that leaves decades of destruction in its wake. Private prisons step into the mix in a big way, and the prison industrial complex, seeing an opportunity to suck money out of even more people behind bars, begins to spread its tentacles into the detention and deportation mass industrial complex. This time it's immigrants, and it appears no one cares whether they are put behind bars. NPR documented how the private prison lobby helped write anti-immigration law in Arizona in order to guarantee a steady stream of bodies.[20] For each body in a cell, there is a profit to be made. Black bodies. Brown bodies.

One day, a well-dressed white man from Nevada shows up in Raymondville, Texas, one of the country's poorest counties. What does this good-looking businessman want from Raymondville? He wants to talk to the county commissioner about a proposal.

Eddie Chapa was a third-generation US citizen from Raymondville, though he spoke English with a Texas Mexican accent. He had returned from Vietnam and Korea a war hero and then went to college as part of the GI Bill, graduated, and years later became the county chairman of Raymondville.[21] The nice businessman pitched Chapa a deal that sounded like it was too good to be true. Except it *was* true, and the savvy businessman brought irrefutable, government-issued data with him.

Here's how the deal worked: Using bonds, the county would go into business with the private prison company and together they would build a facility to hold immigrants. The county would get a percentage of the profits from each immigrant they held in custody. That's when the businessman showed Eddie the sleek charts. Chapa didn't need to look at the graphs, though. All he had to do was look around his community. He knew what I had been reporting on since the 1980s. Here on the border, they kept finding ways to hold more and more migrants. It started in the hundreds. Now it would be in the tens of thousands.

It was a guaranteed profit, the businessman explained, because there were so many "illegals," you could keep the place full. Then you increase the profit margin by spending the least amount necessary on each detainee. The government pays the company $120 per day to house the immigrant, so if you find a way to only spend $50 a day on housing that immigrant, you are making a $70 profit per immigrant per night. The way things are looking, these places can stay full forever because you have 11 million of these people running around the country. I guarantee these places will stay full and your little county is finally gonna start making money. Plus, the detention camp will create hundreds of entry-level jobs, so your county just got another added benefit. We're bringing jobs to Raymondville, where 35 percent of people live in poverty.[22]

The county commissioner saw himself as a hero here, finally able to bring something to his community, an 86 percent Latino population that was always forgotten by the federal government for the sin of being too far from DC and too close to Mexico.[23] He felt bad knowing that his profits would increase by cutting corners in caring for the thousands of lives his county would now be responsible for. But the guilt didn't last long. Maybe they would only have one doctor on site each day instead of a full staff of medical professionals, 24/7. They could also save lots of money buying expired food, because that brings down the cost considerably. Giving detainees used uniforms and underwear also saves money. Stocking the library with the minimum required number of books. Hiring guards who only have a high school diploma so you can save money by paying them minimum wage.

The county commissioner hadn't realized that those same guards might end up overseeing their own undocumented family members. That was a risk he said his county was prepared to take if they had a chance of moving up from one of the ten poorest counties in Texas. Once the Willacy facility was up and running, that nightmare was exactly what happened. Sobrinos became the jailers of tíos and children the overseers of their grandparents. No one was watching when they transported the first group of immigrants to be held at Willacy in tents with no heat or air-conditioning.

———————

Planned raids on workplaces suspected of employing undocumented immigrants have been a strategy of Border Patrol and immigration enforcement agents since the 1950s. This practice only intensified once employer sanctions were formalized with the passage of IRCA in 1986.[24] Ever since then it's been a handy tool in the anti-immigrant arsenal. There are always companies that hire people without papers. They are the best workers, hands down, because they never complain (they can't, because they're undocumented) and they always work hard. They also guarantee a higher profit margin because they are cheap. They can't demand top dollar because they have no labor rights, and if they get tired of the conditions they will simply get replaced.

In 2006, as the government sprang into action to fast-track the development of detention camps like Willacy (imagine a series of white circus tents with no windows), ICE began a years-long crackdown on employers who knowingly hire undocumented immigrants. An increasing number of workplace raids, arresting thousands of people, were carried out across the country, including in states like Colorado, Nebraska, Iowa, Mississippi, Minnesota, Utah, Texas, Oregon, and Florida.[25] On December 12, 2006, US immigration officials, using the pretext of suspected ID theft, swept through meat-processing plants owned by Swift & Company across six states.[26] Nearly 1,300 people were arrested and hauled away, making it the largest immigration enforcement action against a single company in American history.[27] "Illegal Workers Arrested in 6-State ID Theft Sweep"—that was the headline in the *Washington Post*, which made the incident sound more like an assault on identity theft than on immigration.[28]

The raids got little attention nationally—the press was more interested at the time in the trial and execution of the deposed Iraqi leader, Saddam Hussein. Didn't I just tell you that sweeps like this have been happening for more than half a century now? Editors ask, what's the news here? But the trend was undeniable. During Bush's second term in office, from 2005 to 2008, more than 15,000 immigrants were arrested. In contrast, only 845 immigrants were arrested in 2004.[29]

The 2008 raid in Postville, Iowa, however, finally got some people to pay attention not only because of the sheer number of people taken into custody—389 were detained in a town with a population of 2,200 people—but also because of the kind of place where it occurred—Agriprocessors, a kosher slaughterhouse and meatpacking plant.[30]

A place where food was supposed to be its holiest, blessed by a rabbi on the spot, paid $7.25 an hour to immigrants who worked twelve- to seventeen-hour shifts. Twenty-seven of their employees were under eighteen; the youngest was just thirteen.[31] Agriprocessors had been recruiting immigrant workers, many from Guatemala, for years. The immigrants had formed a tight-knit community of believers in the American dream. Everyone in the small town of Postville knew exactly what was happening and no one said anything.

The day of the raid, ICE showed up with one thousand agents, while helicopters circled the plant from above. Out of the 389 detained, 297 were convicted for document fraud and other criminal charges and sentenced to five-month prison sentences. Postville was devastated and lost half its population after the raid.[32] The plant had been the town's main economic engine; by November 2008, Agriprocessors had declared bankruptcy and its CEO, Sholom Rubashkin, had been arrested.[33] The raid operation cost taxpayers $5 million, but what did it actually achieve?

Then it got worse. It was as if ICE and the Department of Justice were testing each other to see how far could they go: How many laws could they violate? How much due process could be denied? Even Linda Chavez, a Latina conservative who worked for Reagan, said on *Latino USA* that these were "gestapo-like tactics" because it didn't stop with the roundup. Entire groups of immigrants were taken to court almost immediately and they were essentially forced to plead guilty to felonies all at the same time without knowing what they were doing. None had been read their rights individually, none had been asked if they spoke a language other than English or Spanish, none had signed for their children to be taken from them.

Inside the Bush administration, the issue of workplace raids was creating rifts like none other. Matthew Dowd, who had been the chief strategist for the reelection of W and one of the quiet leaders of the Bush inner circle, famously left the administration with a story on the front page of the *New York Times*.[34] It wasn't only that Dowd was opposed to the Iraq War. Left unspoken were his qualms with Bush's ramped-up immigration raids. He saw how the party's future success would depend on the Latino demographic explosion. Dowd was also a deeply spiritual Catholic who believed jailing people whose only crime, like Jesus, Joseph, and Mary, was being strangers in search of shelter and safety was unconscionable.[35]

Chapter 13

The New Power of "INMIGRANTE"

For every action, there is an equal and opposite reaction. Around the same time the raids began in 2005, there was a rustling in Congress about passing new legislation that would be tough on immigration. Republican Representative Jim Sensenbrenner introduced H.R. 4437, also known as the Sensenbrenner Bill, which would not only militarize the border and criminalize violations of immigration law, but also make it illegal to assist undocumented immigrants by providing them with food, housing, or medical care. The bill actually passed in the House of Representatives at the end of 2005 and was headed to the Senate next.

Galvanized by the threat of this legislation and invigorated by syndicated Spanish-language radio talk show hosts, immigrants from all over the country took to the streets spontaneously in the spring of 2006. It started in Chicago when more than 100,000 protestors showed up to walk Chicago's Loop on March 10. A record-breaking 500,000 people strode through downtown Dallas on April 9. Then,

on May 1, Los Angeles launched "Day Without Immigrants" and another 500,000 hit the streets en masse, making themselves visible and
asking for a pathway to citizenship for undocumented immigrants.[1]
The movement spread to every corner of the country, spurring millions of immigrants to demonstrate in 140 cities across 39 states.[2]
At every march, the same empowered chant could be heard: "¡Sí se
puede!"[3]

The marches—the largest mass mobilization of people since the
civil rights and antiwar protests of the 1960s—were all peaceful and
celebratory.[4] The profound power of radio and radio personalities was
new to the mainstream English-language media, but not to anyone
from Latin America or who speaks Spanish. Radio hosts followed in
the Latin American tradition of journalists being public advocates
and artists and, in some cases, activists, because they were under
authoritarian regimes and for them democracy was activism. Their
influence had a massive national and political impact in the US. It's
as if immigrants had been waiting for this moment to wear their
Sunday best, take out the American flag, and walk in favor of their
visibility and legitimacy. It was their people-power response to being
labeled an "illegal" people. That's why these demonstrations were so
joyful. They were saying, LOOK AT US. SEE US. See us with our families, see our high school teenagers, see our toddlers carrying American flags. See that we aren't dangerous. Believe what you see, not
what they say about us.

They asked that people wear white and bring plastic bags and leave
no waste behind. And because they were so massive and continuous,
these stories were leading the news cycles for days. They had taken
control of the narrative, and the Sensenbrenner Bill never passed in
the Senate.

The last immigrant march had been in 1996 just before Clinton
signed his regressive reform, the IIRIRA. Twenty-five thousand pro-

testors showed up to no avail.[5] He saw the march but he didn't listen to the people in it and signed the bill anyway.

Hundreds of thousands of people in peaceful protest became the easiest way to dispel the idea that immigrants were criminals. Downtown Manhattan, right in front of the tall, white Municipal Building at the end of the historic Brooklyn Bridge, was packed with immigrants waving American flags as well as flags from everywhere: Mexico, Pakistan, Colombia, India, the Dominican Republic, Ireland, Ghana, and Kenya. There were little boys with American flags tied on their heads the same way bikers wear bandannas.

"Are you afraid now?" I asked Raúl.

"Mom, this is the happiest protest ever. Everyone here is smiling. Even the police are smiling."

I changed his image of protests forever by making him see one with his own eyes.

It felt like the world was waiting for the US to attempt to live up to its name as a country of equality and elect its first woman president. The more people talked about this in the US, the more it extended worldwide, and then it began to feel like a massive feedback loop in terms of women owning their power and feeling inspired to do more. I was now a part of the loop.

Except there was something about the inevitability of Hillary Clinton that concerned me. Early on there was an assumption that it was "her time" and that the nomination would be hers for the taking. Years before, I had received an email from my Columbia pal David Hershey-Webb telling me about a guy named Barack Obama who we had gone to school with. He was running for senator of Illinois, and then he gave the DNC speech. He had that unforgettable smile.

It turned out that we were elated and excited by how progressive our country truly was—that it could overcome race and Islamophobia to support a guy named Barack Hussein Obama. Yet we were equally and deeply disappointed by how sexist and misogynistic it still was at the same time.

My sister, Bertha Elena, called me screaming and crying and sniffling and giggling with happiness when the race was called for him. "I always knew he was going to win," she said to me excitedly. "I could feel it in my bones." After years of not doing anything political, my sister from the suburbs was getting back involved through electoral politics.

I did not feel it in my bones at all, not after the drama of the Florida recount and hanging chads. But the country had done it. It had looked racism in the face and said there is nothing to fear. That message of change was writ large across every mountain and hill in the US, like the Hollywood sign, only this one said: CHANGE! IT'S REALLY HERE! HAVE NO FEAR!

I felt like I could finally let go of the breath I had been holding in since I watched Martin Luther King Jr. speak in the sixties. I was waiting till we got to that mountaintop of having a black man as president, which I first saw a glimmer of when Jesse Jackson ran and won the Michigan primary. Fast-forward twenty years and here was the son of an immigrant with the most beautifully photogenic family since the Kennedys.

For journalists, Obama's presidency was a turning point, and no one could have foreseen the confluence of forces that were about to have a deep impact on American journalism forever. The stock market was about to implode and the country was about to go into a serious recession. Media companies would shrink and journalists would be laid off and not rehired.

There was also a seismic shift in the American psyche. The headlines were so self-congratulatory. Collectively, we felt as if our country had solved one of its biggest problems with just one election. Now everything had changed for journalists. Government was no longer the enemy under Obama—it was going to be a part of the solution. Under Obama, the corruption, insider trading, warmongering, lies to the UN, and human rights abuses like Abu Ghraib were all things of the past, of the corrupt Bush administration. The issues of the day were health care and, activists hoped, immigration. This was a time to rally for progress.

The media criticized the Bush administration and characterized its corruption as part of a larger Republican legacy—Watergate, Iran-Contra, the Iraq War. Republicans talked about small government, but bloated it under George W. Bush. They talked fiscal responsibility, but it was Clinton who paid down the public debt by $452 billion, while the Republicans under Bush doubled it to $11.9 trillion by the time he left office.[6] No one wanted to hear about that now. The slate was wiped clean as it usually is in this country when a new administration comes into power.

By this time, John Siceloff had been producing *NOW* for almost a decade and wanted a change. *NOW* on PBS, the sturdy, independent guiding light he had built, was reduced to a withering, lone match trying to survive the positive winds of "change." *NOW* was a hard-hitting, critical, often depressing show to watch, and that wasn't the vibe anymore, if there is such a thing as a national vibe.

The political winds at PBS were shifting, too. Why rally behind a show whose mission was to challenge governmental institutions when we should give those institutions a chance under this fresh and creative president who represented change? *NOW* had been pointing toward change. Mission complete.

Sonia Sotomayor came to a LIPS meeting in 2000 wearing a purple skirt suit. She sat in a corner and ate pastelitos and talked to all of the

Latinas gathered that night in a big apartment off Central Park West. The LIPSters were thrilled to have this powerful Puerto Rican woman as a guest at our meeting. She was just a few years older than most of us, but served on the most powerful state appeals court in the country. Back then, Rose and I were still working together at CNN. Rose told me we needed to keep our distance, while friendly, from the judge, because she had heard she was on a short list of possible SCOTUS nominees.

"We might be covering her in the future, so we need to keep that in mind," she suggested. And that is why I loved Rose, my fellow journalist, because in our core that's who we were and are: geeky American journalists who live by their ethics.

"Ha! Do you think they will actually confirm a progressive Puerto Rican feminist for the Supreme Court? I would love to see that happen," I said, incredulous that the buzz would lead to anything but more buzz and no action. A Latina on the Supreme Court felt like landing a woman on Mars in my lifetime. Why spend time thinking about it? "They would never let that happen," I scoffed, still unclear as to who "they" were.

Sonia told some hilarious stories about growing up in the Bronx, like being unaware of how poor she really was and learning to dance salsa as an adult by taking classes, and then more private feelings about growing up with a father who was an alcoholic. We immediately made her an honorary LIPSter because she understood what we did when we were together—create a safe space for Latina journalists to let down their guard and feel heard, seen, and validated. And loved. We expected and demanded nothing of anyone. We told dirty jokes, laughed with each other, got a little tipsy, danced, and talked about sex, love, marriage, health, finances, work, and our kids.

Many years after that dinner, in 2009, it happened. Obama nominated Sonia Sotomayor to replace Justice David Souter on the Supreme Court. After she had been confirmed to the court, she was honored at the Congressional Hispanic Caucus Institute's annual gala in DC. The event was attended by a who's who of Latinx power people from media, politics, and activism circles, including stars like Jennifer Lopez and Marc Anthony.

There Sonia was, standing right in front of me, smiling and laughing. I knew I was looking at the most powerful Puerto Rican and Latina in the world. People were rushing up to Sonia to take pictures—her line was longer than J-Lo's! She laughed with her mouth wide open in each photo, hugging people close to her, enjoying life fully, which is not at all what we expect from a justice of the Supreme Court.

I was with my husband, son, and daughter, all glammed up for a pre-event reception in a crowded VIP tent. I had finally made it to the inside of the tent after eight years of distance from the White House and Congress under W. Even so, I was forced to remain distant enough to be critical and suspicious of it all. But this was one thing I couldn't hold back.

"You're a rock star, Sonia!" I whispered in her ear.

"It's crazy!" she said and gave me a bear hug. Then she stood for pictures with my family and hugged my daughter particularly warmly. A few minutes later, I was onstage to emcee the program, which was the high point of Hispanic Heritage Month in the Capitol. It was my job that night to introduce President Barack Obama to a crowd of thousands of electrified Latinos and Latinas who had overwhelmingly voted for him. Their presence in the streets at those immigrant rallies in 2006 had paid off. Obama had made Latinos and immigration a key part of his campaign pitch.

Some of the mainstream media questioned whether Latinos would vote for a black man, which was hard to hear. The punditry were disproven by turnout numbers. Obama carried 67 percent of the Latino vote in 2008.[7] Latinx voters had been an essential part of the coalition that delivered his victory. Obama owed Latinx voters a return on their investment, and tonight was the first time he would address a crowd of Latinx influencers as large as the ones he campaigned to before he had taken office.

I had been so nervous about this event that I lost five pounds and was the skinniest I had been in ten years. Still, it was hard to compete with the dresses at the gala because my fellow Latinas never miss a chance to go all out. Coño, what else is life for if you can't party and dance? There were dresses of all colors with low-cut backs and curves hugging our bodies. We had been taught by our mothers to love our bodies. My pink satin halter dress was stunning. I felt like I was giving off an actual shine, I was so happy inside.

As I introduced the man considered the most important president in history (even though he had voted as a senator for the Secure Fence Act of 2006 that included funding for the wall), I had to stay independent.[8] I am a journalist, not a fangirl for any politician. I decided to remind the president of something.

"Sir, there is no such thing as an illegal human being. We are not illegals; we are not illegal immigrants! See us for who were are!" I said to the crowd, some of whom, but not all, cheered and applauded. I immediately worried whether I had crossed some sort of line. They had told me to not make the event "political." But then I said to myself, *Remember Elie Wiesel and call it what it is. You are repeating the words of a survivor of Auschwitz, the closest thing you have to an angel of history on your side.* Obama may have been the most powerful man in the world, but as a constitutional expert, I had to make sure he knew that I knew that legally and grammatically there is no such thing as an "illegal immigrant."

The president skipped onstage like a guest on a late-night TV show, and then swept in with his tall and lanky frame to hug me tightly. He gave me a dip and said, "I miss hearing your show. I listened all the time in Chicago."

The crowd screamed with delight when he began to speak, while I disappeared backstage, which was crawling with Secret Service. He spoke of Sonia Sotomayor as "our own royalty," and reminded the crowd that he had hired more Latinos and Latinas, including two in his cabinet, than any previous administration. He promised to help the Latinx community and push for immigration reform, saying, "Todos somos americanos" (We're all Americans), but at the same time he acknowledged that his plan to overhaul health care would not provide benefits for people in the US illegally.[9] When he ended, Obama got a massive celebratory ovation. That night was magical, and it was precisely because it felt so magical that I was instantly worried.

What none of us could see was that Obama's big talk about passing immigration reform in his first year in office was just that—talk.[10] A bill was not proposed in Congress until the end of 2010 and it died unceremoniously on the Senate floor. The DREAM Act—a bill that would create a pathway to citizenship for undocumented children brought to this country by their parents—failed to get the sixty votes it needed to stop a Republican filibuster. It came down to five Democrats who blocked the bill because they worried about reelection in 2012.[11]

Here's what also happened: Rahm Emanuel, the grandson of Jewish immigrants and Obama's White House chief of staff, steamrolled the idea of passing comprehensive immigration reform legislation from the very beginning.[12] He saw it as the "third rail of American politics"; anyone who touched the issue would likely lose reelection. Yet the number of undocumented immigrants in the US was on the decline after peaking at around 12 million in 2007.[13] Emanuel made immigration the issue that Obama would use to prove that he was a tough president—just like he had advised President Clinton in the nineties when he served as a top aide—but not too tough to be considered an angry black man.[14] Because if you take that anger and direct it at the "illegals" over there, then that's okay. "They aren't really supposed to be here" was more the Obama ethos than "Welcome to America."

Out of sight from everyone, except for immigrants, community activists, and Spanish language media, the deportation system was becoming a well-oiled machine. Congress got busy allocating money in the domestic budget to keep 34,400 beds filled with immigrants across 250 facilities every single night. The 2009 policy became known as the "detention bed mandate" and went into effect without a lot of fanfare.[15] The impact on actual people's lives, however, was huge. The bed mandate intensified the hunting of immigrants not only by requiring a minimum number of immigrants detained, but also by furthering the development of detention camps and growing our reliance on private contractors to operate these prisons. Worst of all, it took money out of American taxpayers' pockets for this cause. By 2013, it cost $120 a day to keep an immigrant in detention, which, multiplied by the number of people detained, adds up to more than $2 billion a year.[16]

Anyway, does it really matter? They are illegals. They must have done something wrong to deserve this, right? Remember thinking this at any point along the way?

Down in Raymondville, Texas, the detention camps the city helped pay for and build in collaboration with the private prison companies were now chock-full of migrants whose only crime often was simply crossing the border to return to their home in Kansas City, Omaha, Cheyenne, or Chevy Chase. That dream was their crime. But forget about that. The city was already paying itself back for the investment and that's what mattered here. Though a return was still years away, the camps were profitable and they kept on chipping away at expenditures for detainees. No one was coming to these camps anyway. Books? Games? Soccer balls? Why spend money on things like that when it could go into the county coffers instead?

———————

On the day before Thanksgiving in 2009, I was called down from my windowless office at *NOW* to the glass-walled office of a senior executive at Thirteen, New York's local PBS station. He welcomed me into his office and said he wanted to deliver some news to me in person. I needed some good news.

A few weeks earlier I had been told by phone while I was away on a shoot that the funding for *NOW* would not be renewed. John Siceloff was climbing the Himalayas. No one came to rescue the show or fight for it. The executives at PBS had heard that news and public affairs were not where the fundraising dollars were. Those were with *Downton Abbey*. And *NOW* was no *Downton*.

This executive said to me, "I wanted you to hear it from me directly. You will have a role in the new show we are creating." The network was going to kill *NOW*, a successful show, and replace it with a new show produced by the local station Thirteen.

It felt like an act of betrayal to take a job from the show that was created to replace you. But I needed work and I was even a bit flattered that they liked me enough to make me an offer, although it was just the promise of an offer on a handshake. I had been burned like this in the past by promises that came with no contracts. *This is public TV*, I told myself. *We don't play those games here.*

A few months went by without hearing anymore from that executive about the job at Thirteen. In mid-February, a colleague called me into her office and told me the anchors had been named for the new show. I wasn't one of them.

Me puse fría. No wonder why that executive never called me back! The rug had been pulled from under me, and essentially, I had just gotten fucked.

Since I had taken that job promise seriously, I hadn't been looking for work, and I knew how hard it was going to be for me to find another job at this stage of my career. I was over forty and an outspoken Latina. Though I was an award-winning journalist, to most men I was likely perceived as a difficult hire. In other words, a woman who would be intellectually and culturally challenging because women over forty are more centered in their power. I had fired my agent to save money when I took the salary cut at PBS. Without an agent, I had an even tougher road ahead of me. No one operates at this level without an agent.

I ran through my options. NPR had not asked me to try out for any anchor positions, so a full-time gig with them was not happening. Besides, I didn't want to move to DC, where they are based. *Latino USA* was a small part-time thing, so maybe I could try to get a New York correspondent position with one of the television networks, but I'd have to jump through hoops for years to get on the air. Plus, the evening news is only twenty-two minutes long once you account for commercials, and each story is a minute and thirty seconds; very few stories actually end up on the air every night, and the competition can be bloody. I'd have to go back to square one and set my family aside one more time. I had done it with CNN and PBS, but could I afford to do it again? I was done doing breaking news and live weather updates in snowstorms. I couldn't go backward, but I believed I would be perceived as too old to move forward in any meaningful way. I wasn't sure how I was going to survive this.

With my tickets already booked, I headed down to Punta Cana at the beginning of March. My job would be gone in a month and I was overflowing with anxiety. Sandy, who has always been my rock in times of need, met me down there. She walked with me through the sand, her purple-tinged dreads waving gently in the early-morning breeze, to the edge of the light blue water and told me to tap my hands in the lightly shivering waves and speak to Yemaya.

"You need to focus on gratitude," Sandy said softly. "You need to be calm and thankful. Things will fall into place. You're going to be okay, but you have to start from a place of gratitude and abundance, not fear and scarcity."

She said this to me so often that she began to sound like a broken record. I didn't dismiss her words completely, but I kept insisting to myself that I was grateful. I was thankful for my kids and our health and for my husband, even though he always felt that I prioritized him after everything else—a deadline, a flight to somewhere else, an interview. *I am already grateful*, I said to myself impatiently, *but I have real worries and gratitude is not going to solve them.*

———————

I remembered a conversation I had with my friend Deepa in the spring of 2000. Deepa and I met when she was a budding journalist and producer who worked in Austin for *Latino USA*. She had then gone on to work as a TV news producer and married a tech genius and fellow Indian American, Vinay. He had made it big, so now Deepa was on her way to becoming an independent film producer and philanthropist.

I revealed to Deepa how worried I was about surviving in journalism. Back then, things were shaky at CNN. I faced so much uncertainty and the always-having-to-prove-myself thing that was my shadow.

Deepa turned to me and smiled. "Maria, you don't need any of them. You are your own brand. You're Maria Hinojosa!"

I looked at her and started laughing.

"You can't be serious! A brand?"

"You have a name and you have a brand. Your brand is beautiful journalism and storytelling. *Latino USA* is loved by thousands and you are the anchor of that," Deepa said in a businesslike tone that she didn't usually take with me. "You could do your own thing. You should think about that. I'll help you."

I was at the height of my career and on the verge of being unemployed. I had nothing to lose. I had no job, no prospects, no agent, and no job interviews set up. I barely had an updated résumé. The truth is that for most of my career I hadn't had to look for work. I always had something cooking on the back burner even when I was a newbie freelancer.

There was only one place I ever really dreamed about: *60 Minutes*. I worked my contacts and found someone who connected me to one of the senior executives at *60 Minutes* via email. He asked to meet at a Starbucks. Maybe that should have been my first hint, but I was so giddy with excitement that *60 Minutes* would even consider speaking with me. They saw me.

Over coffee, the executive told me I had an outstanding career. We hit it off and did the journalist banter thing, filing down the names of people we knew in common and exchanging war stories. I could tell the meeting was going so well. I told him that Ed Bradley had told me back in 2001 that he hoped I would one day become a *60 Minutes* correspondent. I explained what the show had meant to me as an immigrant kid and how it taught me the role of journalism in a free society and democracy. After about twenty minutes, he said, "Maria, you are a really talented journalist and in so many ways you are just right for *60 Minutes*. The right demographic with solid journalist chops and interviewing skills . . ."

There were fireworks going off inside of me, huge, multicolored explosions. These were the words I had dreamed of hearing. I held my breath and waited for the part where he would tell me he wanted me to come in and meet his bosses so they could find a way to bring me on. I might have a job after all! All of this was happening in my head in triple speed.

"But . . ."

Oh no. My chest sank a tiny bit, but inside, the fireworks were extinguished, flooded by doom.

"The thing is, we have this long list of old white guys on the show. Can you wait until one of them gets sick or dies and then we can talk?"

Wait. Was this a joke? I think I laughed and said okay. We wrapped things up and I gave him a quick hug, a weird expression of passive-aggressive anger and forgiveness. (I wouldn't want *him* to feel awkward, now would I?) I walked to the Columbus Circle subway station in a daze, got on the A train and sat down. I cried as the break-dancers performed and rapped, tears streaming down my face, carrying years of hope that now, poof, was gone.

Things had been so tense with Gérman that when I got home I went into Yurema's room, closed the door, and called my sister to confide how badly it had gone.

"I'm going to have to go on unemployment," I sobbed. "I've never had to do that. Dad will be so disappointed. I'm so disappointed! I can't believe this is happening."

The kids had come home from school, so I wiped my face and dabbed on some concealer.

"¿Que pasó?" Gérman asked in his now usually stern voice.

"Nada," I mumbled back.

No one could take care of this for me. Not Gérman or my parents or my kids or my nonexistent agent. I was going to have to eat my goddamn fear.

At the *NOW* goodbye party, one of the assistant producers, a young Canadian Pakistani woman, practically pinned me up against a wall outside the champagne bar. She pulled out something I had never seen, a one-hit pipe, took a deep drag, and passed it to me, since we were no longer coworkers (she had never done that before because, well, we have rules, and one of them is you don't ever smoke with a coworker).

"*You* need to create your own company," she said while I took a drag. "You are that pit bull, Maria. We would all love to work with you. You should do it for you and for all of us."

I had been smoking more pot than usual as a way to cope with my nerves, a remnant from learning how to effectively manage my 9/11 PTSD. (This also brought me guilt and shame, but mother earth was healing for me.) Over the next few days, I cried in the shower several times because I could not let my family see me so defeated and terrified. I couldn't freak them out about money the same way my father had done with me and my siblings, counting every penny and never, absolutely never, being in a place of abundance. I was worried about how we would survive, and I was doing all of this alone because I was too prideful and sensitive to share it with my husband. Gérman came from nothing. He was a survivor. Me being upset about this would upset him even more. Couldn't I see how privileged I was? Here I was feeling sad for myself. Ay, please, no!

The rock bottom wasn't going to budge. I was the one who was going to have to move and take action.

Okay, fuck you, rock bottom. Now that 60 Minutes *is gone, what is your craziest dream?*

Without thinking, the words tumbled out of my mouth in a whisper: "I want to have my own company."

I had often told people I wanted to have my own company, but I never took myself seriously when I said that. In my mind, I was like, *Girl, please.* It had simply been a beautiful illusion. More Mars fantasies. But hitting this breaking point changed everything.

I'm not going to wait for someone to get sick or die. I'm hitting rock bottom and, guess what, motherfuckers? I'm coming back up for air, cabrones.

That's how I started talking to myself. The very first person I told about this new dream was my daughter, Yurema. That weekend she had asked me to take to her to Boca Chica, our cottage in Connecticut, just she and I. Spring was beginning to say, *Wassup*, with tiny little buds sprouting like green beans on the branches of trees and yellow chirping chickadees excited about the full bird feeders. Yurema must have instinctively known that one way to deal with the dark tension clouds swirling over our heads in our apartment was to get the heck out of Dodge and separate me from Gérman to give us a breather.

"Go for it, Mom. I support you. I know you can do this," my lovely brown-eyed girl said to me and squeezed my hand as we walked one of our favorite trails in the hills of Connecticut.

I didn't think this big dream of mine would go over well with Gérman, so I prepared myself to do it without my honey, mi joni, a mi lado. I had asked for a lot of sacrifice from him in the years I spent climbing the ladder for my career and he had always been patient. Now I was going to say, "Hey, guess what? I'm building my own ladder from scratch and I need your help and patience again."

I told him the day we officially incorporated the company. He was happy and relieved I wouldn't have another boss. He was proud of me, but there was a distance between us now, a by-product of my overwhelming anxiety. About a job. I couldn't see that I should have been more worried about my marriage.

A colleague from *Latino USA* offered to figure out the basics for launching a nonprofit media company. I had decided to create a nonprofit because that's what I mistakenly thought John Siceloff had done for *NOW*. I had also come to understand that foundations and philanthropists like to give money to nonprofits, especially because their donations are tax deductible. I was so basic at this.

In allowing myself to dream my wildest dreams, though, I thought about who could support me immediately with funding and I started making a series of connections.

When I needed thirty thousand dollars to finish my PBS films on women, power, and politics, including covering the expense of flying my team to interview the first female president of Chile, Michelle Bachelet, I had turned to Fiona, my Reiki healer. Fiona did so many things: investment banker, mom of three, healer, entrepreneur, and she was also a philanthropist who funded media. "Name it and claim it and it will be yours," Sandy always said to me. When I finally got Fiona on the phone, we spoke for nearly two hours and I explained my detailed plan for my dream company. And in that phone call, it turned out Fiona needed me to listen to her as much as I needed her to listen to me. She was hurting and needed counsel. I heard her and understood. She heard me and understood. And then she said yes.

In April of 2010, we sent out our first-ever paychecks from Futuro Media. I purposefully gave my company a bilingual name and some-thing forward-looking that did not have my name in it. Even though I had come face-to-face with the power of my own voice and vision, this was a bigger venture than just me. The creation of Futuro Media validated me and everything I represented in a way I never could have imagined. I would have a job with a salary and benefits. I had an angel and her name was Fiona. Years before, she had taught me to trust my heart and be patient and loving, primarily with myself. Fiona was letting me live out my dream. Ask for things. Be open. Be truthful. Be humble, she was saying, but also be a badass, a pit bull, a fearless woman who isn't afraid to take on a challenge.

The first official offices of Futuro were underneath a slanted stair-well in a converted firehouse in Chinatown rented to us by DCTV, another community-based media company. Our desks were made of glass, the kind you would buy for a high school student, compact and teen friendly, but that was what we could afford. I now understood what *start-up* meant and gave thanks for the term that an entire generation embraced and of which I was now a part.

It was in these cramped offices that I found out we had gotten our first grant as a nonprofit. Soon after I had formed Futuro, I called Luz Vega-Marquis, the first and only Latina president of a major national foundation, the Marguerite Casey Foundation based in Seattle. I had met Luz at *NOW* and had helped get a substantial multiyear grant for *NOW*'s beat on women and families that I established. She put me in contact with a program officer, and by then I had taken some of the money Fiona had contributed and used it to hire someone to write grants. After weeks and weeks of concern, I could finally exhale. For a second.

At home Gérman softened a bit. He tried to hide it, but I think it was a major turn-on for him to see me become a fearless, self-starting woman. It made him fall in love with me again, and now no boss was sending me away from my family. I was the boss, la jefa. I couldn't believe it, but it was true.

Meanwhile, in American cities, suburbs, and small towns everywhere in 2010, immigrants who had come to the US as kids were growing into adolescence and beginning to understand how being undocumented forced them to confront a huge set of challenges—it would start with their parents telling them to never discuss immigration with anyone; then, at sixteen, when they would try and get a license they would come face-to-face with the limits. Then they would realize they couldn't get financial aid, and couldn't travel. And it went on and on. Like good American kids, they started channeling that anger into activism. Perhaps their immigrant mothers took them to protests to teach them about civic responsibility and the First Amendment just like mine did.

They were DREAMers—undocumented youth organizing for immigration reform who took their name from the DREAM Act, a piece of legislation that was first introduced in Congress in 2001. The Development, Relief, and Education for Alien Minors Act was sponsored by a bipartisan coalition and designed to create a pathway to citizenship for undocumented immigrant youths who were brought to the US by their parents or adults as minors before age sixteen. Of course, the bill contained additional stipulations. In order to qualify, DREAMers had to be below the age of thirty-five, have lived in the US for five consecutive years, have completed high school, be enrolled in college or the military and, finally, possess "good moral character."[17] The bill failed to pass in the aftermath of 9/11. Since then, nine other versions of the legislation have been introduced in Congress, but none of them have been successful in passing both houses.[18]

Every time the act came up, so many feelings were tied to it. How many people were hanging on the threads of this particular legislation? I worried about these kids. How many other American teens were hooked on and hopeful for a law? Immigrant communities certainly were. Estimates put the DREAMer population at 3.6 million, or nearly one-third of the undocumented people in this country.[19] Each time the DREAM Act didn't pass, I worried about how many of these kids or their parents would be pushed into depression. I was tired of seeing members of Congress prey on their emotions.

Speaking out on immigration reform as an undocumented person was a risky move, and not everyone was on board with the DREAM Act. Old-school activists insisted that the push had to be for comprehensive immigration reform, like Reagan's IRCA, which granted everyone who had entered the US before a certain date eligibility to apply for citizenship and therefore all family members could gain the same status. Giving legal status to some in the community, but not all, would inevitably lead to families being broken up.

I didn't say this at the time because it wasn't my job to do so, but

I also wanted bold, all-encompassing legislation that would generate a new narrative around immigrants. The anti-immigrant sentiment was spurred by Clinton's IIRIRA legislation in 1996. It had been a little over a decade since then. We still had time to turn the narrative around before it cemented itself further.

In 1986, Mexicans made up 70 percent of the people who bene-fited from Reagan's IRCA, who, by the way, helped pull the American economy out of a recession because of their immigrant work and new capacity to buy houses, cars, etc.[20] Immigration reform in the Obama era would ideally include people from Africa, the Middle East, Eastern Europe, and Asia. Focusing on the global, intergenerational nature of immigration would shift the entire conversation and fashion an im-migrant story that was more complex, truthful, and visible across the country. This wasn't just about Latinos and Latinas anymore.

The window for action in Congress felt like it was closing, though. Almost ten years after the bill was introduced, the DREAMers em-braced the name that had been bestowed upon them by legislators and decided to take action. They studied past civil rights move-ments and learned from the LGBTQ community that the internal-ized fear and shame around being who they were was the first step they needed to overcome. As undocumented youth, they needed to be comfortable in their own skin and become visible to themselves before they could become visible to others. People who identified as LGBTQ came out of the so-called closet by making the most intimate and personal part of themselves political. Undocumented people chose to do the same—"come out" and make their status pub-lic in an act of fearlessness.

They learned from the people who crossed that bridge in Selma; they learned from Sitting Bull at Standing Rock in 1890; they learned from the trans women of color at the Stonewall Inn. As good Ameri-cans they learned that in our democracy, the only thing we ultimately have is our people power—our bodies and putting them where they need to be. And like the suffragettes who took to the streets, these activists presented themselves to the public to be judged. They had to kill their shame.

The DREAMers' first big action began on January 1, 2010, with the Trail of Dreams, a 1,500-mile protest walk from Miami, Florida, to Washington, DC.[21] College students Juan Rodriguez, Gaby Pacheco, Felipe Matos, and Carlos Roa walked across the American South carrying banners that said EDUCATION NOT DEPORTATION.[22] Carlos and Felipe, who were both undocumented, exposed themselves to authorities in this act of political protest, which took ganas and chutzpah, the most patriotic kind possible.

In March, the Immigrant Youth Justice League held a "coming out" rally where DREAMers shared their stories of being undocumented.[23] The slogans printed on signs and shouted by the crowd were UNDOCUMENTED AND UNAFRAID! and NO PAPERS, NO FEAR! When the Georgia Board of Regents voted to ban undocumented immigrants from enrolling in the state's top five universities, seven undocumented youth sat down in the middle of a busy street to protest the ban. They were arrested for their act of civil disobedience and became known as the "Georgia Seven."[24] In May, five undocumented students staged a sit-in in Arizona senator John McCain's office to advocate for the DREAM Act.

Local governments were going back to the 1990s and Governor Pete Wilson's failed attempts to block all aid to immigrants in California. I guess they convinced themselves that Prop 187 was a success even though it had been struck down by the courts. They tried first in the new century in the small city of Hazleton, Pennsylvania, which tried to pass ordinances in the summer of 2006 that would penalize landlords for renting to undocumented immigrants and employers who hired them. Six other towns across the US passed similar ordinances.[25] The Hazleton story was in the Spanish-language news several times a week, but the rest of the country barely knew about the racism behind the attempted laws in Hazleton. The ACLU challenged the ordinances in court, where it was ruled unconstitutional by the Third Circuit Court of Appeals in 2013; SCOTUS refused to hear the case, leaving earlier rulings in place.[26]

As the DREAMer movement galvanized undocumented youth, initiating "coming out" actions and protests across the nation, politicians continued to push anti-immigrant legislation at breakneck speed. The most controversial of these was the Support Our Law Enforcement and Safe Neighborhoods Act, or SB 1070. The law, originally introduced to Arizona's State Senate by Republican senator Russell Pearce, made it a crime to reside or work in the US without legal permission. It also required police to determine the legal status of anyone they arrested, meaning they could demand papers from anyone, aka all brown people, and allowed them to arrest individuals they suspected of being undocumented without a warrant.[27] SB 1070 became known as the "Show Me Your Papers" law by everyone except its supporters. Once, that phrase would have been considered a slur. Now it was an attempt at a law.

Nine undocumented activists chained themselves to the doors of the Arizona Capitol to express their opposition to SB 1070. The Capitol police had to use bolt cutters to forcibly remove them as hundreds of others continued their protest on the state house lawn.[28] The bill passed anyway and was signed into law in late April 2010, around the same time that I was launching Futuro Media. We made an executive editorial decision to go down to Arizona and cover the story.

We met one family in which the mother was the only undocumented family member. Under SB 1070, her teenage son could no longer drive her to work because, if pulled over, he could be charged with "criminal transport of an alien." The entire family cried when we interviewed them in their kitchen. The tears streamed from my eyes, too.

Outside on the streets, activists continued to fight. People from political as well as faith-based groups came out at the end of July to demonstrate against the new legislation. Protestors clogged the streets and blocked traffic; dozens were arrested.[29] The undocumented among them put themselves at risk for deportation.

The local papers and television displayed images of the DREAMers as angry and screaming, but in our interviews they were soft-spoken and to the point. I had to ask them to speak up because the mic wasn't picking up their voices. These were hardly hardened activists. More like kids who had learned the lessons of American history and democracies the world over. They were twentysomethings leading change. Few were calling them what they were: patriots.

Many outside of the immigrant community simply didn't get what the commotion was all about. *I'm a citizen*, the thinking went, *so I'll never be stopped and asked to show my papers. And shouldn't people have to show IDs? Those immigrants deserve it, right? They're illegal anyway.*

When I asked anyone who was not an immigrant how they would prove their citizenship, they became noticeably uncomfortable. The passage of SB 1070 meant that anyone, even white people, could be stopped and asked to prove their citizenship. How exactly do you do that if you are not wealthy enough to pay for a passport? Do you carry a copy of your birth certificate with you everywhere? And this is the question that would make many nonimmigrants quite queasy: Do you even know where your birth certificate is?

––––––––––

By April of 2011, I was thankful that Futuro had made it through one full year, which had been painfully rocky because everything—

staffing, office space, workflow dynamics, money—is more complicated in a start-up and I had to figure out how to run one.

Oh, and the money thing. For someone who doesn't care about
money and never felt propelled to make a lot of it or judge myself by
the number of zeros in my salary, I now had to worry about money
every day, and not just for myself but for others. I was scared almost
all of the time, but compared to the days when I was struggling with
PTSD and had toddlers at home, this was easy. I learned how to calm
myself by repeating the words "It will be okay, it will be okay" as I
breathed in and out. I reminded myself that I had made it through
9/11, so I could make it through this.

"No one is dying," Gérman would say to me. "It's just a business.
Don't forget that."

I managed and lived with the low-grade but constant anxiety. If
something went wrong, it wasn't just me who would suffer. If I couldn't
meet payroll, for example, I would be the one responsible for someone
else not being able to pay their rent. The thought of this horrified me,
and I realized I needed to hire an executive director, someone who
knew exactly how to manage a small nonprofit. I did like New Yorkers do when they are apartment hunting. I told everyone I knew that I
was looking to hire someone and that's how Elena, a proud and distin-
guished lesbian from Maine who spoke with a tinge of a Mid-Atlantic
accent, came into the life of Futuro. Elena had managed nonprofits,
understood how media worked, had experience writing grants, and had
a knack for start-ups—she would work with us three days a week and
use the rest of her time to launch her lobster roll food truck in SoHo.

I exhaled a bit more, but almost every day it seemed like another
shoe was going to drop. Every. Day.

"Did you know our contract with NPR is coming up for renewal,
like right away?" Elena said to me when I walked into the office one
day. My stomach was now at my feet.

"What?" I wheezed.

When I formed Futuro, the main property I had to acquire was *Latino USA*. Maria Emilia Martin, the creator and producer of *Latino USA*, had left the show early to move to Guatemala and start her own company. *Latino USA* was, frankly, floundering without her.

Latino USA had survived all these years because it had a dedicated, though small, audience, and KUT, the show's home and Austin's NPR station, cared about it. But after more than seventeen years, even KUT was focusing on newer, shinier things in their lineup, and more money to produce *Latino USA* had to be raised.

I negotiated with KUT to let me take over *Latino USA* as executive producer and move the show to New York, where we would continue to produce, staff, and fund it. I also had plans to grow *Latino USA*'s footprint. We were seen as a "minority show" and that had to end, especially since I had asked my staff to stop using that word in our newsroom. I hate the entire disempowering message of it.

Still, many of the local public radio stations aired the program from five to seven o'clock on weekend mornings, what I jokingly called POC Ghetto Hours. I assumed they booked us for those hours because that's when they thought Latinos and Latinas were coming home from partying or getting ready to go to church. Otherwise, how else do you explain this?

The show needed some TLC. For too long, it had been far away from me, and as the anchor, I needed to step things up. I needed to be more present on the air and behind the scenes. There was no way I was going to let *Latino USA* disappear. I knew what the show meant to people, and not just Latinx listeners. African Americans were our second-largest block of listeners after white listeners. The show had a heart because it had a mission: to humanize Latinos and Latinas by airing stories that no one else was telling.

Plus, I knew the numbers. Latinx, not just people of color, were the audience that every media company had to attract if they wanted to compete in the future. A 43 percent Latinx demographic growth was the only number I needed to know in business.[30]

Elena set up a meeting with senior executives at NPR in DC to determine the future of *Latino USA*. I was so excited to share my vision as a new media owner, anchor, and producer. In many ways, NPR helped to create the journalist I had become and, after many years and growing pains building my career, I was coming back to helm *Latino USA*. I thought NPR would be so proud of me, an entrepreneur and now media executive.

Instead, they told me they were ready to shut it down. They told me to cancel *Latino USA*.

Elena saw how devastated I was after we left the meeting. I didn't speak for an hour; if I did, I would have broken into tears in the airport. The next day, when I finally made it to the office at noon, Elena took me into the private conference room. Her gray, wavy hair framed her stoic face. I suddenly felt small and worried that I was going to be reprimanded for something I did wrong at the meeting, something I shouldn't have said. I was so used to getting slapped on the wrist.

"Maria, you're our leader," Elena began, "you set the tone. You can't wait for anyone else to do it because this is your company. This is your voice. This is your power. You know what you're talking about. You are a savvy media entrepreneur."

She paused for a moment and then took my hand.

"It's your time, dear, as a Latina, as a woman, as a leader," she said, again with a hint of an old-timey British-tinged accent.

That evening on the subway ride home from Chinatown, I thought about what Elena had said. *You need to be that badass pit bull again*, I said to myself as I looked around the subway car. *You've come this far and now you need to get ready for another fight*. Vámonos pues.

How many times had male executives said no to me and I had to fight my way back? Many. Yet, how many times had some of those men been great allies? Several of them had gone to bat for me. I had to grow up and make my case without emotion and back it up with lots of data.

We sat down and wrote up a business pitch using market data to make the argument that killing a Latino media property in the current climate would be a stupid business decision—though we didn't use the word *stupid*. I thought about who I knew at the top and took my request for an appeal to the then–NPR president, Gary Knell. I remembered he was a big *Latino USA* fan and a smart media executive. He allowed us to make a last-minute pitch to keep *Latino USA* alive.

We got a meeting one week later in New York City. Over bialys and bagels at Barney Greengrass on Amsterdam and Eighty-Seventh Street, we made our case to two senior NPR executives. At the end of the week we were told *Latino USA* would remain on the air and NPR would renew our contract. But the one-hour expansion would be a Futuro project.

Our little show was about to turn twenty and had raked in so many awards over the years, but it didn't change the fact that we had to audition all over again. We had two years to prove ourselves. No one, not even our staff, knew how close *Latino USA* had come to disappearing into thin air.

Since *NOW* was off the air, there were no Latinos or Latinas on PBS. I looked at Henry Louis Gates Jr., who every two years produced a high-profile prime-time series with an expensive budget, and realized I needed to be doing the same. I wanted that kind of visibility for Latinx issues.

Name it and claim it and it will be yours.

———

Like clockwork, the DREAM Act was reintroduced in Congress in May 2011, this time by the Gang of Eight. The headlines, like "A Second Try on Immigration Act" in the *New York Times*, were hopeful before any legislation had been passed.[31] On *Latino USA* we talked about the impact of the ups and downs of the unpredictable legislative game on the mental health of immigrants.

"Fool me once," I said on air, "but fool me twice? Take care of yourselves. Try and keep your minds busy. You are more than an act of legislation."

I was adamant that I was not going to get my hopes up. Especially since I had just interviewed former Clinton labor secretary Robert Reich, who said that if the DREAM Act didn't pass in 2010, it likely wouldn't have a chance again until 2017, due to the timing of presidential elections. My son would be out of college by then. It felt like an eternity away. No, I was not going to let my hopes get high. Instead I got high with my husband and made love.

In the eleventh hour, the DREAM Act was passed by the House of Representatives in December, but fell short by five votes to end a filibuster in the Senate.[32] Once again, it died. Immigrants. Thrown. Under. Bus. Again.

Most Americans probably had no idea this was happening. In 2010, immigration legislation was seen as a splinter issue—important to just a splinter of the population. Even so, polls showed that 66 percent of American voters supported the DREAM Act.[33] Middle America was supportive of the DREAMers, but they were also low-key anti-immigrant at the same time.

They cared. Ish. They were taking their cue from the leader of the country. He cared. Sort of, too. Under Obama, the official line (which was not that different from the official line of the George W. Bush administration) was that ICE was deporting "felons, not families" and focusing on "paper raids" by looking into employers hiring undocumented workers rather than workplace raids of employees. Under the direction of Janet Napolitano, the former governor of Arizona, the

Department of Homeland Security would make this subtle shift in policy under a kinder, gentler Obama administration.

Activists on the ground never accepted this language or many of its promises. The Obama administration began to see them as ungrateful.

On the ground, people shared the things they witnessed: ICE taking fathers from their homes at six in the morning. Families were being broken up, but we only heard about it on Univision and Telemundo. Activists were fed up. Every legislative hope had been burned down, and they felt the burn, severely.

On June 5, 2012, in the middle of Obama's reelection campaign, a group of DREAMers that had lost patience took on the president himself. Three dozen activists descended upon Obama's Denver re-election headquarters. Javier Hernandez and Veronica Gomez, both undocumented, went a step further and staged a sit-in inside the office. They refused to leave until the president signed an executive order ending the deportation of DREAMers.[34]

And that is how DACA, the Deferred Action for Childhood Arrivals program, was created. It was not a gift from a benevolent leader. It was the result of a public shaming of a president who didn't understand the ire and disappointment and heart of these determined activists. On June 15, 2012, ten days after the demonstration began, Obama released a statement on immigration and signed DACA into existence.[35] His executive order deferred deportation proceedings and offered work authorization for qualified applicants—primarily immigrant children like the DREAMers who were brought to the US by their parents.[36] The order included many restrictions and intensified the false dichotomy between good immigrants and bad immigrants. If you had ever been charged with smoking pot, you might not even be allowed to apply for DACA. Only "perfect" immigrants got to apply.

These young activists had taken the risk of putting their bodies on the line and they had been seen. Their efforts had inspired actual tangible change finally. Their invisibility had made them fearless and willing to take on Obama directly, which is ultimately what forced him to respond.

DREAMers would have to take a new kind of risk. The government was ready to "see them" in an official capacity, but that would require them to put their private and personal information in the hands of the same government that could deport them. DACA had its pitfalls as an imperfect, stopgap measure to protect DREAMers. Had it not been for those activists, those radicals, esos comecandelas, DACA never would have happened.

But the headlines made it seem like Obama deserved all the credit: "Obama to Permit Young Migrants to Remain in U.S."; "Obama Administration to Stop Deporting Younger Undocumented Immigrants and Grant Work Permits."[37]

It was Obama who told the American public, soon after he won the presidency, to hold him accountable. "Push me," he said. The DREAMers pushed. As hard as they could.

Chapter 14

What I Cannot Unsee

In 2009, a producer had told me there was concern over the treatment of immigrants at detention camps.

"No one is thinking about that right now. What they are thinking about is the threat of getting picked up in a raid and summarily deported." That's what I said, which I find shocking in retrospect. I could not have been more wrong.

The public anguish over raids and deportations was a story we were hearing in immigrant communities. The phenomenon of detention was more secretive. People were ashamed to talk about this part of the story.

Sandra Cisneros, who became a dear friend after I reported for CNN on her purple house in San Antonio, gave me some writing advice once. "Write about the things you wish you could forget," she told me. "Not the things you remember. But the things you try but can't forget about."

When I think about the most terrible thing I've witnessed in all my years as a journalist, Willacy immediately comes to the fore. The first image is of the women huddled together to stay warm because the facility had no heating.

They were human beings being held on US soil, the most advanced nation in the world, and they were freezing. Not just for a couple of hours or even one night. No, these were people being held under government supervision, desperately trying to stay warm. For days on end.

I had been contracted by *Frontline* to anchor an hour-long documentary on immigration called *Lost in Detention*. It would be the first time they took on the issue of immigration, which then–executive producer David Fanning had not been much interested in covering in the twenty-five years he ran the show. It had taken me years to break into *Frontline*. In the business, they have a reputation for being exclusive and controlling, so I was excited and scared. The project had assigned a small team of investigative journalists to look at how rape and abuse had become systemic in one detention camp.

But first, let me clarify my use of terms. The government, ICE, and the private prison industry refer to these places as "centers." I can't in good conscience call these places a benign thing like a center. Not after what I have seen. All of this is happening before our very eyes to people because of one thing and one thing only: they weren't born here. History will attempt to absolve me. But I am sure eventually, and after much resistance, these places will one day be called what they are: camps. Just like the history books wanted us to believe that American citizens of Japanese descent were "interred," not incarcerated against their own will. They were jailed with no charge, then told it was for "the good of the country."

When Janet Napolitano was still the governor of Arizona, she had tapped Dora Schriro to head up the state's Department of Corrections. As the new head of the Department of Homeland Security, Napolitano again turned to Schriro, this time to direct an overhaul of the immigrant detention system. Schriro was one of a few women who had made a career in corrections with her PhD in education.[1] She would be a game changer in the narrative around immigrant detention.

The Willacy County Correctional Center in Raymondville, Texas, didn't even start with actual brick walls when it began housing immigrants in 2006. It was run by Management and Training Corporation (MTC), whose company slogan is "BIONIC," or "Believe it or not, I care." They needed to fill those beds fast in order to start making money right away, so they put up Kevlar tents. Pretty soon it earned the nickname Tent City, or as locals referred to it, Ritmo—short for "the Gitmo of Raymondville."[2]

After the bed mandate was green-lit in 2009, money was made available—almost overnight—to round up and house the millions of people we had always talked about and knew were in our midst. They were our neighbors, coworkers, delivery people, and nannies, but there were those 34,000 beds that were waiting to be filled.

How do you house thousands of people quickly and without drawing too much attention? At Willacy, someone came up with the brilliant yet horrible idea to use these structures that are like small airport hangars, or something you might see at a circus: long, windowless tents that looked like a menacing blimp or a nondescript storage unit if it was holding pounds of coffee or rice, TV sets or even computers, or maybe dogs in a kennel, but human beings? It would be like housing people in an icebox, boiler room, or greenhouse—it doesn't fit together.

But if you are in the business of turning a profit, then you build a place to house people anywhere as fast as you can because every day that passes where you aren't housing 34,000 human beings is a day that millions of dollars are being left on the table. More than likely your member of Congress voted for this if they were in office back then. It was not a big deal.

Those tents were not meant for human beings because they are huge and impossible to heat or cool sufficiently. They were not meant for human beings because they have no windows. They were not meant for human beings because they don't have toilets or plumbing. Willacy was not built for human beings.

That's how I came to see the huddled masses of twenty-first-century America. They were not the Irish, German, and Swedish immigrants in long skirts and crumpled suits in 1900 waving from the boats on their way to Ellis Island. For me, they were the brown women who were thrown into the massive, unheated tents in the middle of a South Texas winter, when the days can give you sunstroke but the nights drop into icy, bitter cold. They were terrified strangers who clung to each other for survival. They wore used underwear, orange jumpsuits, and oversized jackets that didn't keep them warm.

The camp was later transformed into state-of-the-art holding cells that had an appearance of professionalism but hid the true inhumanity of what was happening behind those walls with no windows. Even after they had built the massive concrete structures, they kept the tents going.

The vested interests behind Willacy—the private contractors, the local city government, the ordinary citizens who were promised jobs—were in such a rush to fill the place up and start making money that they barely fed them. They yelled at them, insulted them, beat them because, at the end of the day, everyone housed there was reduced to being one thing.

You're an illegal.

No one cares how we treat you.

You're an illegal.

You don't deserve anything.

You're an illegal.

You don't get to ask any questions here.

You're an illegal.

Shut the fuck up. Turn around. Bend over. Fuck me. Fuck you.

You stupid illegal.

If you say anything, I'll get you deported.

Fucking illegal alien.

That's how the detainees were spoken to. We uncovered that in our work at *Frontline*. I saw it in the detainees' own handwriting in the surveys they filled out after all hell broke loose.

The dirty truth unraveled because of the many people who stood up and spoke honestly about what they had witnessed. Even though they were fearful—some had power and some were victims—they did not stay silent. One whistle-blower in particular stood out.

Her name was Twana Cooks-Allen, and she was a registered nurse who was originally from the Midwest. Because of the economic downturn, she moved her whole family to Raymondville, where she got a job as a mental health worker inside the Willacy Detention Center. From the moment she got there, she sensed a strange vibe. It was a very militaristic environment for civil offenders, first of all. The people who ran the place had military titles like *commander* or *captain*, but they were not in fact military. Many of the people doing the on-the-ground guard work were quite young and had very basic training. They were being paid minimum wage, $7.25 an hour, to babysit grown people, many of whom were business owners themselves.

She noticed people were getting the most cursory medical treatment and were often told to take a Tylenol and drink water for symptoms that appeared to be more serious. In some cases, detainees were overwhelmed with depression because living in a tent not meant to house human beings can fuck with your head. The light at the end of the tunnel was dim and far away for them. At the same time, they were never going to sign their own deportation order because their whole family and livelihood were back in the city they had been taken away from. They identified as American and were going to fight to stay here, despite being locked up in a windowless room. These stubborn complainers who would not shut up and sit down would be more heavily medicated than the rest.

We uncovered the story of a Jamaican man who had been detained even though he had a green card. He lived in the Bronx, where he took care of his ailing mom and his sick wife. When he was a kid in his late teens he had sold drugs on a street corner, pleaded guilty, and spent sixteen months in prison. He was now in his forties with a clean record. This was the threatening guy ICE decided to go after—a middle-aged Jamaican man with a bit of a belly who spends most of his time caring for his mother and wife and hasn't been stopped by a police officer in decades.

He couldn't stop crying. He happened to have some controllable mental illnesses; he battled depression and bipolar disorder. It had been a year since he was imprisoned inside the tent and no one could give him a straight answer as to how long he would be there. They moved him to the middle-of-nowhere Texas, and his family in New York could not afford to come to see him. He was yelled at and insulted by the young Latino guards who called him the N-word and an "illegal." He heard the guards beating up on other detainees for no reason at all. He couldn't complain to anyone because the guards threatened to deport him if he did. He wasn't suicidal because he had to stay alive for his wife and his mother. But he couldn't stop crying and worrying.

One day the psychiatrist prescribed him something another nurse thought was too strong. The doctor overruled the nurse. The crying man took the medication, which was so strong he slept for thirty-six hours straight, rolled off the top of his metal bunk bed four feet off the ground with no railing, and fell flat on his face. He broke his eye socket and cheekbone, and one of his testicles, which he also fell on, exploded. He was taken into surgery. After he threatened to speak out and the inspector general inquired about his case, he was released from Willacy.

The whistle-blower nurse was trying to stay low-key and keep her job. She had two kids under the age of ten and she really needed to work. Plus, no one in her family had wanted to leave St. Louis and move to Texas, but she had made them. Now, imagine this. She was witnessing human rights abuses daily. There were thousands of immigrants with legal green cards and visas who had already served time for whatever small-time crime they may have committed. Now they were facing double jeopardy—being tried twice for the same crime, but instead of serving time, they were being detained and deported.

She listened to so many people complain about the food and dismissed them or simply didn't believe them, but then one day an immigrant came into her office carrying a napkin with something wrapped inside. She opened the napkin and said, "This is what they fed us for breakfast." Twana looked into the napkin and saw live maggots wriggling in mush. She guessed that it was expired oatmeal infested with bugs and then served as a meal to people who are less than human beings because they weren't born in the United States. Because they're just "illegals."

Then one day the whistle-blower came to work and a young Guatemalan woman sat down in her office; she was so distraught she couldn't speak. All she could do was cry. Twana got an interpreter on the phone once she figured out what indigenous language she spoke. After a long while, the woman was able to communicate that she had been raped by a guard. And, she said, so had others. That day a total of eight women came forward to say they had been sexually assaulted while in detention.

The shit had hit the fan when Dora Schriro heard about the rape allegations. She got on a plane from her air-conditioned DC government office to the border the next day. The saga of this one detention camp called Willacy run by Management and Training Corporation that was built almost overnight on a promise to make money for an impoverished city on the backs of people whose only real crime was not having been born in this country was coming to a head, on the backs of raped women. Dora Schriro saw what was going on at Willacy with her own eyes and wrote a scathing report that showed how ICE was in no way equipped—underscore, IN NO WAY equipped—to be in the business of housing people—any people. Specifically people who were NO CRIMINAL THREAT. More specifically, people who had arrived in this land traumatized and seeking asylum, but were put into a prison-like structure. Schriro pointed out the mental health challenges this kind of environment created and emphasized the competence and compassion it takes to run any kind of massive housing or detention system, especially when the people you are holding are not criminals. In conclusion, she recommended that ICE and DHS rethink their entire detention policy. Within months of delivering this scathing report, Dora Schriro resigned and became the Commissioner of Corrections of New York City.[3] Apparently there had been a pissing match between the Obama administration and the Bloomberg administration over Schriro, and Bloomberg won.

She may have left DC because I had heard that people inside DHS and ICE hated Schriro. She was helping to uncover the shocking abuses and rampant corruption that we had reported on in *Lost in Detention*. Detention camps had quotas to meet. The motivation behind ICE raids was about more than picking up "criminal aliens."

"If the numbers weren't high, we would get a call from Washington and this wasn't a friendly call," a former ICE employee, who was a high-level policy person and had helped write the Secure Communities guidelines, told us. "This was a call to summon you to DC to explain your numbers. . . . Once we were inside someone's house we would take the low fruit, the high fruit, and any fruit in between in order to keep those numbers up."

Schriro's report also brought up one of the BASIC tenets of professional detention: know who you are housing with who. Yet in her many visits to Willacy and other detention camps, she saw actual violent criminal immigrants being housed with immigrants who had never even received a parking ticket.

Her report discussed the quality of the food, or lack thereof, served at the camps. At *Frontline*, we exposed the fact that private prison contractors saved money by buying and serving expired food. Detainees wrote that they were hungry because the food was spoiled and inedible. So many detainees, in fact, that Schriro asked for a weight survey, too. She compared the weight of immigrants when they were first taken in to their weight on the date of the survey. On average, each detainee had lost a minimum of ten pounds.

At Willacy, we had heard that women were given one pad a day. Guards yelled at women who asked for a second. If the allotted rolls of toilet paper were used up, that was it; there was no more to be had. The two small windows that did exist in the massive tents were taped off so that no one could actually stand at the window and look outside. In the beginning, when Willacy was being built, detainees were not allowed to go outside, ever.

In the survey forms requested by Schriro and collected by Twana, detainees described over and over again the verbal abuse that was directed at them. They wrote in perfect and labored Spanish or English that the guards constantly yelled at and insulted them, calling them "illegals," "dirty Mexicans," "n*****s," "towel heads," "stupid," "MFers," and "assholes."

They said they were afraid most of the time with the threat of deportation hanging over them. The guards played mind games with the detainees, sometimes forcing them to sign their own deportation orders under coercion. Both men and women were being raped and nothing was being done about it. Guards would take women to an area behind one of the tents where there were no cameras and rape them or trade sex for extra food and phone calls. We heard about three suspected pregnancies caused by rape but couldn't verify any of them. We couldn't verify it independently, but more than one detainee had said the women had all been deported after it was discovered they were pregnant.

The men were taken out and beaten as punishment for any infraction, from talking back to asking for more food. Once, all the men were taken to a room and made to run like cattle. One person said it felt like Abu Ghraib inside the United States. Another said he had to fight with a rat that tried to eat his Cheetos from commissary. He had left them in the drawer under his bed.

Although the conditions at Willacy and other detention camps were deplorable, they were merely a logical extension of the abuse of power that began the moment ICE agents put on those baseball caps that say POLICE in block letters. ICE agents are not actually police. In fact, it is illegal to impersonate a law enforcement official, yet the government maintains it's perfectly fine for ICE agents to deceive people in this way.[4] Los Angeles mayor Eric Garcetti, along with other city officials and civil rights groups, has been one of the few voices urging ICE not to use such unethical tactics.[5]

While I was down at Willacy, we connected with a woman on Facebook named Sigrid who took a temp job at Willacy as a guard since she had worked in the Texas jails before and she needed work. She quit after six months because she said she couldn't handle the abuse she was seeing on a daily basis. Sigrid came by the ornate bed-and-breakfast filled with antiques that we were staying at in the nearby town of Harlingen. As she sat near a particularly beautiful Tiffany lampshade, she told us about the time she walked in on a supervisor and a guard beating a detainee to a pulp for speaking out of turn. Once they finished, she had to ensure that the same detainee was put on the first plane out the next day. I remember listening to her and feeling as I did during the eight-hour-long interview we did with Twana—it was an out-of-body experience.

I'll never forget when one young immigrant named Maria, who had been detained and released after alleging in an official complaint that she was sexually assaulted by a female guard, and who we interviewed for *Frontline*, said to me, "You know the movie *Schindler's List*? I felt like I was in it." She proceeded to describe the day they discovered lice on one of the detainees. In the middle of winter they forced all of the immigrants to strip down their beds and then strip down themselves. They stood in line for the showers naked. Their skinny bodies—the women holding their breasts with one hand and covering their crotches with the other—reminded her of the movie about Nazi concentration camps. My obsession with the Nazi era followed me everywhere.

After *Lost in Detention* ran on PBS, things appeared to get slightly better. The Obama administration had some people in place who appreciated the push and pull between NGOs, activists, and the government. But in general, not much changed. The play was not to slow down the pace of immigrant detention but to ramp it up—to prove to Republicans that Democrats could also be "tough on immigration." *We'll show you who can be a bigger bully to immigrants!*

What started out on clunky wooden wheels was now operating like a bullet train from Japan. The ICE industrial complex was whizzing along, keeping those tens of thousands of beds filled every night with people you are told are terrible criminals but they are not. These people are all around you and yet they are being whisked up and taken away, oftentimes in the early morning, sometimes when they are dropping off their kids at school, sometimes when they are going into or coming out of surgery, now sometimes when they are in a courtroom, getting on a bus or off a train, waiting tables or waiting for an ambulance. It has not gotten better. It has gotten worse.

Just before our *Frontline* documentary ran, the Willacy Detention Center was closed and reopened under the Federal Bureau of Prison's management to house criminal immigrants. Basically, the private contractors at Management and Training Corporation handed over the keys to a new owner who would only hold immigrants charged with a criminal offense. *Well, now, that makes sense,* you are probably thinking. *Keep the "real" criminals in prison and away from the immigrants whose only real crime is that they weren't born in the US.*

I wish I could say you are right. Being a "criminal immigrant" can mean as little as crossing the border more than once and getting caught or getting caught crossing the border after having been deported once. If it all feels too confusing, that is also part of it.

My husband says that the reason this is so hard for me is because I believed in the promise of this country. I bought into the exceptionalism. It's hard to accept how ornery and normal and mediocre this country really is. I thought we were better than this. But we aren't.

Now detention camps are called la hielera, "the freezer," for short. It's hard to show remnants of torture from freezing. And now they are also called perreras, dog cages. It's getting worse.

I had a day or two at home before our *Frontline* team flew out, this time to Los Angeles to record in another facility. I listened to the song "Jailer" by Asa on repeat.

> *I'm in chains,*
> *You're in chains, too*
> *I wear uniforms*

And you wear uniforms, too
I'm a prisoner
You're a prisoner too, Mr. Jailer . . .

How do you go "back to normal" after you have seen the things I saw at Willacy? The hugs with my kids were necessary and tender, but inside I felt nothing. I was falling back into the PTSD numbness.

I was so very hurt by what I had seen, but all I felt was anger and, sadly, Gérman got the brunt of it, as it spilled out of me unconsciously. I was doing exactly what we had made a vow never to do—bring the war outside into our home.

I didn't know what else to do. I was feeling compressed by anxiety like a smashed car in a junkyard, but it didn't show outwardly. Maybe if I had gone down to the subway and screamed at the top of my lungs when the screeching train pulled into the station, maybe if I had been able to do that I would have gotten better. But I couldn't.

The subway train of horrible images was coursing through my body, up and down, up and down. Shaking me. Testing me. And then I had to get back on a plane, this time to Los Angeles to film a ride-along with ICE.

We arrived in the late afternoon and had a production meeting before calling it a day. Our call time the next day was going to be 3:00 a.m. ICE did not give us a reason as to why we had to meet that early. We knew we were going on a ride-along with agents, but they didn't want to provide any other details. It's rare that journalists agree to a scenario with so little information provided in advance, but we had been trying to get ICE to say yes to us for more than six months. We essentially had to say yes to everything they asked from us. They knew we needed this material desperately.

All we were told was to show up in the parking lot of a fast-food joint wearing comfortable, dark clothes. That's exactly what we did.

We circled around the parking lot until we saw them. They were unmistakable.

Ten men in bulletproof gear, which made them look even more buff than they were. They were wearing baseball caps that said POLICE in big white block letters, so at first I was confused. We were there to meet ICE, not the police. As the producer and photographer got our equipment together, I tapped one of the guys on the shoulder and asked him, "Hey, are you guys the police? We're looking for our ICE contacts."

The guy looked at me in disbelief. I was talking to him? They had been warned, of course, that we were coming. I realized they were under strict orders not to speak to us at all.

"I can't talk to you," he said, "I'm sorry."

"Okay, cool," I said. "I get it. But I'm just making sure we are in the right place. Is this ICE or police?"

"It's ICE," he hissed back and turned away abruptly, lest he get reprimanded in front of all his guys.

The word I saw on their uniforms most clearly was POLICE. It was emblazoned on their hats and on the fronts of their jackets and vests. When that agent turned away from me, I saw that it said ICE in smaller block letters on the back of their jackets.

I followed him to where the group of agents was clustered together. They basically ignored us, which was great in terms of filming but also weird because they didn't even say good morning. About eight or ten men stood around a map that was splayed across the hood of a car. They circled two locations in East Los Angeles where we were going. They talked quietly, mumbling so that we could barely hear, about the plan of action, and then quickly filed out into cars. We were shuffled into a huge black Escalade-type car. We still didn't know what was happening, but our cameraman never stopped shooting.

I couldn't help it anymore. I had to start asking questions.

"Where are we going and why are you guys wearing almost full SWAT gear?"

The PR liaison then handed us pictures of two men that were in manila files, but it was pitch-black in the car and hard to see their faces as we bumped along.

"I need you to understand we are on a very dangerous mission," he explained. "Your safety is our primary concern and I need you to follow my orders so you don't get hurt."

Holy shit, what did I get myself into? Do these guys plan to take us to an encounter where there might be gunfire just to fuck with us? Or are they surprised by this, too? I told myself this was a rare experience, but I was suddenly terrified and thinking about how I didn't want to die for this story.

They put the fear of God into the three of us. We had no choice but to keep our heads down and dodge the bullets that were clearly coming our way. They said the two men they were picking up had outstanding warrants for deportation and that they were convicted criminals with possible gang affiliations.

"Sir, how often does one of these ICE pickups end in violence?"

"Well, you never know. Anything can happen. These are dangerous people and our job is to remove them from the country. And now I need you to be quiet and stay in the car. Your cameraman can follow from behind when we cue him. Understood?"

"Yes, sir. Understood."

The streets of LA were still empty when we left the parking lot. It took us thirty minutes to get to East Los Angeles, the soul of the centuries-old Mexican community there. The houses were small but well kept, with little white fences around some of them, gardens, wooden rockers, and hanging plants. The neighborhood seemed picturesque. There was the sound of gallos and barking dogs in the distance. Everyone was probably cozy and asleep with no idea that two stealth vans were creeping through their neighborhood like sharks out for blood.

We pulled up to a house with a statue of the Virgen Maria with her light blue shawl pulled over her head and shoulders. The house also looked well tended to, clean and tidy, which didn't really mean anything, I told myself. Murderers can be clean and tidy, too.

Five agents ran out of one of the ICE vans, quietly opened the dog gate, and then walked up the three stairs to the front door. They banged on the door the way that only the police bang on your door. Everything had been silent until this moment. The sound was unmistakable, loud and forceful. They did it again, even harder this time, and a dog barked in response, maybe sensing the anger in the knock. A middle-aged lady in a flowery housecoat answered. The heavily armed agents looked a little silly now staring down a groggy lady in her pajamas. She let them in and they were suddenly polite as they walked into the house. Within less than a minute, they came out with a fifty-five-year-old who was a pizza delivery man.

His outstanding crime? A DUI that destroyed a bicycle and left the cyclist with a few scrapes. He had paid his fine, though, and even served a few months in prison. Since the accident he had started going to AA; he had been clean now for decades. The DUI was from when he was twenty-five. He was fifty-five and a grandfather with no criminal record.

These were the criminals they were targeting? Maybe I was getting ahead of myself. They said the next person was more dangerous.

The same scenario played out again at the second house of a "possible gang member." The banging at the door. Confusion about who it was and what they wanted.

"It says 'police' on their jacket, and everyone knows you have to open your door to the police," is what the señora told me when I interviewed her before the van drove away with her common-law partner of forty years. He also had a DUI. He was a gardener, also over fifty, with no record except for a DUI from twenty years ago.

I stood on their manicured lawn. It was small, maybe three feet wide on either side of the front door, but it was their little patch of green in East Los Angeles. I saw beyond their front door that they had a huge rug version of the Virgen de Guadalupe hanging in their foyer. The outline of the rectangular rug was lined with twinkling Christmas lights, even though it was the fall.

The patron saint of immigrants looked over this man as ICE handcuffed him but never told him why they were taking him or where or whether he got a phone call or a lawyer. He didn't get a phone call or a lawyer. Immigrants don't. There is an entirely separate legal system for immigrants. A whole separate part of the law that only applies to people who were not born here.

Wait, what?

––––––––––

The public relations executive, a real company man, was excited to show us the better side of detention. He knew we had seen some horrible conditions at Willacy, so he kept telling us how great the James A. Musick detention facility was in Irvine, Orange County, California.

There, instead of closed-in barracks, the doors were open. There was a dusty soccer field and a basketball court. The detainees had more freedom of movement, but the bunk beds were about two feet apart from each other. They had fresh air and the chance to see the sky, but they had no privacy.

I was horrified to confirm another dirty truth of the deportation/detention machinery that was essential to keeping those beds full and paid for. Dozens of men at the Musick facility had green cards! They were business owners and suburban soccer dads, and now they were here, dirty and smelly and wearing stained orange jumpsuits that were too big. One man from Egypt started to cry as he spoke to me about his daughters, three teenage girls who were alone because their mother had gone back to Egypt to care for a sick relative.

"I have twenty employees in my small business, but who cares about that? It's my daughters! How can they leave me here when they know my American citizen daughters are all alone in Los Angeles?"

One man wiped away tears with the sleeve of his jumpsuit, while another openly sniffled. These men had nothing to lose. Crying in front of a stranger, a woman, might be something they would never do, and yet here they were, looking me in the eye, telling me their stories, even briefly touching my hands for some sort of human contact. I was not afraid. These were not criminals.

We wrapped in Los Angeles and then flew to Miami to visit the Krome Service Processing Center, a notorious place that had seen a violent uprising in 1982 and again in 1992, the conditions were so horrendous. Our call time to meet at Krome was four in the morning. There was no real need to make us get up so early, but it was an easy way to get a groggy reporter instead of a fully alert one. This industrial-looking detention camp in the tropics was run by a nice Puerto Rican man who had started out in Border Patrol, had worked hard, and had come far in his career. He was very proud of himself. After decades in the industry, he had risen to the top of the detention food chain and was running one of the biggest detention facilities, where 87 percent of the detainees were Latino.

I care about them more, he told me.

Perhaps, but he had his assistant follow me everywhere in the camp except the bathroom and take notes of every conversation I had. It was disconcerting to be sure, but I put on my New York City bitch attitude and I think she respected me because of that. At the end of the shoot, she told me that she, too, was a badass Latina from NYC.

Along with his assistant, this man stayed at my side the entire time and was shocked when I out of the blue asked him to show me the solitary confinement units. He thought he had befriended me and connected with me as a fellow professional Latino, so he wasn't prepared for that. In order to save face, he walked me over to an area apart from everything else that looked like two separate trailers. Inside one of the trailers I saw several tiny white rooms, maybe seven by four feet. In them men were sitting with their heads down; one man paced back and forth like a caged lion.

As we were walking back toward the offices to wrap up, I saw something that stood out. It was a tall, blond-haired twentysomething. I asked if I could speak with him because he was the only white person I had seen in detention after visiting three of the largest detention camps.

He was a Russian-born high school dropout from Coney Island who had no idea he didn't have papers until he got arrested for selling pot on a Queens street corner when he was nineteen. He was twenty-two now and had never visited Russia since his parents brought him over when he was two years old. He was getting ready to be deported to Moscow and he was visibly worried. "I don't speak any Russian at all," he said, his New York accent solidly from Queens. Here we were in the USA with a smart Puerto Rican running a massive detention camp and deporting white kids from New York City. Part of our agreement with DHS was that we could film as much as possible at Krome up to the actual deportation of detainees. The camp director and his assistant led us to another building, where a group of gaunt, sad men, all brown or black, were standing against a white cinder-block wall. They were getting ready to be flown to a country they didn't see as home anymore. This was what the immigrant industrial machine looked like operating on a daily basis, removing people from the USA.

The men were ordered to look at the floor and one of them caught my eye as he did. He looked like a preppy dude so he stood out with his light brown wavy hair and horn-rimmed glasses. He looked like he could be my cousin or classmate. I watched as the armed guard pulled a long heavy chain off a hook on the wall and wrapped it around the man's feet, snaked it up in front and between his legs, and then around his small waist. The guard pulled the chain tight and locked the man's wrists to it, making it almost impossible for him to walk without falling. Single file, heads down, their chains clanking loudly with every movement, they were loaded onto two buses, one for men and one for women. We followed the buses to an unmarked back-door entrance of the Miami International Airport that led right onto the tarmac. A hundred feet from where we entered was a huge plane and four men with black wraparound sunglasses and machine guns guarding it.

The men and women were all wearing chains. Did the guards really think these prisoners were going to try to escape? Or was it to show us, because we would be putting this on TV, that these immigrants were mighty dangerous and even when being removed, they had to be treated like violent felons (though they were neither)?

It's hard to describe the feeling I had observing this scene. Unless you are in a horror movie, this is something that shouldn't happen— the thing you fear most is suddenly confirmed to be real. It's like learning the boogeyman does exist. What do you do with that?

I thought back to the outdoor detention camps with barbed wire that I saw with Scott Simon back in 1986. We saw the dehumanization of immigrants then, how refugees were treated like animals and left in the sun all day. But that was nothing compared to this.

This story wasn't going away. The story of immigration, I was horrified and convinced, was going to be the story of my career, of my lifetime. The situation wasn't getting better with every year that passed. It was getting sickeningly worse.

I couldn't say it publicly because I knew I would lose my credibility as a journalist forever, but I was sure I was seeing the beginnings of concentration camps in the US. My obsession, my nightmare was coming true.

Chapter 15

Trauma Inherited

Images flashed in my head from the interview I had just taped in Toronto with a former detainee, a Canadian Afro-Caribbean immigrant. My team and I had gotten on a plane and crossed the northern border to meet her because she had agreed, after weeks of conversation with one of our patient and determined *Frontline* producers, to meet us in a hotel in Toronto. By the time we arrived that morning, she had reneged. She'd gotten scared and said she didn't want to relive those terrible memories. Here we were, though, a producer, our DP, and myself, all in Canada and she was walking away.

I had to do something—I told myself I had no choice but to try to convince this survivor to talk to me about the most horrible days in her life in front of a film crew. I got on the phone and pleaded with her to come and tell me about the male ICE agent who spent weeks stalking her and then touched her between the legs and on her breasts, telling her she liked it, pushing her up against the walls where he knew there were no cameras.

270

"Who are you gonna tell anyways?" he would hiss at her. "No one is gonna believe a stupid illegal."

He said these things in her ear from the moment he started to prey on her. This is what it looks like when a dehumanizing word like *illegal* is normalized. Remember, those of us who said that this word was inappropriate were told we had an agenda by respected media companies and fellow journalists. Year after year, until I banned that word from my own newsroom.

He started by forcing himself on her and kissing her in the camera blind spots. Then he cornered her and put his hands all over her body. She knew what was coming next, so she signed a deportation order and decided she couldn't stay in the US and fight her case if it meant staying in this detention hell where she had no one to turn to and was about to be raped, perhaps multiple times. She left behind her business and five American-born children in Florida.

Her "crime"? A check for less than $300 that had bounced. Because she had moved, the collection notices from the big-box store were never forwarded to her new address and the police issued a warrant. When she went in to renew her green card, they detained her immediately. This is what the government means when they say "criminal" immigrants. She had written the check ten years before.

Back in NYC, I was stuck in my head, reviewing a never-ending barrage of horrifying moments. There was the image of her starting to cry, her light brown curls falling over her forehead. The image of her talking about him putting his hand on her vagina. The image of her hands imitating what her assaulter had done to her. The image of her head hanging like a heavy kettlebell in her hands. She was desperate to see her five children; the youngest one was only five years old. Finally, the stark black-and-white image of her arms pinned down by the tall, overpowering guard. This was the image that wouldn't let me sleep. I couldn't get the phrase—*her arms pinned down over her head*—or the image out of my mind.

The stories that *Lost in Detention* aired about the sexual assault of immigrants in detention camps also disturbed one very powerful senator, Dick Durbin of Illinois.

"What is the Department of Homeland Security doing to ensure that immigration detainees are safe from sexual abuse, whether they're in ICE facilities or contract facilities?" This was the question Senator Durbin posed to secretary of Homeland Security Janet Napolitano at the Senate Judiciary Committee hearing on immigration policy oversight held on October 19, 2011.[1] He had watched our *Frontline* documentary and was shocked to learn that immigrants in detention camps—facilities that were only for civil offenses, not criminal ones—had no legal protection from rape. You have more rights if you are raped in prison than if you are raped in detention. As a direct result of watching our work on *Frontline*, Durbin pushed for the Prison Rape Elimination Act (PREA) to be applied to immigrant detainees. That was in 2011. PREA was not officially extended to protect immigrants in detention until 2017; however, the law still does not apply to private or county jails.[2] For six more years after the *Frontline* documentary aired, guards and other personnel could rape or sexually assault immigrants all they wanted. The most sinister of these people knew that if there was ever a threat of an accusation against them, they could simply deport the victim and all evidence of the crime was suddenly out of the country, just like that.

If you are a sadist and a rapist with a high school degree and no criminal record, you know where to go to get work. Any place that detains immigrants: men, women, teenage boys and girls, children, toddlers, babies.

Babies.

What was hardest to believe for some was what Cecilia Muñoz said to me on camera: "There will be parents separated from their children.

They don't have to like it, but it is a result of having a broken system of laws." This out of the mouth of an award-winning immigrant activist who was now a close national adviser to Obama. "What the president is doing is enforcing the law of the land," she said without flinching and with even a bit of attitude.[3]

Cecilia Muñoz and I had never been more than professional colleagues, but like everyone I knew in the world of immigration, I had great respect for her and her work on behalf of immigrants. Born in Michigan to Bolivian immigrant parents, Cecilia had won a MacArthur Genius award. When she invited me to visit the White House soon after her appointment to the Obama administration in 2009, I said yes.

It was my first and only time in the West Wing. As I sat in her tiny office, I remembered that when enslaved Americans constructed that sacred place, they built it to 1792 proportions. Everything in the White House is much tinier than you think.

In 2011, when I was trying to get Obama to give me an interview on camera to answer questions about immigrant detention, the administration offered Cecilia instead, almost like a sacrificial lamb. If the president was unable to defend his actions on immigration, a Latina daughter of immigrants would do it for him. We later heard secondhand that the Obama administration was not happy with our reporting in *Lost in Detention*.

Lawyers, academics, human rights officials, and activists had praised the documentary for being the first to capture detention facilities on camera and expose them to the entire country. Many of those who applauded the work had once been strong allies of the Obama administration, but now no one was happy with what he was doing on the issue of immigration. Instead of trusting his constitutional lawyer's gut and shutting down all of the detention facilities that were popping up across the country, Obama was sending people to detention and deporting them to their home countries around the world in droves, including Cuba, Haiti, and Canada.

Bill Clinton removed 869,646 people (those deported based on an order of removal) and returned 11,421,259 (returns are typically people who are apprehended at the border and returned to their country immediately); in total, Clinton deported more than 12 million people. Under George W. Bush, 2,012,539 people were removed and 8,316,311 returned, for a grand total of 10,328,850. From 2009 to 2014, Obama removed 2,427,070 and returned 1,950,820. All in all, Obama deported more than 4 million people—a number that was significantly lower than his predecessors' totals, but higher in terms of removals.[4] In this sense, the number of ordered deportations have kept on growing, at one point even sweeping up Obama's own uncle who was taken in for a DUI in Boston.

The daily number of noncitizens detained increased from 7,475 in 1995 to 33,330 in 2011. The grand total for the entire year of 2011 was 429,247 people in detention, which is more than the annual number of people serving sentences in federal prison for all other federal crimes. In 2012, the US spent $18 billion on immigration enforcement, which was more than the money spent that year on the Secret Service, DEA, FBI, and all other federal crime enforcement agencies combined.[5] *Combined.*

I saw these numbers provided by the government from their own data, and it made me light-headed and nauseous. As Gary Segura, a former political scientist at Stanford University and the current dean of UCLA's Luskin School of Public Affairs, said, "In the absence of reform, we're left with, essentially, enforcement on steroids. . . . That is our immigration policy," under a progressive Democratic president.[6]

Why couldn't people see where this was leading us? I didn't understand the concept of gaslighting back then. I thought there was something wrong with me because I was so traumatized by what I had witnessed. It didn't dawn on me until much later that what I saw was the truth and others simply chose not to believe me because it was too horrible to accept. Or they accused me of being an untrustworthy journalist.

Janet Murguía saw those numbers, too, and she was done with the promises. A third-generation Mexican American from Kansas City, she was the head of the National Council of La Raza, which is known today as UnidosUS, the most important and historic Latino advocacy organization (that sadly, most other Americans and many Latinx have never heard of). For simplicity, people characterized it as the Latinx NAACP. Janet had taken the organization over from the iconic Raul Yzaguirre, who had founded the organization in the heat of the 1960s. He had been the NCLR's president for three decades. Now that Janet was in charge, she had to navigate that delicate balance of needing to be a DC insider and her responsibility to the organization's activist base across the country. She did this well and, while nonpartisan, was loved and respected by many Democrats.

As she prepared for a huge conference, Janet looked at the suits hanging in her closet and zeroed in on a bright pink one. She was giving an important speech, one she knew would change everything for her, but she was cansada and ready to take a risk.

"Fuck it," she said under her breath, because she would never be caught saying that in public.

Later that afternoon, Janet remembered how angry and powerless she felt after learning about Willacy, Orange County, Krome, and so many others from my *Frontline* documentary—and that this was happening under a Democrat. Today she would take that rage and direct it into her speech. When she got on the stage at the annual NCLR convention, she labeled Barack Obama with three words that have haunted him and his presidency ever since: Deporter in Chief.

The love affair with "hope" was over. The reality of immigrant detention would haunt not only the president, but the entire Democratic Party, for another decade, if not more to come.

———————

The abuses and resulting trauma we uncovered in *Lost in Detention* came back to me years later in an unexpected way. By this time I had begun teaching at DePaul University in Chicago—Ceci had convinced me to try out for a professor position there. It was a job with full benefits and my son wanted to go to school in Chicago. I would spend many days with Ceci in those years, rekindling our love and respect for each other, the hugs flowing freely between us.

In a class I taught on Latinas, mental health, and depression—a subject I have reported on in depth—my students mentioned a Netflix series called *13 Reasons Why*. They basically instructed me to watch it. People argued the series promoted teen suicide, but what I saw was a show about teen girls who are the victims of slut shaming, verbal bullying, and rape.

In the final episode, Hannah, the main character and an emotionally vulnerable teen, goes to a house party and a boy she knows coaxes her into a hot tub. After all of the name-calling and bullying, Hannah thinks she has found a kindred spirit in a boy who invites her nicely to join him. He seems so sweet to her.

Then, suddenly, the full weight of his body is pushing down on her. His hand movements are fast and dramatic, a forced undressing. As I watched this on my iPad, I was seeing something else. It was me. But I wasn't in a hot tub, I was on a new mattress that still had the plastic on it, so it hurt my back. I remembered how he grabbed my hands and held me down. That's why I hadn't fought back, which in my mind was the reason I had convinced myself that I had never really been raped— because I didn't remember fighting back. Seeing the close-ups of her hands being held down I realized that that was exactly what had been done to me. My hands were held down on top of my head, against my will. I was fighting back but I was, as I had always been, too small. All I ever had was my voice, but he chose not to hear my screams of *NO*.

Hannah said no to the boy and kept on saying no, just like me. I watched her visibly disconnect from reality. I knew that feeling. The pain is so great that if you were to think about it you would scream, but you just did scream no and he kept on going. Why scream now?

This is your fault. ¡Te lo merecias! (You deserved it!)

I had never seen anything like this and now I had a visual of my own rape. What happened to Hannah on *13 Reasons Why* was exactly what happened to me years ago. I had come to understand I had 9/11 triggers—the towers burning, the color-coded security threat system, the sound of bagpipes. But I never knew I had a rape trigger till I saw this.

The twenty-four-year-old who had danced with me, made me feel butterflies in between my legs, and kissed me romantically, or so I thought, knew that he was going to force himself on me from the moment he thrust his tongue down my throat on that first kiss. And yet, I kept kissing him and dancing with him. That didn't mean he got to fuck me. But I didn't know any better.

I didn't know that I had the right to say no to him from the moment I realized he was going to force me no matter what I did, when he got back in the car with the condom he had just bought. I didn't stop him then. Is that my fault?

Isn't it his fault? Just because he bought a condom he assumed he could use it no matter what? It was a premeditated assault. And I was a kid.

He never kissed me again after that night, even though I saw him for two more days. Never danced with me again. Never sent me a letter or called. He knew exactly what he did. I was a hole he stuck his tiny, hard dick in. Nothing more or less.

I was on my own lonely path. I had done what I never set out to do purposefully. I had distanced myself from my husband so much that he wasn't there for me. I had convinced myself I needed to prove that I could face anything alone. Some of my closest friends and family had died. I had held my best friend's dying hand in my own hand.

Ceci didn't know it when she told me to apply for the DePaul Sor Juana Ines de la Cruz visiting scholar position that we would be spending her last years on earth seeing each other on my frequent trips to Chicago.

After our having been friends for almost twenty-five years, ours was a ripe, mature, delicious friendship that brought us joy and confidence. We would lie on her big sofa and my godchildren, Ana and Andres, would plop there, too. It was a liberating, loving, no-judgment zone between two women who have been through so much together. We didn't know this would be our last journey together.

When the breast cancer had spread to her brain, Ceci cried with me that she wished we could stop feeling insecure and anxious and instead focus on finding joy in our lives.

I held her hand, telling her she could let go, that I would be there for Ana and Andres and her husband, Gary.

But off she went. Alone.

And so, I had to confront the reality of my rape alone. Carry your own fucking cross!

When I got back from whatever city I had just been to, Gérman had moved out of our bedroom. He said he was having back problems and was going to sleep in Raúl's bed. At least that's what we decided we would tell the kids. The intimate details of the argument we had that night were not pretty and no one needed to know the specifics. We had to be sure the kids were okay. That is what mattered now, not me.

It looked like I was going to get my wish. You want to deal with this alone? Here you go, sister!

I asked my therapist, Cristina, to meet me in the park. It had become our custom to do therapy sitting in the park, in a café, or while walking. People would see me crying and I would go on without stopping. We sat looking at a little pond in a Harlem park. There was a white egret perched on a protruding rock in the pond, ready to hunt a small fish. There was a yellow tabby cat resting on the rocks. Circling above was one of the famous Harlem red-tailed hawks.

I burst out crying as I went into detail describing the scene in the Netflix show to her. I held my tiny wrists out in front of her and told her how I remembered this man holding me down. Cristina immediately took my hands, with the same hands she has used to comfort young women from around the world who have been trafficked and raped multiple times, and then slowly pulled me to her so I could feel rooted to something at that moment. She could tell I was surprised by being triggered. I hadn't expected it, but she remained calm at my side, allowing me to feel whatever was coming up for me as I looked at my own rape now without the filter of secrecy and shame. What had happened was so buried that I hadn't even allowed myself to be triggered.

I was feeling it. Identifying it. Seeing it. Seeing myself there. I had dismissed it for so long, diminished its importance, brushed it off, taken the blame, forced myself to forget, and convinced myself that a "baby rape" could actually be an acceptable term for what had happened to me.

"You are a survivor, Maria," Cristina said.

Oh shit, I thought when she said those words. I had always been clear, intentional, and proud about my multiple identities. I was a chingona, a badass Mexican, born in Mexico, raised on the South Side of Chicago, an NYC Harlemite, a Latina, indigenous, spiritual, an intellectual, a feminist, a chaparra. But a survivor?

I internalized the misogyny and subconsciously equated survivor with weakness. I thought about how I would have another strike against me now as a journalist if I discussed my rape openly. I paused and looked at my hands intertwined with Cristina's. She was a gift from Ceci, another brilliant Argentine hermana to help guide me through life.

And then I thought, *Hell yes. I am a fucking survivor. I didn't let you destroy me, you motherfucker, even though what you did to me almost killed me. And I'm just beginning to realize it now. You killed something in me that night on that cold plastic bed. You killed my trust in intimacy and I didn't even know that because of that my marriage is now dying.*

Chapter 16

Owning My Voice

In the worlds of media and Latinos and women taking charge of things, I was applauded for creating one of the only nonprofit newsrooms run by a Latina in the US. I was in *Crain's New York Business*, cited by *Hispanic Business* magazine as one of the most influential Latinas in the country, and I received a commendation in San Antonio for International Women's Day from a Texas mayor no one had heard of yet named Julián Castro. We had made it through five years at Futuro, many months of which had been rocky with several close calls. The possibility of failure hounded me constantly.

I spoke to women entrepreneurs every chance I had and they told me this was all par for the course. "Coming close to the breaking point? That's normal. Oh, it happens so many times when you are just starting!" By now I had also become friends with some very high-profile, very wealthy women of all races and backgrounds, some older, some younger. I figured they all knew more than me, so I continued living with imposter syndrome, always surprised by my own success.

One Latina CEO who was a triathlete told me she looked to the tenets of scuba diving for advice on running her company. "The basic lesson of scuba diving is never stop breathing," she said. "And that's what you need to do. Just breathe through every moment of pain and growth for your company."

Regardless of how Gérman and I were doing in our relationship, he always gave great advice and perspective.

"If your Futuro goes away now, it doesn't mean you are a failure. You created and ran a company for almost six years! Congrats on that! So if it disappears now, it doesn't reflect badly on you," he said. I exhaled a lot when he said that.

What Futuro has always had is integrity, authenticity, and an unpretentious approach to storytelling. People who value and make these qualities the hallmark of their career want to come and work with us; we choose the most excellent and committed journalists with ganas. If you never give up, sometimes beautiful things can happen.

In 2014, *Latino USA* won an award I coveted from afar, the Peabody. The award was for a piece called "Gangs, Murder, and Migration in Honduras" that looked at how decades of poverty and exploitation had led to rampant gang violence and the decision of many Hondurans to leave their country.[1] Marlon Bishop put his life on the line to report and produce it. And then Ethel Kennedy came calling again. "The Strange Death of José de Jesús" had won the Robert F. Kennedy Award![2] It was a piece that exposed the death by suicide of José de Jesús while on "suicide watch." He swallowed and choked on a knee sock he wasn't supposed to have.

To reach those highs, there were so many lows: great staffers who were poached away, deals that fell through, money promised that never came, interview requests that were passed on. I began to see the perpetual give-and-take of being a media entrepreneur, a title that I now took on because I was one; I needed to own it and not be afraid to compete with the men. I knew I was connected to an audience they wished they had.

We had proven NPR wrong. After relaunching *Latino USA* in an hour-long format in 2016, the number of public radio stations airing our show increased by nearly 20 percent and our digital numbers began to explode. This demonstrated exactly what I had been saying not for years, but for decades: the audience is there and they will respond to quality journalism that is authentic and understands their POV on the world. We had cornered two important but very different markets. On NPR, *Latino USA* had an older, nearly all white audience, but digitally, we had younger, nonwhite, and a majority of women listeners, mostly Latinx and African American. The best news was that both audiences were listening to the entire show and our audience numbers kept on growing. We had become a jewel in the NPR crown.

When it was tough running a small nonprofit, it was really tough. I was burned out from the anger and trauma, and the emotional ups and downs were unsustainable. This could not go on anymore. I was going to start losing staff because people were losing their patience with me. Yes, I had experienced death and loss and tragedy. My dad had died, my prima, too, and my best friend, who was only fifty-three years old, damn it! I was in mourning but I needed to see I was acting out. There was a shit ton of ego mixed up in this, too. I was angry because after being invited to be on *Meet the Press* multiple times in 2015, they suddenly and without telling me why, stopped inviting me. I was wounded after being ostracized by the one percent. How faux humble of me.

My team had a solution: "We believe Futuro should lead the political conversation in this country. If the networks won't invite you to be on the Sunday politics talk shows, we'll create our own. In keeping with our mission, we will feature mostly journalists and experts of color to give them a voice and make them more visible nationally."

Most network talk shows treat voters of color like some kind of unique specimen, when in fact, people of color talk politics at home all the time because we are often the most impacted. Yet we are rarely asked to give our analysis or opinion. Our show would be Futuro's own version of the politics talk shows, but it would come out twice a week and not on Sundays.

We called it *In The Thick,* and with this new media property, we plunged into the world of self-distribution. Even though Futuro had a big footprint, our numbers were still small compared to more established media. Big distributors often passed on us. This happened a lot and it always made me doubt what I was doing. I mean, look at BuzzFeed, Gimlet, or ProPublica. Compared to them, Futuro was a tiny fried catfish on the side of their whale plate.

In order to save my company, my soul, my staff, and to save face, we took a huge risk and launched *In The Thick,* the first national politics podcast to focus on journalists and experts of color. And we made our first acquisition: LatinoRebels.com.

Yes, we were doing this. Aw, hell yes.

———————

Gérman had told me that I was attacking him out of my fear of losing him. Attacking? I was prepared to show what an attack from me really looked like. I would hit back like a taunted poisonous viper. Everything in our relationship had become tit for tat.

If I couldn't open my eyes, maybe my ears would help me. Sandy had always told me, "Listen. You will hear the voices of your ancestors speaking to you if you are quiet enough." That morning as the sun was rising over Chicago before I started my day of teaching, I looked into the infinity of the waves and fell into a momentary trance. I receded into silence and began to hear Papi. *Es el amor de tu vida. El papá de tus hijos. Te ama. Te ama. Lo amas.*

And then there was Ceci . . . *Malu, it's not the end of your relationship with Gérman. Make it a new beginning.*

They both said a phrase to me that I have said on a weekly basis for close to three decades at the close of each *Latino USA* show. I've said it so much it's become one of my unofficial trademarks.

No te vayas.

No te vayas.

Stay with us.

Don't be afraid. It's going to be okay.

So I didn't leave. Months later, I told my mom and sister the harrowing tale of my rape over the summer, when my marriage was finally healing and being tended to lovingly. They both felt terrible hearing about my rape because they had been there and had never realized what had happened. I was a good actress and had been convinced they would blame me and say it was my fault, so instead I said nothing like a frightened kid.

It was around our family table in Chicago that I realized I had been getting a central part of the story wrong. When we looked at a calendar side by side so that we could go back and piece it all together, we realized my timing was off. I had told myself it happened on New Year's Eve of 1978, but it was actually 1977.

I had convinced myself this happened to me at the same age my mom lost her virginity and got married, as if that somehow made it better in my mind. I wasn't seventeen when he raped me. In fact he was twenty-four years old and I was just sixteen. I was a five-foot, one-hundred-pound child, a child who had been on this earth for just sixteen years. We found photos of me, sunburned and sad, sitting next to my rapist with a forced smile on my face.

In a conversation over café con leche and bagels for desayuno that spilled into an afternoon of tequila and quesadillas fritas, Mom talked about her own sexuality, abuse, and sex life with my dad. When Mom was six years old, her mom took her to a neighborhood movie theater in La Colonia Narvarte. She went to use the girls' bathroom, and there was a man with his pants down and an erection. He gave my mom a strip of satin and told her to tie a bow on it. My mom did and then she left. There were three or four more incidents we knew nothing about until right then. She talked about almost being raped at her job twice by male coworkers in the seventies.

"Mom! You are a survivor!"

"Ay, no, mijita. It just happened. That's all."

I told this to Cristina, my therapist, and she helped me make the connection. She freed me from guilt.

I had every right to be hot, horny, and desirous the night I was raped, she told me. I had the right to choose desire and trust.

"Lust, the same one your mother had for your father on that first night and the lust you had for your rapist, were in many ways the same. Your mom got a marriage and a healthy relationship with sexuality. Your sense of trust and intimacy was impacted and because you were violently raped your experience with sex was hurt, but not forever."

Could this be why I often recoiled from sex? Was this why having an orgasm took so long to conquer? Was this what my shame looked like? What my self-blame looked like?

"Sex is about trust and you trusted this man and you were not wrong to trust him," Cristina continued. "He was wrong to violate that trust and assault you. You had every right to want sex then and anytime you want. Your sexual desire is a beautiful, powerful thing. Expressing it is not only a form of self-love, but also a way to return to intimacy with the man you love and who you know now deeply loves you back. And he has always been able to express it by making love."

"El te quiere, Maria," Cristina said. "Gérman called and we had a chance to talk. He loves you, Maria. He adores you. He doesn't want to leave you.

"Maria. You have so much. But it's your turn to give. And you have to give of yourself to the people who are around you the most, your family. You have to give lovingly and without ego to yourself. Then you give to everyone else."

Cristina told me to think about fighting for my marriage, my family, and for my relationship with my husband as if I were fighting for my last breath. She didn't know that was one of Gérman's favorite sayings about life.

When you have nothing to lose, you'll keep breathing and fighting until the end. Cuando no tienes nada que perder, seguirás respirando y luchando hasta el final. As with everything else, I didn't give up. I kept on breathing. In and out. Slow.

"This will be one of the greatest lessons you can teach your daughter and son," Cristina said. "You love your husband, you love your family. You are going to show them what it looks like to fight for the things that truly matter."

I had to stop fighting against everyone and every institution. I had to change the way I was fighting. Needing constant validation from the men and institutions around me in order to feel enough was tiring. I never felt good enough, always like an imposter. I had to go through hell to get to the other side.

Now with Cristina's help, whenever I think of that scary night at the top of a sea cliff, I have an image of myself with a superpower: arms strong enough to push away an elephant if one tried to crush me. I came out on the other side of pain being a better lover, a more erotic woman, a more present and romantic human being because I was able to look at what that man took away from me. Because to him, I was nothing.

But I claimed my power and took it back. And now I fully own my sex and my passion.

Chapter 17

Illegal Is Not a Noun

When the Bush administration opened the T. Don Hutto Family Detention Center in Taylor, Texas, in 2005, even the young children being detained there who had arrived in the US with their parents were forced to wear prison-style jumpsuits.[1] But this wasn't the first time the government had detained families. The Berks Family Residential Center in Leesport, Pennsylvania, began housing detained immigrant families in 2001. It had already been holding children since 1998.[2]

A report compiled by the Lutheran Immigration and Refugee Service and the Women's Commission for Refugee Women and Children in 2007 reported that the "policy" at detention camps was that if a child woke up at night and left their bed to look for their parents, the alarm would sound and only guards were allowed to respond.[3] A follow-up report in 2014 revealed that, in many cases, small children in detention lost weight due to malnutrition, lacked adequate access to medical treatment and mental health services, did not attend school, and could not keep toys in their cells.[4]

Everyone acted surprised about the children being picked up crossing the border, but the numbers were there. The arrival of unaccompanied minors who were fleeing violence, poverty, and abuse in countries like Honduras, Guatemala, and El Salvador had been increasing steadily since 2011. That year, 24,120 children arrived. By 2016, it had increased to 58,819 children.[5] Some of us were waving our hands and telling those stories. Yeah, people were "tired" of immigrant stories in the 1990s and 2000s. That's one of the reasons why George W. Bush and Obama got away with so much. Remember Elián González? The child refugee crisis started under Clinton, but the government didn't seem to care enough.

Under the direction of Obama, secretary of Homeland Security Jeh Johnson turned up the screws on immigrants in what he insists was a deeply humanitarian decision: detain the entire family instead of releasing them! He claimed it was a humanitarian decision to end something called "catch and release." As in fish.

The "catch and release" policy had originally been embraced by Obama's administration as a way to avoid massive detention (the federal government spent north of $3 billion for the 2018 fiscal year to detain and house all of these people—that is what your taxes are paying for). Immigrants were "released" because historically these migrants posed no threat and data showed they would actually appear for their court dates. It was the more humane way to deal with them.[6] Not to treat them like fish but to treat them like what they are: desperate people, families, children alone who are escaping for their lives. Wait, doesn't this country advertise that on its website? Release them.

As disgusting and dehumanizing a term as "catch and release" is, it was actually the more compassionate thing to do. They hadn't yet realized the new formula for making a shit ton of money, i.e., house and detain immigrants + private prisons = kaching! The consequences of this policy shift were tragic. Most detained families, often mothers and their children, were subjected to prison-like conditions in camps rife with abuse and denied basic rights like due process, before being fast-tracked for deportation.[7]

On April 6, 2018, Jeff Sessions announced a new "zero tolerance" policy toward "criminal immigration enforcement" as US attorney general. Citing a 203 percent increase in "illegal" border crossings from March 2017 to March 2018, Sessions argued, "The situation at our Southwest Border is unacceptable. Congress has failed to pass effective legislation that serves the national interest—that closes dangerous loopholes and fully funds a wall along our southern border. As a result, a crisis has erupted at our Southwest Border that necessitates an escalated effort to prosecute those who choose to illegally cross our border."[8]

The policy of taking kids and babies away from new immigrants hadn't been labeled a policy per se until this announcement. Parents had to be separated from their children, it was alleged, so that they could be prosecuted for "illegal entry." They could end up serving their sentence in Willacy, the place where hell existed in 2011.

The message was clear. Since we didn't build the wall and Mexico didn't pay for it and you brown people insist on coming here, we are going to take away your kids to punish you and make you never even think about coming to this country. Stay the fuck out or we will keep your kids and you will never see them again.

In June 2018, the government began "housing" unaccompanied minors (they call them UACs for short, which stands for *unaccompanied alien children*, a term I still refuse to use) who had crossed the border, as well as children separated from their families, in tents at Tornillo, Texas. The facility opened with the capacity for four hundred children; by the time it was condemned and closed in January 2019, it was holding nearly three thousand children.

———

The *New York Times* has used the term *illegal immigrants* in a headline as recently as 2017, despite the fact that the Associated Press revised its usage guidelines on the term in 2013: "Use illegal only to refer to an action, not a person: illegal immigration, but not illegal immigrant."[9] The *Times*'s own style guide admits that the term is contentious, though they do not reject its use completely. Instead, it suggests to writers: "Without taking sides or resorting to euphemism, consider alternatives when appropriate to explain the specific circumstances of the person in question or to focus on actions: who crossed the border illegally; who overstayed a visa; who is not authorized to work in this country."[10]

Yet the use of the term *illegal* to refer to immigrants, propagated by the almighty USA, is alive and thriving. Look at some of the most widely read and watched news publications and TV channels, and you see it everywhere: "ICE warns **illegal immigrants** facing murder, child sex offense charges could be released in North Carolina sanctuary cities," says Fox News.[11] In 2018, a writer in *The Atlantic* asked, "How should the United States treat **illegal immigrants**?"[12] A 2019 op-ed in the *Washington Post* was titled "**Illegal immigrants** have rights. Shaping American democracy isn't one of them."[13] "Bipartisan House Deal Opens Path to Citizenship for **Illegal Immigrant** Farmworkers," read a headline in the *Wall Street Journal*.[14]

When Donald Trump got elected, ICE agents said they were finally unshackled, and they were. They took parents dropping off their kids at school, attempted to deport a child on life support, seized people who were going in for their legal marriage visas, and even took people out of courtrooms for the first time. They continued to apprehend people from their cars, buses, airports, private homes, jobs, parks, playgrounds, factories, etc.

There was a pattern to their raids. I thought back to what I learned in my studies of COINTELPRO in the 1960s. The most effective strategy is to target leaders so that you can bring down organizations. That's what ICE was doing.

The first immigrant journalist they detained was Manuel Duran, who was born in El Salvador. He was arrested in 2018 while covering a protest in Memphis, Tennessee; he was detained for 465 days. Some of his previous work had reported on alleged cooperation between law enforcement and ICE.[15] The first immigrant rights activist targeted was Erika Andiola, a leader in Arizona's DREAM coalition. On January 11, 2013, under the Obama administration, ICE raided her home and took her mother and brother.[16] Andiola later became a spokesperson for Bernie Sanders's 2016 campaign.

Now it was as if they had come and broken into the hunger strike of Central American refugees at Riverside Church that I covered as a college student and taken everyone. Back then the government took Reverend John Fife and charged him with felonies for helping the refugees. Now it was beginning to look like fascism. ICE agents were hanging out on street corners in front of Hostos Community College in the South Bronx, a predominantly Latinx community college. Just standing there as a show of force. In New York City. So imagine Omaha.

They were taking away people's US passports and not reissuing them unless they could show more proof that they were American born. ICE was doing this to Spanish speakers who were born on the US-Mexico border and delivered by a midwife, not in a hospital. Cristela Alonzo, the comedic actress and activist, has a brother whose passport was taken away; he was told to come up with more proof he was really an American. And then President Trump ordered US Citizenship and Immigration Services (USCIS) to go back into the records and find people who should be stripped of their citizenship based on inconsistencies in their files via Operation Second Look.[17] In 2020, the Department of Justice went one step further and opened an office dedicated to denaturalizing immigrants.

None of this is normal. None of it. Just like it wasn't normal to have a blacklist during the McCarthy era. It wasn't normal for American citizens of Japanese descent to be incarcerated "for their own good." It was never normal to lynch black men and Mexicans and Chinese for minor infractions, or worse, for simply existing.

I think about the death threats I received from the right-wing, CIA-sponsored Omega 7 when I was a WKCR DJ. I remember when my Dominican neighbor up in Washington Heights told me the FBI had rung her door and asked for me in 1983. I think about the *X* I always get on my passport paperwork when I'm coming back from international travel.

I'm not that important. Don't take yourself so seriously, I mumble to myself. Bajale, bajale, *come down from your high horse.*

But my application for citizenship was done in pen, not on computer. That's how old it is. The truth is, I have to ask myself, what's to stop them from coming after me?

I talk myself down by telling this joke. If this president comes after me it's because I am five things he hates the most: I am Mexican, an immigrant, a journalist, a woman, and pause—wait for it—I am flat-chested.

I laugh because otherwise I'll cry.

These are the things that tumbled forward in a kind of nausea of thoughts: my student who is a citizen gets punched in the nose by his noncitizen older brother, a drug-crazed mistake or the accumulated rage of not having what your brother has, those ten numbers on a Social Security card. Uziel, a young man from a neighborhood store, is questioned while getting on a bus in Rochester; even though he had his DACA card, he is not allowed to board the bus, as if he were some kind of human threat; his detention is stayed because his mom happened to be by her phone in NYC. My students, several of them, have to deal with court dates and ICE check-ins. Parents who used to take their family out regularly for a meal to celebrate being together now won't leave the house even to go to the corner store. Undercover ICE agents ripping a mother away from her kids, who are screaming in horror in front of an ice cream truck. (The real thing sounds so different from a horror movie. You cannot imitate the sound of this kind of pain.) Deporting a child from her hospital room.

Since when did the Constitution say, *Hey, by the way, this document is only for those of you who have papers*? If you can't prove you were born here, no constitutional rights for you. Says who exactly?

I will never forget when I interviewed Mark Krikorian, the executive director of the Center for Immigration Studies, in 2011, and he looked me in the eye and explained, *Immigrants are part of our country's past. We were that country that needed immigrants. We aren't that country anymore. That was in our country's adolescence. We are a mature country now. That immigrant narrative isn't us anymore.*

That is exactly where we are today. Even immigrants and the children of immigrants and the grandchildren of immigrants think undocumented immigrants should be deported.

Chapter 18

The Power of Standing in the Light

There was only one cousin who really saw me for who I was during those annual trips from Chicago to El DF.

On those rainy Mexico City summer afternoons when there was always a guaranteed downpour, Sergio would pull out his worn guitar and sing the classics to me: "Cielito Lindo" and "Piel Canela," among others. On one particular rainy Monday he sang a song I didn't recognize.

"It's called 'La Golondrina,'" he whispered to me, "and that's what you are to me." A swallow.

"You are a little bird that flies back and forth, crossing borders and states every year. You travel far and see many things, but you always come home to me and Mexico, just like the golondrinas do."

Sergio was the first member of the family who told me that my border crossings were what made me special and magical—like a bird who can fly thousands of miles. Not like a dirty specimen who doesn't fit in in either country and often feels like the borders slice her apart from the family and person she wants to be.

Around the end of winter 2019, Mami was wrapping up her extended stay in Mexico, where she lives during the harsh winter months in Chicago. She went to the weekly comida en la casa de la tía Gloria, a meal that typically gathers together as many family members as are available. It's just family, which means that anything can happen— a verbal spit fight, dramatic tears, exuberant declarations of love, or long, pensive moments of silence.

After the comida, during the sobremesa, Mami started talking about the Mexican presidential campaigns and her thoughts on the Mexican electorate being tired of the stagnant, corrupt politics of the PRI and the PAN, two of the longtime major parties. She said she believed Mexicans would vote for the left because they were exhausted by the status quo ping-pong between these two parties that had produced little structural change.

Sergio became enraged when my mom spoke with such ownership about her fellow Mexicans and their voting patterns. My mom was the tía he always loved most because she changed his diapers and fed him as an infant. They had a special bond, but in that moment Sergio could not contain his anger. He yelled at my mother and told her she had no right to express her opinion about Mexican politics. She was a gringa!

Over the years, my cousin Sergio and his family had become devout Opus Dei Catholics, the most strident wing of an already conservative spiritual tradition. They resisted traditional PRI party politics in Mexico (the party that held power for seventy-one years) by becoming supporters of the once-outsider-party PAN, which is also very right wing. Mom has always been politically progressive.

When Mami told me about this incident, I remembered how my dad was bullied and called a vendido for having moved to the US. My mom, however, is still a Mexican citizen, since she reclaimed her citizenship after she had to give it up to become a US citizen in 1996. My cousin lashed out at Mami for having an opinion on Mexican politics because she lived in the US. His version of nationalism was

Mexico for Mexicans. She and her "gringo" opinions were no longer welcome in his house.

The argument culminated with Sergio, who is very tall, looking down at Mami and telling her she should leave Mexico and go back to where she came from: Los Estados Unidos.

This hatred and suspicion of the other is a sickness that is spreading everywhere. Every one of us is responsible for trying to stop its expansion and dissemination; that much is within our control.

A few months later, I saw Sergio in person and told him the story of "La Golondrina"—it was he who gave me my freedom to be joyous about myself, instead of focusing on my never-enough-ness.

You, primo, made me whole. How can you let rhetoric fill you now, with fear of the person I was and am? A happy, fluttering golondrina who sees only endless clouds, not finite walls.

He was deeply moved. Before I left his home, as my cab waited outside, he began to sing "La Golondrina" to me a cappella with tears in his eyes.

On many mornings—when the sun is beaming down on my head from the east side of Manhattan, or when in the dead of a winter Sunday the silence is so heavy you can hear the snowflakes falling, or when the birds are up at four in the morning looking for food in the dumpsters of Harlem—I wake with a shudder. My eyes pop open and in the darkness of my room, my heart contracts. All I see are the numb eyes in the pallid face of that little girl in the McAllen airport.

I breathe through the complicated feelings of my own buried anguish, attempting to feel what this little girl might be feeling hundreds of miles away. And yet I realize how impossible, even ludicrous and not helpful, that idea is. I see the face of the little girl and how her lack of expression said it all to me: she had left to escape a horror never realizing she was being placed into another. Here was a horror she never could have imagined, because how could she? Her town was in the mountains. They don't have concrete buildings made to house children in gated crates there, as if children were dogs that need to be put in pens. But that's how it is in the United States of America. We get the message.

Every day the facts get worse. Those millions of dollars and decades spent on the right-wing, white nationalist, anti-immigrant think tanks, giving dollars to closed-border-sympathizing academics, have all paid off. The policies are changing almost daily and the stranglehold on not letting any more people into our America tightens.

Now you cannot ask for asylum from within the US. Now you have to ask for asylum in the country you are afraid to live in. Now you have to wait in line. Now a family can be held indefinitely. Now there is government data that proves the psychological damage done to children who are ripped from their parents' arms. Now children are cavity searched. Now you don't need to pass a background check to become a guard in these places. Now children are being held at privately run detention camps. Now we have records and complaints that show women are raped at facilities, and year after year these places still pass audits because the audits are done internally.

During the period of time I wrote this book—about twelve months—the profits for the private prison industry were projected to grow to $5.9 billion in 2019, even while crime and incarceration rates were falling.[1]

These places that house women, children, and men are hidden in plain sight. They are everywhere: Texas, Pennsylvania, California, Louisiana, Alaska, Michigan, Georgia, Arizona, Colorado, New York, and the District of Columbia. There are now more than two hundred detention camps, centers, facilities, and jails across thirty states. They are tied to business growth in multiple sectors, like transportation, phone and communications, and cleaning and food services, and run by companies with innocuous names like the GEO Group, Inc.; CoreCivic; Asset Protection & Security Services LP; Ahtna, Inc.; and Doyon Limited.

Even the most progressive politicians, like socialist Bernie Sanders, for example, talk about the need for "border security." They say they will focus on deporting only "criminals"—something Sanders said to me in an interview and I pressed him hard. A week later, he finally voiced support for a moratorium on all deportations. Days before the Nevada caucuses, Biden finally spoke to Jorge Ramos (still not me) and said the Obama immigration policies were a mistake. He fell short of apologizing.

If crossing the border without papers because you are fleeing life-threatening danger is a crime, if coming back to the US to see the children you had to leave behind because you were deported is a crime, then who are we to judge?

Sometimes people I meet tell me to my face how they are afraid of being overrun by Mexicans. White liberals unknowingly say similar low-grade discriminatory things about immigration being out of control. They wring their hands and wonder what they can do—to help? Or is it to make themselves feel safe?

Can people just help other human beings? You have got to be pretty self-aware, which often means living in the uncomfortable space of asking yourself—was that right? It's not that I want you to live in imposter syndrome with me, but I am asking you to live like the other in society. Not like the center.

I always go back to the image of my daughter attending that elite private high school in New York City. At the end of her first year, she was having a challenging time there socially and often cried in the privacy of the bathroom during the school day. Sometimes, though, she left the classroom in tears.

The school called me in for a meeting with my daughter and the director of the school, the dean of her class, and the school social worker. The tenor of our polite yet serious conversation was that Yurema was perhaps too emotional to make it in their highly competitive but we-are-so-committed-to-diversity sort of community.

After our meeting, I asked my daughter to give me a moment and wait for me outside the stately hundred-year-old director's office.

"There is something I think you should know," I said to the three school officials sitting in front of me, remembering the sage words of Sandy to put honey on my tongue before speaking. "My daughter has a group of girls here who have befriended her. . . ."

"Yes, such a nice group of young women," one of them said, as if it were a generous thing for a clique of girls to open themselves up and let one more in.

"Yes, those same girls," I continued, "they tell her Mexican jokes. And they berate her for being bilingual. This might help you understand why my daughter cries here."

Their jaws dropped.

———————

There will be great art during the worst times of our lives.

I was standing on the US side of the border fence overlooking the beautiful and expansive Rio Grande, which is always written about as if it were a war zone. Yet it is the river that made this stretch of land—six miles from the US Border Patrol Central Processing Center in McAllen, Texas—one of the most impressive bird-watching areas in the world.

It was late afternoon and instead of a group of bird-watchers with binoculars, there was a small, mostly Latinx crowd watching a full-on protest performance by self-labeled dragtavists. There were toddlers in strollers and college student protesters. There was also an older white couple sitting on two pullout lawn chairs, gleefully applauding the queer men with big hair and over-the-top makeup strutting up and down the border fence in full Mexican drag.

Down the street from the protest, Mike Benavides, a Mexican

American man who works eight to four in the local McAllen school district, was busy shuffling back and forth to Matamoros on the Mexican side of the border with supplies for the dozens of people sleeping outside as they "waited in line" to ask for asylum in the US. Among the people waiting were a four-month-old baby, a pregnant woman who was six months along, and at least ten toddlers and their parents.

By June of 2018, he couldn't take seeing the images of his own city on the news. So he got off his couch and started waking up early at his ranch house in the McAllen suburbs, spending part of his salary to buy breakfast burritos and coffee, and delivering food and other supplies to the people sleeping on the sidewalk in Matamoros. He goes to work all day after making this morning drop-off; he then does the same thing at night, bringing tacos and water so that these humble, desperate people know they are not invisible.

It took our country fifty years of visual reporting on TV to get to the point of a savvy media-heavy construction of immigrants as the most feared people in the country. We are not the legacy of this place, after all. We are its menace.

And now it is on every single one of us, every single day, to deconstruct this bullshit.

There are thousands of daily actions we can take to do this, from the simplest—saying good morning and thank you to the day laborers and gardeners, nannies, and delivery people—to the most engaged and committed—forming a neighborhood watch group to alert your neighbors when undercover ICE agents are around, volunteering in one of the thousands of humanitarian, church-based, or political organizations that strive to make us all feel connected and visible, and supporting independent journalists like me and their noncommercial POC-led newsrooms. As of this writing, I am the only Latina running a nonprofit newsroom in the US.

When I feel low, which is often, I walk through my Harlem neighborhood and sit at the statue of Harriet Tubman or Frederick Douglass. I ponder the challenges they faced, and then after a day of sadness and rest, I get back to it, like they did. Only recently did my French-born colleague and producer of *Unladylike*, a digital doc series, Charlotte Mangin, introduce me to the American journalist, suffragist, and humanitarian Jovita Idar, who was born in 1885 in Laredo, Texas. She was a columnist who criticized Woodrow Wilson's policy in Mexico. The next thing she knew, the Texas Rangers came to her newspaper and tried to shut it down. Tiny like me, she used her five-foot body to block them from taking away her right to Freedom of the Press.

Tubman, Douglass, Idar—I am their legacy. That is the truth of this country. That we see ourselves in the people most unlike us on a daily basis, but most certainly when we are forced to survive and save each other.

When two planes hit the World Trade Towers, no one stopped to ask people their religious affiliation or place of origin before pulling them from the ash.

You help break down the wall when you spend a moment reflecting on your own immigrant roots and talking about them, especially if they didn't come with papers, to others who have forgotten their families were once immigrants, too.

Doing something about this means opening your eyes and asking questions and understanding that people are being denied basic due process on a daily basis: no phone call, no Miranda rights, no lawyer, no date by which they must be released.

Change starts with knowledge: thousands of children are being held and sent across state lines with strangers; people in your own communities are making money off of immigrant detention; universities are invested in private prisons; women and men are being held in concentration camps with no legally binding standard for how they should be taken care of, the quality of food they are served, or the cleanliness and safety of the facilities they're housed in; there are no guarantees that they won't be raped.

Sadly, some of the most abusive guards in these torture chambers on the southern border are Latinx themselves. We need whistle-blowers to speak out and tell the truth about what they see. A paycheck will never erase being a witness to the humiliation of an innocent human being whose only real crime, like me, was not having been born in the US.

In October 1996, after Clinton signed his retrograde Illegal Immigration Reform and Immigrant Responsibility Act into action, there was a massive pro-immigrant-rights demonstration in DC. It was a celebration, but it was also an affront to President Bill Clinton. His anti-immigrant rhetoric was searing and nonstop. Twenty-five thousand people showed up, including Gérman and me. Gérman was carrying Raúl in a back carrier and playing a snare drum to rev up the crowd. There were no arrests.

In 2006, when the pressure cooker was growing, President George W. Bush had decided to unleash ICE, and private prisons were just getting into the game, there was another round of massive nonviolent pro-immigrant demonstrations. The Spanish-language DJs made it happen by telling immigrants to come out to the streets: "Show them who we are. See us! Don't believe what they say about us."

See us.

Half a million people in Dallas. The same in Los Angeles. Another one hundred thousand people in Chicago. Not one arrest. And yet we are labeled as criminals and lawbreakers? Not a single arrest amid the Mexican, Salvadoran, Colombian, Dominican, Ethiopian, Irish, and American flags? Not one.

We were ignored and the detention and deportations sped up, and only because of activists who took on Obama directly in 2012—they chained themselves to his reelection campaign offices—did he create DACA. It was not because he felt like it.

The people at the center of this American story have been taking to the streets, but they can't do it on their own any longer. We all need to speak up.

I have often struggled to see myself as a part of the arc of history in this country, where I arrived in 1962 and was marked as a "dirty Mexican" who needed to be inspected and "deloused." It wasn't by chance that the immigration agent spotted a rash on my skin that day at the Dallas airport. He was, in fact, looking for it. He had been trained to look for someone like me. Imperfect. Had he succeeded in separating me from my mother, he would have then deposited me in a room in the Dallas/Fort Worth International Airport where they quarantined all the "dirty Mexicans."

Immigration officials in El Paso, Texas, launched a disinfection campaign in 1917 to ensure that Mexican laborers who routinely crossed the border into the US for work were not bringing disease and vermin into the country. They did this by subjecting people to full-body inspections, vinegar and kerosene baths, and toxic fumigations using Zyklon-B gas and DDT. Although the various chemical treatments changed over the years, this policy of "delousing" immigrants remained in place until 1964, when the Bracero Program ended.

What almost happened to me, what is now happening to thousands of families every day, was not a chance encounter. It was prescribed immigration policy. But for my mother's voice, I would have been excluded from this country.

So how did I ever find connection to this place?

The writing of this book made me understand the connections I needed to make. It was here, where I delve deep into the stories of the immigrants who came before me, that I found my own story. I now see myself in the Asian women from "China, Japan, and any other Oriental country" who were the first to be excluded from coming here by the Page Act of 1875. The history books written by white men said that these women were prohibited from entering because they were sex workers. The US government used their sex to keep them out, when they were more likely women hoping to escape poverty and oppression, or wives looking to reunite with their husbands, just like my mom.

I am their legacy. I am writing my own American history, not only making these invisible women visible but also tenderly inviting them in to take up space in my heart. Their longing to be here is one I can understand.

For a long time, I looked at those who arrived on Ellis Island and saw only distance between us. They were the "welcomed," "legitimate" immigrants, the ones who came "the right way." I wasn't them. But then, during my research, a Jewish professor connected the dots for me: my almost-quarantine story in the Dallas/Fort Worth airport was related to, in fact followed in the tradition of, those immigrants quarantined on Ellis Island, who were prevented from stepping foot on the island where I now live, Manhattan—an island where the first white pilgrims arrived without papers or permission, and carried infections that killed off tens of thousands of people indigenous to this land.

For over a century, they have quarantined us and searched our bodies for the illnesses they say we bring. Today, as you read this, body cavity searches are being conducted on immigrant and refugee women and children.

Something else haunted me. Since I was a girl, why had I felt a profound yet invisible tether to the Jewish people attacked by Hitler? Why did I feel so strongly when even my DNA confirmed, in spite of my expectations, that I was not a member of their tribe?

It was only after the tragedy of the shooting in El Paso in the summer of 2019 that I realized the same gas they used to "sanitize" the clothing of the "dirty Mexicans" who crossed the border there and throughout Texas would end up being the same gas used to kill Jewish people in the concentration camp gas chambers. The Nazis had been inspired by photographs of the airtight rooms in El Paso used to gas immigrant clothing; they used American ideas to design the rooms they built to gas human beings.

We are tied to each other and we didn't even know it.

I hope I am following in Harriet Tubman's footsteps, because she had the capacity to dream of liberation. Not all of us allow ourselves to fulfill our dreams of freedom. Maybe you dream of being free from a job, a relationship, a city. . . . But acting on freedom can be the scariest thing we do. To believe we are so radically free that we can dream the craziest, wildest dreams for ourselves and then work nonstop to make them come true, no matter the odds. No matter the borders we have to cross. No matter how many glass ceilings we have to crash through. This struggle, the restless determination, the feeling of urgency that comes with working to make things better—it never really goes away.

It was a sticky August evening when I made my way to a church near what used to be the seedy part of midtown in New York City. I was alone. No assistant, no producer, no audio recorder. Just me wearing flats, something I do only when I want to intentionally come off as small and nonthreatening.

Recently, I met a high-powered Latina media executive who now spends most of her days volunteering with newly arrived Central American refugee women and babies. She introduced me to Noemi. When I met Noemi in the midtown church she had a chicle on her left hip stuck to her so hard that he barely budged. His face was nuzzled into Noemi's left armpit. Four-year-old Bobby and his twenty-one-year-old mom had arrived in the US a year earlier, but both remained in substantial and visible trauma.

Bobby was mute and blind when they crossed into the US in August 2018, begging for safety. His mother, Noemi, was a survivor. She said local Mafia had killed her father for his land. Her son was a product of rape. The baby's father had tried to kill her and her brother more than once by trying to run them over with a speeding car. The only place safe for her and her disabled son was far away from everything she knew.

They were in a detention camp for nine long days.

They tried to take Bobby from Noemi but, like my own mother, she began to screech and scream and create a ruckus in the detention facility. The guards worried she would inspire other mothers to do the same, so they let her keep her blind son, who uttered no words or sounds.

If he was taken away, how could he ever be reunited with his mother? That would only be possible if mother and son were each permanently marked, tattooed . . . and so she never let go of the boy.

Was it possible for the horror of life in detention to get worse? Yes. Her account was one I had never heard before. The women and children were woken up every hour to be "counted and checked." As a result, they were beyond sleep-deprived. Not only were they kept in "la hielera," the freezing icebox torture chamber that leaves no permanent marks, but they were also psychologically tortured and told that if they did not physically carry their children in their arms that the guards would take them away. One afternoon, a mother took a nap and her arms had fallen away from around her toddler's waist.

A guard came in and, as the horrified mothers were about to scream to wake her up, he told them that if they did he would take their children away, too. They watched in silence as the guard took the sleeping child. The mother woke up in a panic. She screamed and cried for hours and hours. She pleaded with the guards. They came and got her and she had to get on her knees and beg for her child. Then they returned her alone to her cell without him. Finally, after hours, they returned the distraught child to his traumatized mother. It was punishment and a statement to prove that they were serious about taking their children unless they were like chicle, stuck to your body.

The day I met Noemi and Bobby I didn't bring my recorder, but it would not have mattered. Bobby had never uttered a word in public before. Watching a mute child cry is confusing. The face contorts, the mouth looks like it should be letting out a wail, but not a sound comes out.

I was introduced to Noemi and Bobby by Virginia, a white woman from East Grand Rapids, Michigan, who has lived in New York for the last ten years. Several months ago, as she watched the television, listening to the wails of babies ripped from their mother's arms, she decided she could no longer sit in her living room and do nothing. Some of the separated children and parents, she had heard, might be arriving at LaGuardia Airport, not far from her apartment in Astoria, Queens.

"I live ten minutes away from there. How could I not go?" she told me.

Soon she had linked up with a grassroots organization and began greeting immigrants released from detention at LaGuardia and Port Authority Bus Terminal. Government agencies say they care about the treatment of vulnerable women and children, but once they pass their credible fear interview they are released from detention without any further assistance or guidance. They are not free. ICE tightly clamped a plastic electronic shackle to Noemi's leg and told her she was under house arrest from 6:00 p.m. to 6:00 a.m. They dropped her and Bobby off at a bus station in Texas. She bought tickets to New York City to meet up with an uncle she had never met who lived in the Bronx. After forty-eight hours on the bus, they arrived at Port Authority and that's where Noemi and Bobby met Virginia.

Virginia was raised in a well-to-do family and grew up a theater nerd. She works as a nanny by day and an actress and singer by night.

Virginia is also a survivor. She ran away from home as a teenager to escape the emotional abuse her family inflicted on her. She had the white picket fence, but she also suffered from trauma and suicidal thoughts. Meeting Noemi, she understood her immediately and saw a version of her younger self who had run away from home.

Noemi agreed to let me tell their story on *Latino USA* as long as I changed their names.

The second time I met Bobby, in early September 2019, he had started going to special education school. It was the first time in his life he had ever been in a classroom with other children. He was, miraculously, beginning to say words, in private, only to Noemi, but in English and Spanish. He would never have been allowed in school in Honduras. They said he was incapable of learning.

That day I got close to his ear and I realized he remembered my voice from the first time I met him a month before. I asked him if I could hug him, which I did. Then, in a mom-like way and with tremendous tenderness, I asked if I could tickle him, and he didn't resist when I did, gently, on his sides.

Then Bobby started to laugh out loud in delight and so did I. We fell into a momentary hypnotic lapse of giggles and tickles.

A week later I called Noemi the night before she was going to see the judge in her asylum case. She would be accompanied by Virginia, her lawyer, and six other supporters. I asked if Bobby was there and if she could put him on speakerphone.

After hearing my voice for a few seconds, Bobby, all on his own, started to squeal, just like he did during our trance. I started to squeal back and I was crying because, before my own eyes, I was witnessing the capacity of one child to soften, after a full year of intensive therapy, enough so that he could laugh. Previously he hadn't even been able to make a sound of agony. Now he was owning his voice through joy.

I imagine Bobby will grow up and tell his story in both English and Spanish. He will talk about the group of women who surrounded him and his mother with love, how they got together every week. In the auditorium of a New York City church they would be together, this self-made community of survivors, from Grand Rapids, Michigan, to Tegucigalpa. They played the drums of the Garifuna people, an Afro-indigenous group that historians wrote off but has survived over the centuries.

When people ask me what interview has inspired me the most in my career, it would make sense to say Sonia Sotomayor, the most powerful Latina in the world, or Michelle Bachelet, the first woman president I ever interviewed, who served as Chile's president twice.

Both women did inspire me. But these days it is Noemi and Bobby who shed their light on me. They are flawed, uneven human beings mistaken as misfits, as the miserable. To me, Bobby and Noemi are finding their voices quite literally and I am humbled to be allowed to witness this.

I feel some mystical tie to Bobby. My father wanted to give those who lacked it the gift of hearing. I bet there is a medical doctor out there who will be able to help Bobby regain his sight. And Noemi is like my own mother. She stood up for herself and her vulnerable child. Noemi, like my mom, was a woman born to be an American citizen because she was actually willing to die for her right to speak up and protect her child. My mom was ready to take on a man who looked like a redwood; she was prepared to do whatever it took to never let them take me, just like Noemi did with Bobby.

I am you, Noemi. I am you, Bobby.

I will be your chicle, too. I will attempt to tell your story with respect so you are not silenced and not invisible.

These are my truest inspirations, the ones who may be invisible to you, but who are in fact everywhere around us. Everywhere around you.

If you would just open your eyes and see them.

Acknowledgments

It is January 20, 2020, the day before the Senate impeachment trial of the forty-fifth president. I have just returned from visiting Juarez and Tapachula on Mexico's northern and southern borders. The so-called wall is there now, in southern Mexico! My two countries are actively turning their backs on migrants and refugees, and so the story about immigration keeps getting worse. My heart is heavy but I don't plan on giving up telling these stories.

My thanks first of all go to Deepa . . . If it wasn't for Deepa Donde, who said to me excitedly one fall morning in 2017, "You *have* to write this book," it probably would not have happened. And if it wasn't for you, Deepa, as the chair of the board of my little nonprofit that could, Futuro Media, we wouldn't be celebrating a decade! You are the engine of light that pushes me beyond my fear and for that I will always be indebted.

I am so thankful to everyone who has worked with me at Futuro Media. By now there are so many past and present Futuristas that I could not name them all, but during the writing of this book, the staff pulled together hard for me, especially the teams from *Latino USA* and *In The Thick*. Particular thanks to Erika Dilday, Marlon Bishop, Julio Ricardo Varela, Miguel Macias, Maggie Freleng, Antonia Cerejido, Nicole Rothwell, Charlotte Mangin, Diane Sylvester, Sophia Paliza-Carre, Fernanda Camarena, Julieta Martinelli, Janice

311

Llamoca, Amanda Alcantara, Juan Pablo Garnham, Nour Saudi, Fernanda Echavarri, Stephanie Lebow, Julia Caruso, Luis Luna, Natalia Fidelholtz, Stacey LeMelle, Yolanda Moore, Leah Shaw, Mario Gonzalez, Jared Lilly, Megan Wrappe, and Leta Hallowell. Thanks to my diligent assistants, Jennifer McDowell, Raúl Perez, and Lili "La Pescadita" Ruiz, who doubles as my TA. You make this *all* happen!

Many people I knew crossed over during the last decade. Their spirits came to me in the delightful hummingbirds that visited my desk in Punta Cana, where I wrote much of this book. Que VIVAN: Mi papá, Maritere Marin, Santiago Garza, Elaine Rivera, Dolores Prida, Kris Buxembaum, Mike Gittleman, Chris Kokenes, Madeline Parrasch, Brian Dvorsky, Lorraine and Debbie Godwin, Bob Baillie, Maria Tapia Belsito, mi tío Miguel Angel, mi primo Homerito Peña, mi tío y mi primo Hermilo Ojeda, Michelle Serros, Verta Mae Grovesnor, John Siceloff, Vidal Guzman, la grande Ana Real y mi querida Cecilia Vaisman. They, along with my ancestors, are the shoulders I lean on to find strength.

To my querida LIPSters who have gifted me with friendships that span almost three decades: Rossana Rosado, Rose Arce, Sandra Guzman, Sandra Garcia-Betancourt, Evelyn Hernandez, Lee Llambelis, Neyda Martinez Sierra, Gloria Montealegre, Ana Marengo, Tania Lambert, Edna Negrón, Maria Newman, Mireya Navarro, Maite Junco, Blanca Rosa Vilches, Michele Salcedo, Maritere, Margaret Ramirez, Rose R., Carolina Gonzalez, Laura M., Zulema Wiscovitch, and honorary LIPSter Mandalit del Barco.

For the dream deconstructions, the literary guidance and encouragement, and most of all for una amistad de la buena, my thanks to Sandra Cisneros. Your tender ways with humans and perritos are glorious to witness. I am blessed to have you in my life.

Thank you to la Susan Bergholz for being the first to see the writer in me. Gracias also to Bert Snyder. Thank you to Cherrie Moraga,

Julia Alvarez, Ana Castillo, Denise Chavez, Gabby Rivera, Yesika Salgado, and Elizabeth Acevedo for the inspiration.

To Elena Poniatowska, Blanche Petrich, Guadalupe Pineda, Maria Elena Salinas, and so many other Mexican and Latin American women journalists who are my role models. To Frederick Douglass, Harriet Tubman, Ida B. Wells, and Jovita Idar, who I imagined were sending encouragement my way on so many mornings of writing. To so many brilliant journalists who I have met along the way in my career: María Elena Salinas, Jorge Ramos, Jay Kernis, Scott Simon, Norman Morris, Karen Palmer, Esther Cepeda, Tammis Chandler, Stephen Ferry, Mark Carter, Suzi Schiffer, Gary Knell, Joseph Tovares, Michelle Smawley, Brenda Breslauer, Joy-Ann Reid, David Gura, Michelle Cumbo, and my colleagues at NPR, CBS News, PBS, CNN, and friends at MSNBC.

Thank you to the Latin American and Latino Studies Department at DePaul University, the Harvard Kennedy School Shorenstein Center on Media, and Barnard College for the honor of letting me be a professor. Thank you, Lourdes Torres, Sian Beilock, Linda Bell, Paige West, J.C. Salyer, Nicco Mele, Nancy Gibbs, and to each and every one of my students: remember the writing on the board.

To Cristela, Judy Reyes, Melissa Barrera, Justina Machado, Daphne Rubin-Vega, Diane Guerrero, Edna Chavez, Dascha Polanco, Che Che Luna, and Eve Ensler for your art and activism. Gracias Lin-Manuel and Jon M. Chu for a dream come true.

Futuro is our staff but also our board, so thanks to past and present members of the Futuro board of directors, among them Linda Shoemaker, Roy Cosme, Martha Spanninger, Diana Campoamor, Ingrid Duran, Renato Ramirez, Ken Lehman, Theresa Barron-McKeagney, Hal Strelnick, Phil Schreiber, Priscilla Rojas, Jonathan Garcia, Mariano Diaz, Carlos Miranda, and Carmen Rita Wong.

For the sisterhood, thank you to Nini Ordoubadi, Cat Gund, Sayu Bhojwani, Amy Bucher, Nina Alvarez, Alicia Bassuk, Quiara Alegria

Hudes, Nancy Trujillo, and for decades of amistad, David Hershey Webb.

I give thanks for Suave and Estrella, who have changed my life forever in ways that go beyond words. Thank you for trusting me with your lives and stories. You have given me light in darkness and made me understand that a prison doesn't limit us unless we let it.

My gratitude to Virginia, Noemi, and Bobby for bringing light and esperanza into my life today. For Suzi, Zoe, and Josue, thank you for telling me your stories.

I am deeply grateful for the joy given to me by my godchildren, Ana Rosa, Andres Vaisman Marx, and Liliana Marisela Chavarria. Thanks to Marina LaBarthe, CJ Strauss, and Sam Davis for teaching me the all-encompassing beauty of they/them.

Gracias to mis terapistas Andaye and Cristina Kartheiser. You saved my life and so many other parts of me.

Thank you to Vardit Buse and Sidney Liang. Thank you to my dear lawyer Neil Rosini for the small-print reading and patience during fifteen years. Gracias to Maria Belen for mi joyeria and to Flor de Cielo for my dresses.

Thank you to Leatress Tice, Xavior R. Qvistgaard, LaTonya Bynum, and Paul Thomas for pushing me beyond my physical limits. Thank you Myra Livingston; Pamela Kuma; Dragon Brown; and Hieu Thi Nguyen, or "Mimi," who was made from love during a war. Thank you for your inspiration.

Thank you to the founders of *Latino USA*, Maria Emilia Martin and Gilberto Cárdenas at the Center for Mexican American Studies at the University of Texas at Austin.

Thank you to my extended familia of listeners and staff of my favorite politics podcast, *In The Thick*, including Jamilah King, Wajahat Ali, Bill Ong Hing, Imara Jones, Christina M. Greer, Eddie Glaude

Jr. Michael German, Terrell Jr. Starr, Tina Vazquez, Jenni Monet, and LaTosha Brown.

Thanks to Dr. Joseph Tait, Larry Johnson, Latonya Jones, Arlene McCalla, Ramon de Jesus, Tameika Halliman, Wendy King, and Ericka Powell.

Shout-out to my Cambridge peeps: Amanda Matos, Mariangely Solis Cervera, and Maria Peniche. And to my Chicago hermanitas, Tanya Cabrera, Cindy Agustin, and Lulu Martinez. To my NYC reina Marta Moreno Vega, gracias for showing the path. Ashe.

Thanks to my "let's keep her healthy" team: Johanne Picard at Harlem Chi, Gregory Castro, Marvin Cooper, Larry Levitan, Cameron Rokhsar, Frank Lipman, Laurie Polis, Mark Nesselson, Elmo Randolph, and Shawn Shields.

Thank you to my speaker's bureau APB, to Bob Davis, all of the agents, and especially to Constance Wine.

Thank you to Patricia Alvarado, Catherine Pino, Nely Galan, Raquel Cepeda, Elena Scotti, Luis Moreno, Sean Collins, Jennifer Argueta, Jon Abbott, Denise Dilani, Daisy Rosario, John Guardo, Nadia Reiman, Yasmeen Querishi, Leda Hartman, Nusha Balyan, Andres Caballero, Flo Hernandez Ramos, Marea Chaveco, Zoe Malik, Los Penchazadehs, Michael Simon Johnson, Sayre Quevedo, Steve Meehan, Waltaya Culmer, Mario Diab, Carmen, Hazel, Antonia, Silvia, Rodrigo, Gonzalo Aburto, Virginia Frias, and Ornella Pedrozo.

Thank you, Kevin Abosch, for the beautiful portrait.

To my philanthropic family Darren Walker, Margaret Morton, Farai Chideya, Brian Eule, Beatriz Solis, Stephen Heintz, Tamara Kreinin, Luz Vega Marquis, Norris West, Lauren Pabst, Kathy Im, Geri Mannion, Vartan Gregorian, La June Montgomery Tabron, Arelis Diaz, Helena Huang, Ana Oliveira, Richard Besser, Maryam Elahi, Abigail Disney, Jordan Reese, Tanya Barrientos, Luis Ubiñas,

Michael Stubbs, Bill Resnick, Barabara Bridges, Elizabeth Alexander, Agnes Gund, and so many others who have believed in my vision, thank you deeply.

Thank you especially and forever to Fiona Druckenmiller.

Thank you to the team that brought *America By The Numbers* to TV and may we soon return: Paul de Lumen, Titi Yu, Sue Ding, Emily Harold, Paola Piers-Torres, and the dozens of people involved.

In Punta Cana, muchas gracias to Bienvenida Beltre, Florencio Castillo, Pedrito Guzman, Bolivar Gomez, Maria Hernandez, Ricardo Dalmasi, and Nestor Castillo, and to Oscar Imbert and la Confusa Bendecida for getting us to Punta Cana in the first place.

To Misha Baryshnikov and Lisa Rinemot, thank you for your lasting friendship.

To my readers Ilana Benady and Raúl Castillo, you were there at the start and finish and I relied on you more than you know.

To my researcher and reader Maya Doig-Acuña, and to your mom, Eugenia Acuña, por la amistad.

Thank you to Katie Salisbury, who was my daily writing boss for seven months. Your editing is precision, but it's your writer's soul that I love most. This book would not be here but for your assignments!

So much love and respect for Adriana Dominguez, my dear agent, who found solutions to my multiple problems and not once was frustrated by anything. Ever. ¡Que ejemplo de mujer! You helped bring this to fruition and I will always be grateful.

Michelle Herrera Mulligan is my book queen. MHM, you saw what this project could become and you touched us with your vision and you have been at my side throughout. You are my partner in this and more. Gracias for the work and the friendship. Te quiero.

I would be lost in so many ways were it not for Sandra Rattley. Thank you, Sandy, for being my sister forever. I love you.

To my family—Berta, mi mamá, Bertha Elena, Raul y Jorge, Scott,

Christen, Mark, Daniel, Anna, Sophia, Giulia, and Marcel. THANK YOU FOR EVERYTHING! You are the roots and branches to the story. I love you very much. Abrazos para la tía Gloria y los primos Marin, Peña, Ojeda, and los del lado Hinojosa, especialmente el primaso Pancho Hinojosa.

To Safiya and Miko, and to Walter—woof and meow.

My son, Raúl Ariel, and my daughter, Yurema, are like miracles to me. They actually came from me? These extraordinary human beings? I see them and the future looks more exciting. I hope you both will forgive me for the many times I asked you to wait to speak to me until I finished writing a sentence. And for being away too much. I love you both to the moon and back and forth to infinity.

And to my husband, Gérman Perez, who just this morning as I set out to write these last words took my hand and danced a little bachata with me. Gracias, joni, for always, always trusting in me and for teaching me to comerme el miedo.

And to all of you I say: No te vayas—stay with us. Don't you leave and I won't, either.

Notes

CHAPTER 1: LAND OF FALSE PROMISES

1. "Chinese Exclusion Act," the African American Policy Forum, https://aapf
.org/chinese-exclusion-act.
2. Peter Shrag interview with Maureen Cavanaugh and Megan Burke, "The
Long View on American Attitudes Toward Immigration," audio file, KPBS,
May 10, 2011, https://www.kpbs.org/news/2011/may/10/long-view-american
-attitudes-toward-immigration/.

CHAPTER 2: HOW I BECAME AMERICAN

1. Warren Kozak, "George Wallace 1968 Presidential Campaign," History on
the Net, https://www.historyonthenet.com/george-wallace-1968-presidential
-campaign.
2. "Trends in Migration to the U.S.," Population Reference Bureau, May 19,
2014, https://www.prb.org/us-migration-trends/.
3. Diane Bernard, "President Hoover Deported 1 Million Mexican Americans
for Supposedly Stealing Jobs During the Great Depression," *Washington
Post*, April 13, 2018.
4. "About," Bracero History Archive, http://braceroarchive.org.
5. Muzaffar Chishti, Faye Hipsman, and Isabel Ball, "Fifty Years On, the 1965
Immigration and Nationality Act Continues to Reshape the United States,"
Migration Policy Institute, October 15, 2015, https://www.migrationpolicy
.org/article/fifty-years-1965-immigration-and-nationality-act-continues
-reshape-united-states.

CHAPTER 3: IS THIS WHAT DEMOCRACY LOOKS LIKE?

1. Rian Dundon, "Photos: The L.A. Zoot Suit Riots of 1943 were a targeted
attack on Mexican and nonwhite youths," *Timeline*, February 8, 2018,

https://timeline.com/zoot-suit-riots-of-1943-were-a-targeted-attack-on
-mexican-youths-8e5b34775cff.

2. Derek Hawkins, "The Long Struggle over What to Call 'Undocumented Immigrants' or, as Trump Said in His Order, 'Illegal Aliens,'" *Washington Post*, February 9, 2017.

CHAPTER 4: NOWHERE TO HIDE

1. Angie Galicia, "The Beautiful Face of Courage: The Adelitas," Inside Mexico, October 11, 2018.

2. Farah Mohammed, "Who Was La Malinche?" *JSTOR Daily*, March 1, 2019, https://daily.jstor.org/who-was-la-malinche/.

3. "La Malinche," don Quijote, https://www.donquijote.org/mexican-culture /history/la-malinche/.

4. Wallace Turner, "First Wave of Southeast Asian 'Boat People' Arrives," *New York Times*, September 21, 1977.

5. "Boat People and Hill People," op-ed, *New York Times*, December 23, 1977.

6. Shane Croucher, "California Governor Jerry Brown's 'Sanctuary' Law Under Fire as Poll Finds Majority Backs Deportations," *Newsweek*, April 19, 2018, https://www.newsweek.com/california-backs-more-deportations -jerry-brown-refuses-trumps-mexico-border-892211.

CHAPTER 5: EMBRACING A NEW IDENTITY

1. Larry Rohter, "4 Salvadorans Say They Killed U.S. Nuns on Orders of Military," *New York Times*, April 3, 1998.

CHAPTER 6: FINDING MY VOICE

1. Wesley S. McCann and Francis D. Boateng, *National Security and Policy in America: Immigrants, Crime, and the Securitization of the Border* (Taylor & Francis, 2019).

2. Ronald Reagan, "Following is the text of President Reagan's speech Wednesday," UPI Archives, speech, May 9, 1984, https://www.upi.com /Archives/1984/05/09/Following-is-the-text-of-President-Reagans-speech -WednesdayMy/7055452923200/.

CHAPTER 7: YOU CAN TAKE CARE OF ME A LITTLE

1. Melissa Muriente, "Mexican migration to NYC: The social, economic, and cultural characteristics in comparison to traditional Mexican migration to the Southwest."

2. David A. Badillo, "An Urban Historical Portrait of Mexican Migration to

New York City," *New York History*, vol. 90, no. ½ (Winter/Spring 2009): 107–24.

3. Mario Diaz, "Mexican Community Increasing Strength by the Numbers Is the Real Story This Cinco de Mayo in NYC," PIX 11, May 5, 2016, https://pix11.com/2016/05/05/mexican-community-increasing-strength-by-the-numbers-is-the-real-story-this-cinco-de-mayo-in-nyc/.

4. June 7, 2017, and Pm, "Flashback."

5. Robert McCoppin and Susan Berger, "25 Years—and a Surge in School Violence—Since Laurie Dann Shootings," *Chicago Tribune*, May 19, 2013.

CHAPTER 8: A TASTE OF THE ACTION

1. Francis X. Clines, "The Twin Towers; After Bombing, New Scrutiny for Holes in Immigration Net," *New York Times*, March 12, 1993.

2. Thomas Lippman, "Lenient Visa Rules Permit Terrorists to Enter U.S.," *Washington Post*, July 23, 1993.

3. Steven A. Jensen, "No Room for Sentiment on Immigration," Letter to the Editor, *New York Times*, April 29, 1993.

4. Joseph P. Fried, "Oct. 1–7: Another Verdict; 10 Militant Muslims Guilty of Terrorist Conspiracy," *New York Times*, October 8, 1995.

5. Elena Goukassian, "Delicate and Detailed Paper Sculptures by Chinese Migrants Detained in the US," *Hyperallergic*, February 23, 2018, https://hyperallergic.com/423666/golden-venture-paper-sculptures-chinese-migrants/.

6. Patrick Radden Keefe, "A Path Out of Purgatory," *New Yorker*, June 6, 2013, https://www.newyorker.com/news/daily-comment/a-path-out-of-purgatory.

7. Goukassian, "Delicate and Detailed Paper Sculptures."

8. Robert D. McFadden, "Smuggled to New York: The Overview—7 Die as Crowded Immigrant Ship Grounds off Queens; Chinese Aboard Are Seized for Illegal Entry," *New York Times*, June 7, 1993.

9. Opinion, "The Golden Venture, Plus 100,000," *New York Times*, June 9, 1993.

10. Ian Fisher, "A Town's Strange Bedfellows Unite Behind Chinese Refugees," *New York Times*, February 21, 1997.

11. Julio Ricardo Valera, "The Latino Vote in Presidential Races: 1980–2012," *Latino USA*, October 29, 2015, https://www.latinousa.org/2015/10/29/the-latino-vote-in-presidential-races/.

12. "1996 Clinton vs. Dole," The Living Room Candidate: Presidential Campaign Commercials 1952–2016, the Museum of the Moving Image, http://www.livingroomcandidate.org/commercials/1996/next-century#4175.

13. Marian Burros, "Bill Clinton and Food: Jack Sprat He's Not," *New York Times*, December 23, 1992.

14. Joel Brinkley, "A Rare Success at the Border Brought Scant Official Praise," *New York Times*, September 14, 1994.

15. Timeline of Important Dates, Latino Americans, PBS, https://www.pbs.org /latino-americans/en/timeline/#y1900.

16. German Lopez, "The Controversial 1994 Crime Law That Joe Biden Helped Write, Explained," *Vox*, June 20, 2019, https://www.vox.com/policy-and-pol itics/2019/6/20/18677998/joe-biden-1994-crime-bill-law-mass-incarceration.

17. Carla Rivera, "Stigma of Welfare Hampers State Push Toward Jobs," *Los Angeles Times*, May 9, 1997.

18. Mark Z. Barabak, "On Politics: Pete Wilson looks back on Proposition 187 and says, heck yeah, he'd support it all over again," *Los Angeles Times*, March 23, 2017.

19. Gebe Martinez, "Learning from Proposition 187," Center for American Progress, May 5, 2010, https://www.americanprogress.org/issues/immigra tion/news/2010/05/05/7847/learning-from-proposition-187/.

20. B. Drummond Ayres Jr., "Anti-Alien Sentiment Spreading in Wake of California's Measure," *New York Times*, December 4, 1994.

21. Martinez, "Learning from Proposition 187."

22. "California Proposition 187, Illegal Aliens Ineligible for Public Benefits (1994)," Ballotpedia, https://ballotpedia.org/California_Proposition_187, _Illegal_Aliens_Ineligible_for_Public_Benefits_(1994).

23. Eleanor Acer and Olga Byrne, "How the Illegal Immigration Reform and Immigrant Responsibility Act of 1996 Has Undermined US Refugee Protection Obligations and Wasted Government Resources," *Journal on Migration and Human Security*, vol. 5, issue no. 2, 2017: 356-378; Dara Lind, "The Disastrous, Forgotten 1996 Law that Created Today's Immigration Problem," *Vox*, April 28, 2016, https://www.vox.com/2016/4/28/11515132/iirira-clinton-immigration; Bill Clinton, "1995 State of the Union Address," C-Span, video file, January 24, 1995, https://www.c-span.org/video/?c4774500/bill-clinton-immigration.

24. David M. Grable, "Personhood Under the Due Process Clause: A Constitutional Analysis of the Illegal Immigration Reform and Immigrant Responsibility Act of 1996," *Cornell Law Review*, vol. 83, 1998: 820–66.

CHAPTER 9: WORKING MOTHER

1. Juleyka Lantigua-Williams, "40 years later, U.S. invasion still haunts Dominican Republic," *The Progressive*, April 21, 2005, https://progressive.org /40-years-later-u.s.-invasion-still-haunts-dominican-republic/.

2. "U.S.-Mexico: A State Dinner," President, George W. Bush, The White House, September 5, 2001, https://georgewbush-whitehouse.archives.gov /president/statedinner-mexico-200109/.

3. Eric Schmitt, "Bush Aides Weigh Legalizing Status of Mexicans in U.S.," *New York Times*, July 15, 2001.

CHAPTER 10: THE END OF THE WORLD WILL BE TELEVISED

1. Greg Morabito, "Windows on the World, New York's Sky-High Restaurant," *Eater*, September 11, 2013, https://ny.eater.com/2013/9/11/6547477/windows-on-the-world-new-yorks-sky-high-restaurant.
2. Congressional Research Service, "The Selective Service System and Draft Registration: Issues for Congress," January 28, 2019.
3. "Selective Service," USA.gov, https://www.usa.gov/selective-service.
4. Brendan Nyhan, "Republican Attacks on Dissent Since 9/11," blog, https://www.brendan-nyhan.com/blog/gop-dissent-attacks.html.
5. Katie McDonough, "A Short, Brutal History of ICE," *Splinter*, February 2, 2018, https://splinternews.com/a-short-brutal-history-of-ice-1822641556.
6. Heather Timmons, "No One Really Knows What ICE Is Supposed to Be. Politicians Love That," *Quartz*, July 7, 2018, https://qz.com/1316098/what-is-ice-supposed-to-do-the-strange-history-of-us-immigration-and-customs-enforcement/.
7. McDonough, "A Short, Brutal History."
8. Franklin Foer, "How Trump Radicalized ICE," *Atlantic*, September 2018, https://www.theatlantic.com/magazine/archive/2018/09/trump-ice/565772/.
9. Edward J. Mills, editor, "Mortality in Iraq Associated with the 2003–2011 War and Occupation: Findings from a National Cluster Sample Survey by the University Collaborative Iraq Mortality Study," *PLOS Medicine*, October 15, 2013, https://journals.plos.org/plosmedicine/article?id=10.1371/journal.pmed.1001533.

CHAPTER 11: CONFRONTATIONS

1. Chad C. Haddal, Yule Kim, and Michael John Garcia, "Border Security: Barriers Along the U.S. International Border," Congressional Research Service, March 16, 2009.
2. "Fact-Checking Dobbs: CNN Anchor Lou Dobbs Challenged on Immigration Issues," Democracy Now!, video file, December 4, 2007, https://www.democracynow.org/2007/12/4/fact_checking_dobbs_cnn_anchor_lou.
3. Matt Apuzzo, "Times Reporter Will Not Be Called to Testify in Leak Case," *New York Times*, January 12, 2015.
4. "Democracy Now!'s 2004 Year-In-Review," Democracy Now!, video file, December 30, 2004, https://www.democracynow.org/2004/12/30/democracy_now_s_2004_year_in.
5. Reginald Stuart, "Minority Journalism Groups Dissolve UNITY Collab-

orative," *Diverse: Issues in Higher Education*, March 1, 2018, https://diverse
education.com/article/111267/.

CHAPTER 12: CITIZEN JOURNALIST

1. Sewell Chan and Ray Rivera, "Property Values in New York Show Vibrancy," *New York Times*, January 13, 2007.
2. Katherine Clarke, "From eyesore to goldmine: The transformation of the hulking former *Daily News* building on W. 33rd St. is well underway," *New York Daily News*, July 8, 2015, https://www.nydailynews.com/life-style /real-estate/hulking-daily-news-building-new-lease-life-article-1.2285293.
3. *NOW*, PBS, September 9, 2005.
4. *NOW*, PBS, November 11, 2005.
5. Griselda Nevarez, "Latino Workers Helped Rebuild New Orleans, But Many Weren't Paid," NBC News, Augusts 28, 2015, https://www.nbcnews .com/storyline/hurricane-katrina-anniversary/latino-workers-helped -rebuild-new-orleans-many-werent-paid-n417571.
6. Michael Martinez, "Big Easy Uneasy About Migrant Wave," *Chicago Tribune*, November 3, 2005.
7. "Louisiana: European Explorations and the Louisiana Purchase," Geography and Map Division of the Library of Congress, presentation, https:// www.loc.gov/static/collections/louisiana-european-explorations-and-the -louisiana-purchase/images/lapurchase.pdf.
8. Lesley Kennedy, "Building the Transcontinental Railroad: How 20,000 Chinese Immigrants Made It Happen," History.com, May 10, 2019, https:// www.history.com/news/transcontinental-railroad-chinese-immigrants.
9. Terry Gross interview with Francisco Balderrama, "America's Forgotten History Of Mexican-American 'Repatriation,'" *Fresh Air*, NPR, audio file and transcript, September 10, 2015, https://www.npr.org/2015/09/10/439114563 /americas-forgotten-history-of-mexican-american-repatriation.
10. Alex Wagner, "America's Forgotten History of Illegal Deportations," *Atlantic*, March 6, 2017, https://www.theatlantic.com/politics/archive/2017/03 /americas-brutal-forgotten-history-of-illegal-deportations/517971/.
11. "The Bracero Program," UCLA Labor Center, 2014, https://www.labor.ucla .edu/what-we-do/research-tools/the-bracero-program/.
12. Doris Meissner, "U.S. Temporary Worker Programs: Lessons Learned," Migration Policy Institute, March 1, 2004, https://www.migrationpolicy.org /article/us-temporary-worker-programs-lessons-learned.
13. "About," Bracero History Archive, http://braceroarchive.org.
14. Pam Belluck, "Settlement Will Allow Thousands of Mexican Laborers in U.S. to Collect Back Pay," *New York Times*, October 15, 2008.

15. Maclovio Perez Jr., "El Paso Bath House Riots (1917)," Texas State His-
    torical Association, July 30, 2016, https://tshaonline.org/handbook/online
    /articles/jce02.

16. Kuang Keng Kuek Ser, "Data: Hate crimes against Muslims increased after
    9/11," PRI, September 12, 2016, https://www.pri.org/stories/2016-09-12
    /data-hate-crimes-against-muslims-increased-after-911.

17. Congressional hearing before the Subcommittee on Immigration, Border
    Security, and Claims of the Committee on the Judiciary House of Represen-
    tatives, "War on Terrorism: Immigration Enforcement Since September 11,
    2001," May 8, 2003, serial no. 21, http://commdocs.house.gov/committees
    /judiciary/hju86954.000/hju86954_0f.htm.

18. Bill Ong Hing, *Defining America Through Immigration Policy* (Philadelphia:
    Temple University Press, 2004), 209–10.

19. Department of Homeland Security, "Table 39. Aliens Removed Or Re-
    turned: Fiscal Years 1892 To 2014," *2014 Yearbook of Immigration Statistics*,
    November 1, 2016, https://www.dhs.gov/immigration-statistics/yearbook
    /2014/table39.

20. Laura Sullivan, "Prison Economics Help Drive Ariz. Immigration Law,"
    Morning Edition, NPR, audio file and transcript, October 28, 2010, https://
    www.npr.org/2010/10/28/130833741/prison-economics-help-drive-ariz
    -immigration-law.

21. "The Latino American Who's Who Recognizes Eddie R. Chapa," Latino Who's
    Who, August 10, 2015, http://latinwhoswho.net/press/tag/eddie-r-chapa/.

22. United States Census Bureau, "QuickFacts: Willacy County, Texas,"
    Census.gov, https://www.census.gov/quickfacts/table/PST045214/48489
    /embed/accessible.

23. "Raymondville, Texas Population: Census 2010 and 2000 Interactive Map,
    Demographics, Statistics, Quick Facts," Census Viewer, http://censusviewer
    .com/city/TX/Raymondville.

24. Hing, *Defining America Through Immigration Policy*, 130, 144, 155.

25. Spencer S. Hsu, "In Immigration Cases, Employers Feel the Pressure,"
    Washington Post, July 21, 2008.

26. Jerry Kammer, "The 2006 Swift Raids: Assessing the Impact of Immigra-
    tion Enforcement Actions at Six Facilities," Center for Immigration Stud-
    ies, March 18, 2009, https://cis.org/Report/2006-Swift-Raids.

27. Spencer S. Hsu, "ICE Sweep was Largest Ever Against One Firm," *Washing-
    ton Post*, December 14, 2006.

28. Spencer S. Hsu and Krissah Williams, "Illegal Workers Arrested in 6-State
    ID Theft Sweep," *Washington Post*, December 13, 2006.

29. Hsu, "In Immigration Cases, Employers Feel the Pressure."

30. Susan Saulny, "Hundreds Are Arrested in U.S. Sweep of Meat Plant," *New York Times*, May 13, 2008.

31. Julia Preston, "After Iowa Raid, Immigrants Fuel Labor Inquiries," *New York Times*, July 27, 2008.

32. "'What Did It Achieve?': Documentary Examines Largest Immigration Raid In U.S. History," *Here & Now*, WBUR, July 30, 2018, https://www.wbur.org/hereandnow/2018/07/30/postville-iowa-immigration-raid-documentary.

33. Courtney Crowder and MacKenzie Elmer, "Postville Raid Anniversary: A Timeline of Events in One of America's Largest Illegal Immigration Campaigns," *Des Moines Register*, May 10, 2018.

34. Jim Rutenberg, "Ex-Aide Says He's Lost Faith in Bush," *New York Times*, April 1, 2007; Jim Rutenberg, "Former Advisor Breaks with Bush," *New York Times*, March 30, 2007.

35. Jim Rutenberg, "News Analysis: U.S. Immigration Bill Tests Bush's Strength," *New York Times*, May 26, 2006; Matthew Dowd on Twitter, December 24, 2016, https://twitter.com/matthewjdowd/status/812604998852968448.

CHAPTER 13: THE NEW POWER OF "INMIGRANTE"

1. "May Day—The Great American Boycott 2006," Industrial Workers of the World, April 2, 2006, https://www.iww.org/node/2307.

2. Mark Engler and Paul Engler, "Op-Ed: The massive immigrant-rights protests of 2006 are still changing politics," Opinion, *Los Angeles Times*, March 4, 2016, https://www.latimes.com/opinion/op-ed/la-oe-0306-engler-immigration-protests-2006-20160306-story.html.

3. Laura Griffin, "Huge Crowd Marches in Dallas in Support of Immigrants," *New York Times*, April 9, 2006.

4. Alexandra Starr, "Voice of América," *Slate*, May 3, 2006, https://slate.com/news-and-politics/2006/05/the-spanish-language-djs-behind-the-new-latino-activism.html.

5. Pamela Constable, "Latinos Demand Rights, Respect at D.C. March," *Washington Post*, October 13, 1996.

6. Louis Jacobson, "Bill Clinton Says His Administration Paid Down the Debt," Politifact, September 23, 2010, https://www.politifact.com/truth-o-meter/statements/2010/sep/23/bill-clinton/bill-clinton-says-his-administration-paid-down-deb/; Daniel Wesley, "The $22 Trillion U.S. Debt: Which President Contributed the Most," DebtConsolidation.com, May 22, 2018, https://www.debtconsolidation.com/us-debt-presidents/.

7. "The Hispanic Vote in the 2008 Election," Pew Research Center, November 5, 2008, https://www.pewresearch.org/hispanic/2008/11/05/the-hispanic-vote-in-the-2008-election/.

8. Allison Graves, "Fact-check: Did top Democrats vote for a border wall in 2006?," Politifact, April 23, 2017, https://www.politifact.com/truth-o-meter /statements/2017/apr/23/mick-mulvaney/fact-check-did-top-democrats -vote-border-wall-2006/.

9. Philip Elliott, "Obama Praises Sotomayor at Hispanic Gala," *San Diego Union-Tribune*, September 16, 2009; Barack Obama, "President Obama at Congressional Hispanic Caucus Institute Awards Gala," YouTube, video file, September 22, 2009, https://www.youtube.com/watch?v=TY tw84RjcH4.

10. Josh Hicks, "Obama's Failed Promise of a First-Year Immigration Overhaul," *Washington Post*, September 25, 2012.

11. Scott Wong and Shira Toeplitz, "DREAM Act Dies in Senate," *Politico*, December 12, 2010, https://www.politico.com/story/2010/12/dream-act -dies-in-senate-046573.

12. Peter Nicholas, "Democrats Point the Finger at Obama's Chief of Staff for Immigration Reform's Poor Progress," *Los Angeles Times*, May 21, 2010.

13. Jeffrey S. Passel and D'Vera Cohn, "Overall Number of U.S. Unauthorized Immigrants Holds Steady Since 2009," Pew Research Center, September 20, 2016, https://www.pewresearch.org/hispanic/2016/09/20/overall-num ber-of-u-s-unauthorized-immigrants-holds-steady-since-2009/; Julia Preston, "Number of Illegal Immigrants in U.S. Fell, Study Says," *New York Times*, September 1, 2010.

14. Ryan Grim, "Maureen Dowd Asked Rahm Emanuel to Weigh in on an Immigration Debate. His Record is Abysmal," *Intercept*, July 17, 2019, https:// theintercept.com/2019/07/17/rahm-emanuel-immigration/.

15. "Immigrant Detention in the United States," United States Conference of Catholic Bishops, JusticeforImmigrants.org, 2016, https://justicefor immigrants.org/wp-content/uploads/2016/11/immigrant-detention-back grounder-1-18-17.pdf.

16. Ted Robbins, "Little-Known Immigration Mandate Keeps Detention Beds Full," *Morning Edition*, NPR, November 19, 2013, https://www.npr.org /2013/11/19/245968601/little-known-immigration-mandate-keeps-deten tion-beds-full.

17. Elizabeth Keyes, "Defining American: The DREAM Act, Immigration Reform and Citizenship," *Nevada Law Journal*, vol. 14, Fall 2013: 101–55.

18. "The Dream Act, DACA, and Other Policies Designed to Protect Dreamers," American Immigration Council, fact sheet, September 3, 2019, https:// www.americanimmigrationcouncil.org/research/dream-act-daca-and -other-policies-designed-protect-dreamers.

19. David Hawkings and Thomas McKinless, "Why Are the Dreamers Called

the Dreamers?," Roll Call, video file and transcript, June 20, 2018, https://www.rollcall.com/video/why_are_the_dreamers_called_the_dreamers.

20. Dr. Raúl Hinojosa-Ojeda, "Economic Stimulus Through Legalization," William C. Velásquez Institute, white paper, http://wcvi.org/intermestic_initiatives/FinalWCVIWhitePaperLegalization.pdf.

21. Ashley Rhymer, "Trail of Dreams Is Trail of Hope," Amnesty International, https://www.amnestyusa.org/trail-of-dreams-is-trail-of-hope/.

22. "A Long Walk for a Cause," *New York Times*, April 28, 2010.

23. Albert Sabaté, "The Rise of Being 'Undocumented and Unafraid,'" ABC News, December 4, 2012, https://abcnews.go.com/ABC_Univision/News/rise-undocumented-unafraid/story?id=17872813.

24. Pepe Lozano, "Immigrant Youth Arrested in Georgia after Civil Disobedience," People's World, April 7, 2011, https://www.peoplesworld.org/article/immigrant-youth-arrested-in-georgia-after-civil-disobedience/.

25. Julia Preston, "Pennsylvania Town Delays Enforcing Tough Immigration Law," *New York Times*, September 2, 2006.

26. "Lozano v. Hazleton," ACLU, February 5, 2015, https://www.aclu.org/cases/lozano-v-hazleton.

27. "Arizona SB 1070," Ballotpedia.org, https://ballotpedia.org/Arizona_SB_1070.

28. Stephen Lemons, "Activists Chain Themselves to Arizona Capitol to Protest Russell Pearce's SB 1070," *Phoenix New Times*, April 20, 2010, https://www.phoenixnewtimes.com/news/activists-chain-themselves-to-arizona-capitol-to-protest-russell-pearces-sb-1070-6500565.

29. Emanuella Grinberg, "Protesters, Riot Police Clash over Arizona Immigration Law," CNN, July 29, 2010, https://www.cnn.com/2010/US/07/29/arizona.immigration.protests/index.html.

30. Jeffrey S. Passel, D'Vera Cohn, and Mark Hugo Lopez, "Hispanics Account for More than Half of Nation's Growth in Past Decade," Pew Research Center, March 24, 2011, https://www.pewresearch.org/hispanic/2011/03/24/hispanics-account-for-more-than-half-of-nations-growth-in-past-decade/.

31. Jada F. Smith, "A Second Try on Immigration Act," The Caucus, *New York Times*, blog, June 28, 2011, https://thecaucus.blogs.nytimes.com/2011/06/28/a-second-try-on-immigration-act/.

32. "HR 5281—DREAM Act—National Key Vote," Vote Smart, https://votesmart.org/bill/12443/32955/dream-act#32982.

33. Marshall Fitz and Ann Garcia, "The DREAM Act by the Numbers," American Progress, December 17, 2010, https://www.americanprogress.org/issues/immigration/news/2010/12/17/8845/the-dream-act-by-the-numbers/.

34. John Ingold, "Immigration Activists Stage Sit-in at Denver Obama Office," *Denver Post*, June 5, 2012, https://www.denverpost.com/2012/06/05/immi gration-activists-stage-sit-in-at-denver-obama-office/.

35. Barack Obama, "Remarks by the President on Immigration," Office of the Press Secretary, the White House, speech, June 15, 2012, https://obama whitehouse.archives.gov/the-press-office/2012/06/15/remarks-president -immigration.

36. Lori Robertson, "The Facts on DACA," FactCheck.org, January 22, 2018, https://www.factcheck.org/2018/01/the-facts-on-daca/.

37. Julia Preston and John H. Cushman Jr., "Obama to Permit Young Migrants to Remain in U.S.," *New York Times*, June 15, 2012; Elise Foley, "Obama Administration to Stop Deporting Younger Undocumented Immigrants And Grant Work Permits," *Huffington Post*, June 15, 2012, https://www .huffpost.com/entry/obama-immigration-order-deportation-dream-act_n _1599658.

CHAPTER 14: WHAT I CANNOT UNSEE

1. Bruce Rushton, "Dora's Darlings," *Phoenix New Times*, June 3, 2004.

2. Reynaldo Leanos Jr., "A Private Prison Company with a Troubled Past Looks to Reopen an Immigration Detention Facility in Texas," PRI, June 13, 2017, https://www.pri.org/stories/2017-06-13/private-prison-company -troubled-past-looks-re-open-immigration-detention-facility.

3. Nina Bernstein, "Immigration Official to Run New York's Jails," *New York Times*, September 8, 2009.

4. Joel Rubin, "It's Legal for an Immigration Agent to Pretend to be a Police Officer Outside Someone's Door. But Should It Be?," *Los Angeles Times*, February 20, 2017.

5. Rebecca Hersher, "Los Angeles Officials To ICE: Stop Identifying Your- selves As Police," *The Two-Way*, NPR, February 24, 2017, https://www.npr .org/sections/thetwo-way/2017/02/24/517041101/los-angeles-officials-to -ice-stop-identifying-yourselves-as-police.

CHAPTER 15: TRAUMA INHERITED

1. Gretchen Gavett, "Sec. Napolitano Questioned About 'Lost in Detention,'" *Frontline*, PBS, October 20, 2011, https://www.pbs.org/wgbh/frontline /article/sec-napolitano-questioned-about-lost-in-detention/.

2. Derek Gilna, "Prison Rape Elimination Act Finally Extended to ICE De- tention Facilities, but Not to Private or County Jails," *Prison Legal News*, April 13, 2017, https://www.prisonlegalnews.org/news/2017/apr/13/prison

-rape-elimination-act-finally-extended-ice-detention-facilities-not-private
-or-county-jails/.

3. "Lost in Detention," *Frontline*, transcript, https://www.pbs.org/wgbh/pages
/frontline/immigration-2/lost-in-detention/transcript-11/.

4. Department of Homeland Security, "Table 39. Aliens Removed Or Returned: Fiscal Years 1892 To 2014," *2014 Yearbook of Immigration Statistics*,
November 1, 2016, https://www.dhs.gov/immigration-statistics/yearbook
/2014/table39.

5. Doris Meissner, Donald M. Kerwin, Muzaffar Chisti, and Claire Bergeron,
"Immigration Enforcement in the United States: The Rise of Formidable
Machinery," Migration Policy Institute, January 2013.

6. " Lost in Detention," *Frontline*, transcript.

CHAPTER 16: OWNING MY VOICE

1. "Latino USA: Gangs, Murder, and Migration in Honduras (NPR)," Peabody Awards, http://www.peabodyawards.com/award-profile/nprs-latino
-usa-gangs-murder-and-migration-in-honduras.

2. Kerry Kennedy, "2017 Robert F. Kennedy Journalism Awards Winners,"
Robert F. Kennedy Human Rights, May 5, 2017, https://rfkhumanrights
.org/news/2017-robert-f-kennedy-journalism-awards-winners.

CHAPTER 17: ILLEGAL IS NOT A NOUN

1. Bill Ong Hing, *American Presidents, Deportations, and Human Rights Violations: From Carter to Trump* (Cambridge, UK: Cambridge University Press,
2019), 96.

2. Colin Deppen and Sarah Anne Hughes, "Why PA's Controversial Berks
Detention Center for Immigrant Families Is Still Open," *Billy Penn*, June
22, 2018, https://billypenn.com/2018/06/22/why-pas-controversial-deten
tion-center-for-immigrant-families-is-still-open/.

3. Lutheran Immigration & Refugee Service and the Women's Refugee Commission, "Locking Up Family Values: The Detention of Immigrant Families,"
February 2007, page 17, https://www.womensrefugeecommission.org/resources
/document/150-locking-up-family-values-the-detention-of-immigrant-families.

4. Lutheran Immigration & Refugee Service and the Women's Refugee Commission, "Locking Up Family Values, Again: A Report on the Renewed
Practice of Family Immigration Detention," October 2014, https://www
.womensrefugeecommission.org/images/zdocs/Fam-Detention-Again-Full
-Report.pdf.

5. Hing, *American Presidents, Deportations, and Human Rights Violations*, 83.

6. Laurence Benenson, "The Math of Immigration Detention, 2018 Update:

Costs Continue to Multiply," National Immigration Forum, May 9, 2018, https://immigrationforum.org/article/math-immigration-detention-2018 -update-costs-continue-mulitply/.

7. Hing, *American Presidents, Deportations, and Human Rights Violations*, 96–9.

8. Office of Public Affairs, The United States Department of Justice, "Attorney General Announces Zero-Tolerance Policy for Criminal Illegal Entry," press release, April 6, 2018, https://www.justice.gov/opa/pr/attorney -general-announces-zero-tolerance-policy-criminal-illegal-entry.

9. Lawrence Downes, "No More 'Illegal Immigrants,'" Taking Note, *New York Times*, April 4, 2013, https://takingnote.blogs.nytimes.com/2013/04 /04/no-more-illegal-immigrants/.

10. Stephen Hiltner, "Illegal, Undocumented, Unauthorized: The Terms of Immigration Reporting," *New York Times*, March 10, 2017.

11. Adam Shaw, "ICE warns illegal immigrants facing murder, child sex offense charges could be released in North Carolina sanctuary cities," Fox News, November 8, 2019, https://www.foxnews.com/politics/ice-lists-release-in -north-carolina-as-administration-ramps-up-pressure-on-sanctuary-cities.

12. Derek Thompson, "How Immigration Became So Controversial," *Atlantic*, February 2, 2018, https://www.theatlantic.com/politics/archive/2018/02 /why-immigration-divides/552125/.

13. Ed Rogers, "Illegal immigrants have rights. Shaping American democracy isn't one of them," Opinions, *Washington Post*, August 20, 2019.

14. Michelle Hackman, "Bipartisan House Deal Opens Path to Citizenship for Illegal Immigrant Farmworkers," *Wall Street Journal*, October 30, 2019.

15. Rachel Frazin, "Reporter Manuel Duran Released from ICE Custody," *Hill*, July 12, 2019, https://thehill.com/latino/452818-reporter-manuel -duran-released-from-ice-custody.

16. Cindy Carcamo, "Relatives of Erika Andiola, Immigrant Activist, Detained," *Los Angeles Times*, January 11, 2013.

17. Seth Freed Wessler, "Is Denaturalization the Next Front in the Trump Administration's War on Immigration?" *New York Times Magazine*, December 19, 2018.

CHAPTER 18: THE POWER OF STANDING IN THE LIGHT

1. "Correctional Facilities Industry in the US - Market Research Report," IBIS World, June 2019, https://www.ibisworld.com/united-states/market -research-reports/correctional-facilities-industry/.

Index

About the Author

Maria Hinojosa's nearly thirty-year career as a journalist includes reporting for PBS, CBS, WGBH, WNBC, CNN, NPR, and anchoring and executive producing the Peabody Award–winning show *Latino USA*, distributed by NPR. She is a frequent guest on MSNBC and has won several awards, including four Emmys™, two Robert F. Kennedy Awards, the Edward R. Murrow Award from the Overseas Press Club, and the Walter Cronkite Award for Excellence in Journalism. In 2010, she founded Futuro Media, an independent nonprofit organization with the mission of producing multimedia content from a POC perspective. Through the breadth of her work and as the founding coanchor of the political podcast *In The Thick*, Hinojosa has informed millions about the changing cultural and political landscape in America and abroad. She lives with her family in Harlem, New York.

"Historical, entertaining, educational, instructive, heroic, honest, and courageously brave. It's a must-read for anyone, especially in this critical time as we try to make sense of how the divisions in our country came to be, but also how to overcome them."

—Dolores Huerta, cofounder of United Farm Workers

"*Once I Was You* throws down, proving that Maria Hinojosa is beyond badassery: *esta mujer es una chingona* to be reckoned with. In warm, journalistic prose, Hinojosa unfurls a map of *una vida extraordinaria* that shows her developing, nurturing, and sustaining a career best described as iconoclastic. Her skills as a writer and reporter enable her to trace the ugly contours of US racial politics as she simultaneously narrates a compulsively readable autobiography."

—Myriam Gurba, author of *Mean*

"Maria Hinojosa tells her own life story to open our eyes to the stories of people, some locked up along our borders, others living underground in our great cities, who want the chance to enrich America in all ways. Her book is a lyrical act of recollection and empathy."

—Scott Simon, host of *Weekend Edition Saturday*, NPR

"Maria Hinojosa has assembled a full arsenal of facts, stats, and deeply complex histories to weaponize a revolution of justice in this country. The courage of Hinojosa's reportage resides not only in her ability to enter the ground zero of a conflict, but to also turn the lens on herself."

—Cherríe Moraga, coeditor of *The Bridge Called My Back*

"As far-ranging and politically illuminating as Hinojosa's memoir becomes, it is also laser-focused and intimate, and at its heart are portrayals of immigrants, especially immigrant children. . . . A fascinating and essential journalist's memoir."

—*Booklist* (starred review)

Praise for *Once I Was You*

"Maria Hinojosa is a national treasure. I always know I can trust her in her reporting. Here, as an author, she steps forward with her usual clarity and a new surge of power to tell us a deeply needed narrative about ourselves."

—Luis Alberto Urrea, Pulitzer Prize finalist and bestselling author of *The Devil's Highway*

"As a POC journalist, feminist, survivor of sexual assault, and truth-teller, Maria Hinojosa is tough as nails. This expressive and captivating book not only reveals how she has fought to tell stories that are so often silenced by the mainstream media, but also lays bare the deep fissures in our politics and our society. *Once I Was You* is essential reading for anyone who wants America to do better."

—Jane Fonda, Academy Award–winning actor and activist

"With frankness, brilliance, and a generous heart, Hinojosa blends intimate experience and professional tales to correct the American story—or, as she puts it, to 'deconstruct this bullshit.' A consummate truth-teller, Hinojosa spares neither political side in doing so. *Once I Was You*, deeply researched and poetically told, will inspire you to create a better world."

—Sarah Smarsh, journalist and *New York Times* bestselling author of *Heartland*

"Maria Hinojosa is a renowned journalist whose observational skills are legendary and on full display in this compelling work. But it's her committed, compassionate, truth-seeking heart that makes this book so timely, necessary, and urgent."

—Bryan Stevenson, founder and executive director of the Equal Justice Initiative and *New York Times* bestselling author of *Just Mercy*